Five Mod

of

Spiritual Direction

in the

Early Church

George E. Demacopoulos

University of Notre Dame Press

Notre Dame, Indiana

Library of Congress Cataloging-in-Publication Data

Demacopoulos, George E.
Five models of spiritual direction in the early church / George E. Demacopoulos.
    p.   cm.
Includes bibliographical references and index.
ISBN-13: 978-0-268-02590-8 (pbk. : alk. paper)
ISBN-10: 0-268-02590-8 (pbk. : alk. paper)
1. Spiritual direction.   2. Asceticism—History—Early church, ca. 30–600.
3. Pastoral theology.   I. Title.
BV5053.D45   2006
253.5'309015—dc22

2006028979

∞ *The paper in this book meets the guidelines for permanence and durability of the Committee on Production Guidelines for Book Longevity of the Council on Library Resources.*

For Katherine, Zoe, Elizabeth, and Eleftherios

Contents

Acknowledgments

This book grew out of a dissertation at the University of North Carolina at Chapel Hill on the pastoral strategies of Pope Gregory I. The decision to expand the study to its present form was based, in part, upon a casual suggestion by my mentor Peter I. Kaufman, just a few days before I left Chapel Hill for New York. To Peter especially, as well as Elizabeth Clark, Lance Lazar, Bart Ehrman, Carolyn Connor, and Nicholas Constas, I owe a great deal. Collectively, they stimulated my intellectual development and provided exceptional, yet distinct, examples of scholarship and teaching.

The original inspiration to study St. Gregory's *Pastoral Rule* stems from my many conversations with Fr. Demetrios Carellas, now the chaplain of the Greek Orthodox women's monastery, the Nativity of the Theotokos, in Saxonburg, Pennsylvania. His love for the fathers of the Church is matched only by his devotion to his spiritual children.

Along the way, I have received assistance from a number of colleagues. In North Carolina, I benefited greatly from a dissertation reading group composed of doctoral students at UNC and Duke. I would especially like to thank Catherine Chin, Stephanie Cobb, Andrew Jacobs, Caroline Schroeder, Christine Shephardson, and Edwin Taite, who all read early drafts of sections that appear in this volume. I would also like to thank the Royster family and the Graduate School of Arts and Sciences, which provided a generous dissertation completion fellowship that enabled me to finish expeditiously.

At Fordham University, I have benefited immeasurably from my conversations and collaboration with Aristotle Papanikolaou. I am also thankful for the insights of Rev. Joseph Lienhard, S.J., as well as the opportunity provided by Maryanne Kowaleski to share my work with the large group of medievalists on campus. And I would be remiss not to acknowledge Rev. Gerald Blaszczak, S.J., who was so encouraging of an Eastern Orthodox perspective when I first arrived. The opportunity to make final revisions to the manuscript was made possible by a Junior Faculty Fellowship from the university. The Graduate School of Arts and Sciences at Fordham University underwrote the cost of the cover art and indexing for the present volume.

I must also acknowledge the generous assistance of David Brakke, who read and then suggested important revisions to the chapter on Athanasius. Both Claudia Rapp and Maureen Tilley shared many thoughts between sessions at various conferences and graciously shared their work in manuscript form, prior to publication. Similarly, Peter Kaufman and Elizabeth Clark made unpublished works available, for which I am grateful. The anonymous readers of the University of Notre Dame Press made many helpful suggestions. The press's editor, Barbara Hanrahan, has been delightful and encouraging from the start. John Gavras, a close friend and exceptional editor (although a geologist by trade), read much of the manuscript and offered many helpful suggestions. Whatever errors remain are, no doubt, my own.

Finally, I wish to express my thanks to my family: to my parents, who not only paid for much of my education but always encouraged intellectual curiosity; to my in-laws, who sacrificed much of their own time so that I could work; and most especially to my wife, Katherine, and three children, Zoe, Elizabeth, and Eleftherios, to whom this book is dedicated.

Introduction

The origins of monasticism predate Constantine's Edict of Toleration. Nevertheless, most scholars of Christian antiquity agree that there was some connection between Constantine's conversion to Christianity and the subsequent rapid growth of monasticism. By ending the persecutions, Constantine and his successors are thought to have invited into the Church persons with less religious ardor than that which was possessed by Christians of the preceding era. The rise of monasticism is seen as an attempt by a rigorous faction within the religion to return to the challenge that the early Christians faced. As the fifth-century author John Cassian understood it, the spread of monasticism was a revival of the purity of the ancient Church.[1]

As a consequence of the widening divide between lay and monastic Christians, a distinction emerged in the patterns of spiritual direction.[2] By *spiritual direction,* I mean the modus operandi by which religious authorities (in both lay and monastic communities) sought to advance the spiritual condition of those under their care.[3] This involved both the criteria by which they selected their successors and the specific techniques that they used to achieve their pastoral goals.[4] Like many things in early Christianity, there was significant variation in the approaches to spiritual direction.

To present monastic and lay communities as distinct entities is risky. At that time, there were theological, social, and even economic interactions between the two groups. What most distinguished monks from lay Christians in late antiquity was the extent of their *askesis*—asceticism.[5] In early Christianity, asceticism was a method of self-control developed by individuals to root out desire for those things that brought "worldly" pleasure (e.g., food, sex, wealth, and fame) and to redirect their energies toward the worship of God.[6] As early as the New Testament, Christian authors had encouraged their readers, married and unmarried alike, to adopt ascetic disciplines (e.g., almsgiving, fasting, and the temporary cessation of sexual activity). By the fourth century, a monk's *askesis* would have been different from his lay coreligionists' in both degree and kind. A monk would be permanently chaste, theoretically poor, and likely to live apart from lay Christians, either by himself or among a group of other professed ascetics. Complicating this distinction is the fact that in the fourth century we also find the first attempts by Christian authorities to standardize and regulate the ascetic practices of lay Christians—further evidence of the close links between the monastery and the "parish."[7]

These links, however, should not keep us from examining how monastic life at this point differed from parish life, specifically in its charismatic as opposed to institutional conceptions of both authority and spiritual direction. As we will see, there was a plethora of opinions about leadership and pastoral care. One of the more useful ways to understand the diversity of opinion and trace the evolution of the ideals is by conceptualizing along the lines of an ascetic/monastic and a lay paradigm.[8]

In recent years, scholars have documented the rise of ascetics to positions of authority in the broader Church. Among other things, these studies have emphasized the emergence of an ascetic discourse that linked the qualifications for leadership to self-denial and have shown how the episcopate eventually came into the hands of former monks. In short, these studies have demonstrated that lay communities either came to adopt or were forced to accept asceticism as a legitimate qualification for authority.[9]

One important aspect of the "asceticizing" of the lay Church that has been neglected by historians is the extent to which the monastic and lay communities had developed distinct conceptions of spiritual direction. The central questions of the present study derive from the encounter of these two pastoral traditions. To what extent did ascetic notions of pastoral care affect the lay Church as monastic leaders gained greater authority? Or, more bluntly, What happened when monks became bishops? Did the new clerics conform to the patterns of pastoral care that were already operating in the lay Church, or did they bring with them the traditions that they had learned in the ascetic community? And if they tried to impose new patterns of supervision on the laity, were their pastoral initiatives met with resistance?

Specifically, this book explores the careers and ideas of five influential Christian authorities: Athanasius, Gregory Nazianzen, Augustine, John Cassian, and Pope Gregory I. Each of the five spent time in an ascetic environment; each was a member of the clergy; each left a literary record of his pastoral anxieties and policies; and each was well known (if not well liked) by other late ancient clerics. These are the authors who shaped the medieval pastoral traditions of the East and the West. Each of the five struggled to balance the tension between his ascetic idealism and the realities of the lay Church. Each offered different (and at times very different) solutions to that tension. The diversity in their models of spiritual direction demonstrates both the complexity of the problem and the variability of early Christianity.

Spiritual Direction in the Lay and Ascetic Communities

It is well known that the number of monks and monasteries grew exponentially during the fourth century.[10] We can contrast the intense life of professed ascetics, many of whom isolated themselves from society, with the progressively institutionalized, imperial, and less rigorous practice of married Christians who continued their various urban and rural lifestyles. To accommodate the increasingly differentiated pastoral needs of these communities, patterns of spiritual direction evolved along two distinct trajectories. The first focusing on the lay community and directed by the clergy, emphasized doctrinal instruction, the distribution of charity, and the celebration of the sacraments. In contrast, the second, which was developed in a monastic setting, took a more personal and interactive approach through the spiritual father/spiritual disciple relationship, typically stressing the specific activities of one's renunciation.

For simplicity, I will refer to these pastoral traditions as the clerical and the ascetic traditions. Such a characterization is not perfect. I am not suggesting that the pastoral initiatives that I associate with the clergy were employed only by ordained priests or that every cleric endorsed them. Likewise, I am not implying that every ascetic Christian (and indeed there were great variations among ascetic communities in late antiquity) understood spiritual direction to comprise the same elements. But if we carefully examine both the criteria for authority and the techniques of religious formation, we find different patterns for how spiritual direction operated in the lay and ascetic communities.

The Basis for Authority

The difference between the clerical and ascetic models is most visible in their understanding of authority and the selection of new leaders. Whether Nicene, Arian, or another sect, most people who self-identified as Christians in the fourth century would have acknowledged the authority of the clergy. The pastoral epistles that were attributed to St. Paul made provisions for the ordination of bishops and deacons, thereby establishing criteria for their election and identifying many of their responsibilities. In the letters of Ignatius of Antioch (who was martyred in Rome in the early years of the second century), we find an emphasis on the authority of the bishop. For Ignatius, the bishop who professed the apostolic faith could discern right from wrong and isolate orthodox truth from heretical teaching.[11] While one recent commentator has suggested that scholars often overstate Ignatius's advocacy of a mono-episcopacy (potentially a later development), it is certain that the bishop of Antioch expected the laity to obey the clergy.[12]

Between the second and the fourth centuries, the theory of apostolic succession emerged to legitimize the authenticity of episcopal teaching and power. Though initially employed to marginalize unacceptable theological positions, apostolic succession cemented the notion that the orthodox clergy possessed the grace of the Holy Spirit.[13] As such, the bishop who was rightly ordained was mystically endowed to serve as Christ's agent among the faithful. By the fourth century, there was little denying that authority lay with the episcopate, but the question at that time was which episcopate (i.e., Nicene or Arian).

It was the rite of ordination that served as the source of pastoral and spiritual authority in the cleric-oriented model. Writing near the close of the fourth century, St. John Chrysostom connected the authority of the priesthood to ordination. "The work of the priest is performed on earth but is recognized in heaven. And this is only proper, because no man, no angel, no archangel, no other created power, but the Holy Spirit itself arranged this succession and persuaded men to make apparent the ministry of angels, though they remained in the flesh."[14] Through the sacraments, especially baptism and the Eucharist, Chrysostom reasoned, bishops and priests conferred salvation upon the whole Christian body.[15] And they alone possessed the ability to bind and loose (cf. Matt. 16:19).[16] The link between the sacraments and episcopal authority went back to at least the third century and probably earlier. The third-century Church order known as the *Didascalia Apostolorum* offers a clear connection: "[B]ut honor the bishops, who have loosed you from sins, who by the water regenerated you, who filled you with the Holy Spirit, who reared you with the word as with milk, who bred you up with doctrine, who confirmed you with admonition, and made you to partake of the holy Eucharist of God, and made you partakers and joint heirs of the promise of God."[17] By presiding over the sacraments, the clergy both functionally and symbolically asserted its leadership within the Christian community.

Though most clerics agreed that ordination was the foundation of their authority, the criteria by which they selected new candidates varied considerably at times. According to 1 Timothy, a bishop "must be blameless, the husband of one wife, temperate, sober, of good behavior, hospitable, able to teach, not given to wine, not violent, not greedy for money, but gentle, not quarrelsome, not covetous; one who rules his own house well, having his children in submission."[18] When Ignatius wrote to Polycarp, he added the criterion of orthodoxy to this list of moral qualifications.[19]

The *Didascalia* records a more lengthy analysis of the criteria for episcopal election. Many of its injunctions are an expansion of the moral requirements listed in 1 Timothy. But by the third century the very nature of clerical service had changed: the bishop now controlled the community's finances and also had the ability to excommunicate those whom he deemed to be in violation of the Church's standards.[20] As Claudia Rapp notes, it is probably for this reason that the text takes such great care in establishing the moral and ascetic qualifications of the bishop.[21]

The *Didascalia* requires that the bishop be able to explain every aspect of the faith to his flock, including the potentially difficult task of harmonizing the Hebrew Scriptures with the Gospels.[22] He must also perceive the distinct needs of individuals and provide the appropriate pastoral instruction (whether it be doctrinal information, admonition, or consolation).[23] To help ensure these qualifications, the text establishes a minimum age of fifty for episcopal election and recommends that the candidate be a man of good education (though exceptions for both requirements are anticipated).[24]

After Constantine's conversion, the issue of education became increasingly important for some Christian authorities. One reason was the perception that the theological debates that had emerged in the fourth century (e.g., over Donatism and Arianism) were more dangerous than those of pre-ceding eras. Because Christian emperors often enforced theological positions as a matter of imperial policy, bishops quickly learned that one faction could be rewarded and another punished according to the ability of each to sway the emperor to its side. Also fueling the interest in higher educational standards was a shift in the demographics of believers. It was during the fourth century that a sizable percentage of the *curiales* (the landowning provincial aristocracy) first entered the Church and assumed roles among the clergy.[25] These men had the benefits of education and wealth. Not only did they use these gifts to their advantage, but many came to perceive them as indispensable prerequisites for pastoral leadership.

Men like Gregory Nazianzen and Augustine of Hippo believed that an educated clergy could not only articulate a response to the challenge of heresy but also minister more effectively to their congregations. As we will examine in chapter 3, Augustine identified rhetorical expertise as the single most important skill possessed by a Christian leader because the priest communicated doctrinal information through public speaking.[26] For him, the surest way to guarantee that the faithful would receive adequate teaching was to employ men already trained in public speaking.

Though a candidate was typically not barred by humble origins, bishops in the post-Constantinian period were increasingly drawn from the nobility, particularly the *curiales*.[27] In part, this was the natural consequence of Constantine's conversion—he enabled other members of the Roman elite to join the religion. It could also be a result of Constantine's establishment of the episcopal court system, which provided an alternative legal venue for Christians who feared persecution from pagan judges.[28] Since every bishop was required to preside over legal cases, it became necessary to consider judicial competence as a prerequisite for episcopal election. By employing the judicial talents of the *curiales,* the Church utilized the resources of the Roman administrative system. However, the extent to which the *curialis*-turned-priest was required to abandon the privileges of his noble life was a matter of debate and varied widely.

There is ample evidence of Christians trying to enforce a more rigorous asceticism on the clergy than that prescribed by 1 Timothy. This was true of both the pre- and post-Constantinian period. The *Didascalia,* for example, requires that the bishop "be scant and poor in his food and drink, that he may be able to be watchful in admonishing and correcting those who are undisciplined. And let him not be crafty and extravagant, nor luxurious, nor pleasure-loving, nor fond of dainty meats."[29]

Part of the anxiety about moral and ascetic purity stems from the perceived connection between the cleric's sanctity and his ability to bind and loose sin. It took time for catholic Christians to arrive at the conclusion that the sins of the priest should not negate the effectiveness of his sacraments. In the third century, we find uneasiness regarding the connection between a bishop's holiness and his purgative powers. The *Didascalia* posits that a bishop who fails to live up to the standards of the episcopate jeopardizes the entire community.[30] And in his *Commentary on the Gospel According to Matthew (Commentaria in Evangelium secundum Matthaeum)*, the great Alexandrian teacher Origen (d. ca. 254) casts doubt on the ability of a sinful cleric to offer effective spiritual leadership. Commenting on Peter's ability to bind and loose, Origen interprets that prerogative as belonging to anyone who is a "Peter" in the eyes of God (i.e., whoever meets the standard of Peter's faith and life).[31] Accordingly, judicial authority (i.e., the ability to punish and forgive sin) is linked to the same qualifications.[32] As Rapp observes, Origen provides for a scenario in which there are two kinds of bishops, those according to man and those according to God. There is overlap between them, but there are also bishops who ultimately lack spiritual authority.[33] The Alexandrian notes, "[A]nd if anyone who is not a Peter, and does not have the same stature as Peter, thinks that what he binds on earth will be bound in heaven, and what he looses on earth will be loosed in heaven, such a one is demented and does not understand the meaning of the Scriptures—and being demented, has fallen into the trap of the devil."[34] In short, Origen offers a tacit acknowledgment of the authority of the bishop in the Church, but he cautions that the dignity of the episcopate guarantees neither virtuous living, spiritual knowledge, nor an effective pastoral ministry. For our purposes, Origen's critique demonstrates that there was a faction within the Church (in the era preceding Constantine) that questioned the extent to which ordination guaranteed a successful pastoral ministry.

By the fourth century, the monastic communities of Egypt and elsewhere understood ascetic experience (and not ordination) to be the standard for leadership. For example, the monastic author Ammonas insisted that authority derived from ascetic progress made in isolation.[35]

This is why the holy fathers also withdrew into the desert alone, men such as Elijah the Tishbite and John the Baptist. For do not suppose that because the righteous were in the midst of men it was among men that they achieved their righteousness. Rather having first practiced much quiet, they then received the power of God dwelling in them, and then God sent them into the midst of men, having acquired every virtue, so that they might act as God's provisioners and cure men of their infirmities. For they were physicians of the soul, able to cure men's infirmities.[36]

Writing to his disciples, Ammonas hoped that they too could come to know the mysteries of the Godhead. This knowledge, however, came "only to those who had purified their hearts from every defilement and from all the vanities of the world and to those who had taken up their crosses and fortified themselves and been obedient to God in everything."[37] Consequently, only a few select leaders possessed an intimate knowledge of the divine and were therefore able to assist others.[38]

Ammonas differentiated between those who possess spiritual authority and those who do not. What distinguished Ammonas and ascetics like him from Christians living in the world was that, for him, ordination had no part in the formula of authority. In fact, he never mentions the clergy or ordination in any of his extant letters to disciples.

While ascetic experience was the most important criterion for Ammonas, like most ascetics he did not believe that it was the lone basis for spiritual leadership. Only those who had also displayed obedience and maintained a powerful prayer life were suited to lead others. Ammonas reminded his readers that he had been a disciple of St. Antony the Great. Ammonas's own rise to the rank of spiritual father was directly related to his subordination to such a holy master.[39]

Discernment (διάκρισις in Greek and *discretio* in Latin) was another marker of spiritual authority in the ascetic community. In many of his letters, Antony writes that he prays his disciples may receive the gift of discernment in order to understand better the difference between good and evil and thereby offer themselves more completely to God.[40] He also relates that he knows of men who pursued asceticism for many years but whose lack of discernment eventually led to their spiritual demise.[41] Going a step further, Ammonas identifies discernment as the spiritual gift that separates the average monk from the elder. "Now, therefore, my beloved, since you have been counted to me as children, pray both day and night that this gift of discernment may come upon you, which has not yet come upon you since you came to the ascetic way. And I too, your father, will pray for you that you may attain this stature, to which not many of the monks have come—save a few souls here and there."[42] How does one attain discernment? For both Antony and Ammonas discernment comes as a result of ascetic progress, trial, and prayer.[43] To these prerequisites, Ammonas adds isolation. "If you want to come to this measure . . . withdraw yourselves from [others] or else they will not allow you to progress."[44]

Within the various ascetic communities of late antiquity, discernment (or the discernment of spirits) was understood to comprise a variety of spiritual gifts.[45] In early texts (e.g., Origen), it involved the ability to differentiate between good and evil spirits. With time, the gift of discernment was also believed to empower a spiritual father to learn the spiritual needs of individual disciples. I will say more about discernment in the pages that follow. For now, let us note that the possession of διάκρισις was another important indicator of spiritual authority for members of the ascetic community.

The Spiritual Father and Pastoral Activities of the Ascetic Community

Within most ascetic communities of the late ancient period, a dynamic relationship existed between a spiritual father and his disciples.[46] A monk's advisor was not always the abbot of his community, and in the fourth century he was rarely ordained.[47] Both Basil of Caesarea and the Egyptian monk Pachomius, two important organizers of monastic communities, envisioned societies of lay monks that were too large for a single abbot to serve as the only spiritual counselor. They divided the responsibility of supervision among several experienced elders who worked under the watchful eye of the abbot.[48] Ideally, advisor and advisee communicated regularly; the novice confessed his sins to his mentor, while the mentor encouraged, taught, and reprimanded the novice as necessary.[49]

Although a thorough comparison is beyond the scope of the present study, the spiritual father/spiritual disciple model that became so active in the ascetic communities of late antiquity was, in many ways, informed by the traditions of teaching and the care of souls that existed in the philosophical schools of classical world. As Pierre Hadot has observed, the philosophical dialogue that occurred in the Socratic schools (and elsewhere) was designed as a "spiritual exercise" practiced for the improvement of the self.[50] In many ways, the same was true of spiritual direction in the Christian ascetic community. Though adapted in a context very different from the philosophical school, the spiritual father of the desert tradition, like the Socratic, Platonic, or Epicurean philosopher, was principally concerned with the advancement of his disciples' souls.

Naturally, in the desert Christian communities of the late antique East much of the spiritual father's instruction was concerned with the discipline of *askesis*. The *Apophthegmata Patrum* (a collection of sayings of the Syrian, Palestinian, and Egyptian elders, arranged alphabetically by their names) is predominantly concerned with the desert monk's praxis. These sayings originated as an elder's response to specific questions or circumstances. Individual monasteries or groups of monks transcribed these teachings for future generations, which eventually circulated the sayings among communities.[51] As Benedicta Ward notes, the disciples did not seek a theological axiom or a dialogue with their elders. Rather, they wanted teaching that they could apply to their life and their *askesis*.[52]

Beyond rudimentary instruction concerning renunciation, the spiritual father was believed to possess a kind of mystical teaching that could not be revealed to everyone or through texts. Ammonas notes in one of his letters that he hopes to visit his disciples so that he can share with them what he is unable to write. "When I come to you I will tell you about the Spirit of joy, and how you should obtain it. And I will show you all of its riches, which I cannot entrust to paper."[53] To receive this teaching, Ammonas instructs his readers to prepare themselves through *askesis* and prayer. To this, Ammonas will add his own prayers.[54] The spiritual rewards, the elder promises, are well worth the effort. "You will become free from every fear, and heavenly joy will overtake you; and so you will be as men already translated to the kingdom while you are still in a body and you will no longer need to pray for yourselves but for others."[55]

For many authors, an important component of the elder/disciple relationship was the absolute authority of the spiritual advisor. For example, Basil of Caesarea insisted that a monk abandon his own will and submit to his superior. He wrote: "[The novice] does not make the choice of what is good or useful, since he has irrevocably relinquished the disposal of himself to others."[56] When some of Ammonas's disciples suggested that they might move to another place, he sternly warned them that they should do nothing without his approval, noting, "[I]f you go out, acting on your own authority, God will not work together with you."[57] Identifying the spiritual father as the oracle of God's will in the life of the disciple, he added, "[D]o not go away until God permits you. I am aware what is God's will for you; but it is difficult for you to recognize the will of God. Unless a man denies himself and his own will, and obeys his spiritual parents, he will not be able to recognize God's will; and even if he does recognize it, he needs God's help in giving him the strength to carry it out."[58] In short, subordinates were not to question the instruction of their superiors, nor were they to act of their own accord. By the beginning of the seventh century, the virtue of obedience so dominated ascetic literature that John Climacus claimed that a truly obedient monk would find salvation even if his spiritual father led him into heresy.[59]

With the authority of leadership came duty and accountability. Antony frequently acknowledged his responsibility to pray for his disciples and to extend spiritual love to them.[60] Ammonas, likewise, noted that a spiritual father was expected to pray continuously for those in his care.[61] For his part, Basil warned that any spiritual father who failed to correct the vice of his disciples would pay for their sins at his own judgment.[62] With this in mind, many authors warned of the difficulty associated with spiritual direction. As we will see in chapter 2, Gregory Nazianzen concluded that spiritual direction was so difficult it was the "art of arts and science of sciences."[63]

As noted, one of the things that separated an elder from ordinary monks was the possession of discernment. For some ascetic authors such as Antony, discernment was a tool sought by a monk for his own enlightenment. In the context of spiritual direction, however, it was the key supernatural gift that enabled effective guidance. Discernment empowered the elder to recognize demons and angels and to understand the spiritual challenges of his disciples. It was believed that individual monks had specific needs.[64] According to Basil, the discerning elder would offer the precise admonition and/or instruction that could lead his disciples to salvation.[65] As we will see in chapter 5, Pope Gregory I believed that Benedict of Nursia could discern whenever one of his monks tried to deceive him. As a result, the saint was better prepared to offer the necessary spiritual medicine. Although a conception of discernment operated beyond the confines of the Christian ascetic community (e.g., it was understood differently by the Greco-Romans), in the hands of the ascetic elder it assumed an unprecedented pastoral importance.[66]

Other pastoral techniques of the ascetic community included οἰκονομία (known in Latin as *condescensio*), the internalization of the spiritual battle, and the use of the saintly exemplar. Οἰκονομία refers to a spiritual father's temporary adjustments to prescribed reprimands. By the fourth century, the Church had established fixed punishments for many specific sins, but the spiritual counselor had the authority to increase or lessen the weight of the penalty, depending on the attitude of the sinner and his ability to withstand it. The goal was to avoid a punishment that did more harm than good. To be sure, the Pauline corpus provided a basis for οἰκονομία, and it was almost certainly employed by some of the clergy, but it was in the monastic environment that its pastoral application developed most completely. For example, Basil of Caesarea established a systematic method of discipline for his monastic community at Pontus. There, an initial infraction generated a reproach; a pattern of misbehavior led to excommunication.[67] The spiritual father, however, was encouraged to season his correction of subordinates with discernment.[68] The pastoral goal of disciplinary action was to return the sinner to proper conduct. If necessary, the elder was to amend the rules, and he was expected to determine the spiritual challenges faced by his disciples, identifying the most constructive path to recovery—a path that would often require a temporary "bending" of the rules.

The spiritual contest was very much internalized in ascetic literature. The legislative enjoinders found in Scripture (e.g., do not kill, do not steal, do not commit adultery) presented a moral imperative. However, through the process of intensive self-reflection, ascetics of the fourth century began to identify sin where it had gone unnoticed in the previous age. For example, they scrutinized the vices (i.e., inner depravations that led to spiritual or physical sin) and created a catalog of spiritual antidotes for their prevention—fasting prevented gluttony, charity assuaged greed, humility protected against pride. There is evidence of these concerns as early as the letters of Antony and Ammonas, but Evagrius of Pontus's identification of eight λογοσμοί and John Cassian's transportation of these ideas to the West best characterize the ascetic's intensive analysis of personal vice and virtue.

Another expression of this interiorization of the spiritual life is heightened concern about demonic activity.[69] Recurring references to demonic activity characterize ascetic literature from the fourth century and beyond. Antony's physical battles with invisible demons and Evagrius's identification of the eight λογοσμοί with demonic assault are prime examples of the spiritual anxieties underlying ascetic literature.[70] Pastorally speaking, the identification of demonic activity reinforced the need for ascetic action. By linking hunger to the demon of gluttony or sluggishness to the demon of sloth, ascetics fostered a self-perpetuating world of spiritual conflict full of suspense and danger. The threat of demonic influence reinforced the need for self-examination, and the detection of vice or the evidence of demons reaffirmed the need for *askesis* and spiritual supervision. The elder did more than instill order and regulate abstinence. He was the only one capable of protecting the average monk from inner temptations as well as external spiritual foes.

A final example of the methods of spiritual direction in the ascetic community is that of the saintly exemplar. The circulation of ascetic sayings and *vitae* in late antiquity provided a paradigm of instruction that was easily communicated to a multitude of audiences. After a monk confessed his sins or doubts to his mentor, the elder was able to offer encouragement and/or instruction through the exemplar. The *Apophthegmata* is the best example of this, but as we will see in chapter 4, John Cassian's *Conferences (Conlationes)* functioned in a similar way. By exhorting a disciple to either a holy saying or pious act, the spiritual counselor could solve any crisis. If a monk suffered from despair, then there was an account to rebuild his confidence. If he suffered from gluttony, then there were dozens of anecdotes to scare him into temperance. These accounts provided practical spiritual advice that reinforced the ascetic imperative — the wide circulation of the lives and sayings of the saints was due, in part, to their pastoral practicality.[71]

Pastoral Activities of the Clergy

Generally speaking, the "parish" clergy of the early fourth century busied themselves with a different type of pastoral ministry that was dominated by the sacramental, doctrinal, and administrative responsibilities of their office. By this time, the sacramental roles of the clergy had been firmly established. As John Chrysostom noted near the close of the century, the priest could literally confer salvation through baptism and the Eucharist — a quality (according to Chrysostom) that placed the priest in a position superior to the angels.[72]

Also by this time, confession and penance had begun to emerge as important "sacramental" functions of the clergy.[73] Even before Constantine, the *Didascalia* provided some detail about the bishop's role in investigating, disciplining, and counseling the sinners of his community.[74] However, the text also acknowledged that the bishop was unlikely to be familiar with every lay person and consequently that the latter should use the deacons as a mediator.[75] According to the *Didascalia,* however, the deacons did not possess the ability to bind or loose sin.[76] As a result, the text did not provide for the type of intimate spiritual relationship that we find in the ascetic community between a spiritual father and his disciples. While some clerics who were unaffiliated with organized asceticism may have cultivated a relationship with members of their flock (a relationship that would have mirrored the more intensive pattern of the ascetic community), there is little evidence from our sources for such a scenario. Not until the second half of the fourth century (when men like Gregory Nazianzen, Basil of Caesarea, and John Chrysostom rose to the episcopate) do we find an endorsement of the ascetic notions of spiritual fatherhood penetrating the lay Church.

For many members and advocates of the cleric-oriented approach to spiritual direction, doctrinal instruction was the most important of the cleric's many pastoral responsibilities. The great influx of converts during the fourth century prompted the call for an articulate, well-trained clergy who could disseminate the teachings of the faith to a large and diverse audience. The priest was expected to convey the doctrinal truths of orthodox teaching to the faithful through either catechism, the public homily, or private consultations. It was not enough for the cleric to understand the tradition—he had to be able to communicate it effectively. Interestingly, every hierarch that commented on the subject during the fourth and fifth centuries bemoaned the paucity of quality preachers.

An essential component of instruction involved the proper understanding of the Scriptures. Many bishops from the fourth century onward devoted an immense amount of time to public exegesis. John Chrysostom provides an excellent example of this. Over five hundred exegetical sermons on various books of the Old and New Testaments survive, clearly demonstrating his moniker as the "golden-mouthed." At least three of our authors, Athanasius, Augustine, and Gregory I, understood the public explanation of Scripture (i.e., preaching) to be the cornerstone of a bishop's pastoral ministry. Through preaching, they hoped not only to promote an orthodox understanding of the Scriptures but also to shape Christian behavior.[77]

It was the administrative responsibilities that seem to have caused the most head-aches for the early clergy. Our sources describe with embittered detail the time and resources that clerics spent caring for the poor and sick, supervising widows and virgins, and building churches and hospitals.[78] By the close of the fourth century, these rather obvious pastoral tasks expanded to include many civic responsibilities that had been previously performed by the Roman *curiales* and other administrative officials.[79] Participating in the institution of the episcopal court was seen by many bishops to be an enormous burden.[80] Moreover, in those regions that were unsettled by the barbarian movements, the ransoming of captives and care of prisoners became important clerical roles. As we will read in chapter 5, by the close of the sixth century the papacy had become so ingrained in the civic administration of Italy that Pope Gregory I found himself arranging for lumber shipments, rebuilding the city's defenses, and negotiating with hostile forces.

Even the more traditional of the bishop's administrative concerns were likely to absorb a great amount of his attention and bring him little satisfaction for his efforts. In urban environments, providing for the poor put the bishop into the businesses of fund-raising, property management, and administration. The same was true of the care of widows, which involved both financial support and spiritual outreach. In describing the anguish that accompanied the care of widows, John Chrysostom lamented: "Widows, as a group, owing partly to their poverty, partly to their age, and partly to their gender, indulge in an uncontrolled freedom of speech (this, I think, is what I will call it). The minister must bear it all politely and not be provoked by their annoying habits or their unreasonable complaints."[81]

Although monastic and lay life would remain distinct, by the fifth century some of the pastoral traditions that had originated with the ascetic community began to take root in the broader Church. A significant change had occurred. Among the many transformations for the Christian community during the fourth century, one of the most significant was the rise of professed ascetics to positions of episcopal power. This began in the second half of the fourth century and continued to gain momentum in the fifth and sixth centuries. For our purposes, this evolution in episcopal recruitment led to a sea change in the practice of spiritual direction in the lay Church because many of these ascetics brought with them the pastoral traditions that they had learned in a monastic setting. For several generations, however, that change was inconsistent, and many authors presented competing ideas about spiritual direction. It was precisely during this period of uncertainty that some of the most influential writers developed a new genre of Christian literature to navigate the choppy waters of post-Constantinian spiritual direction.

Pastoral Literature and the Merger of the Two Traditions

The second half of the fourth century witnessed a new development in Christian writing: the pastoral treatise. Gregory Nazianzen, Ambrose of Milan, and John Chrysostom separately authored substantial treatments of the subject. Their texts defined who should and who should not receive ordination, identified the priest's practical responsibilities, and anticipated many of the priest's pastoral challenges. Each of these men fit the model of the ascetic-bishop, and each struggled to resolve the tension between ascetic idealism and the realities of pastoral ministry.[82] I believe that the pastoral treatise emerged, in part, to resolve that tension.

Unlike any that preceded it, this genre provided its authors with the opportunity to explore in detail both the criteria for authority and the techniques of spiritual leadership. It also offered its authors sufficient flexibility to maneuver between their ascetic ideals and pastoral obligations. Unlike the *Didascalia* or other Church orders, which had issued specific qualifications for leadership and precise rules concerning discipline, the pastoral treatise enabled an author to offer nuanced ideas about spiritual authority and supervision. John Chrysostom, for example, could identify ascetic experience as a prerequisite for leadership, but he could also assert that a successful ministry was not guaranteed by renunciation alone.[83] Likewise, Gregory Nazianzen could encourage his readers to moderate their correction of subordinates according to the needs of individual circumstance (something discovered through discernment).[84]

Moreover, as we will see in chapter 2, Nazianzen used the pastoral treatise to express his deepest uncertainties about his ability to balance care for his flock with his own private meditation. His solution, a middle course between pastoral service and ascetic contemplation, instituted a new paradigm for clerical leadership that eventually came to dominate spiritual direction in the Middle Ages. It was the pastoral treatise that hastened the acceptance of this model.

Not only did Gregory's ideas inform subsequent authors of pastoral treatises (especially John Chrysostom and Pope Gregory I), but the pastoral treatise became the preferred genre for authors who embraced Gregory's basic thesis to circulate their own ideas about spiritual direction.[85]

For example, we find the earliest discussions of how to combine ascetic and clerical duties in the pastoral treatise. Ambrose, bishop of Milan from 374 to 397, understood the priest's duties to include doctrinal instruction, the celebration of the sacraments, the support of the poor and widows, and the supervision of virgins. He also described the need to mentor inexperienced clerics. Referring to the ideal relationship of Joshua and Moses, Ambrose described the bond that a teacher and disciple shared, and he affirmed that spiritual authority could be transferred from the one to the other.[86] Though not fully developed, Ambrose's description of the experienced advisor was similar to the spiritual father/spiritual disciple pattern of direction that was developing in the ascetic community. The bridge between the ascetic and clerical patterns of direction was even more explicit in Nazianzen's "Apology for His Flight" and Chrysostom's *On the Priesthood (De sacerdotio)*.[87]

Although Ambrose, Nazianzen, and Chrysostom each included ascetic standards among their criteria for ordination (e.g., St. Ambrose even insisted on clerical celibacy), this first group of pastoral treatises does not show a whole-scale adoption of the ascetic model.[88] John Chrysostom, for example, continued to locate the soteriological role of the priesthood in the sacraments. And not everyone approved of the infusion of ascetic ideas into the realm of pastoral care. Many members of the clergy resisted the idea of bestowing authority solely on the basis of ascetic experience (e.g., John Chrysostom, Augustine, and Pope Siricius).[89] But the pastoral treatise gave Nazianzen and others like him (in both the East and the West) the opportunity to explore the ambivalence of their pastoral intuitions. As the wide circulation of these texts suggests, pastoral treatises provided subsequent generations of clergy with a map for making the uncertain journey from monastery to parish.

RECENT SCHOLARSHIP AND THE PRESENT STUDY

In the last few years, three impressive monographs have explored the relationship between asceticism, the episcopate, and authority in late ancient Christianity. Conrad Leyser, Andrea Sterk, and Claudia Rapp each offer insightful and provocative interpretations of authors and themes that are explored in this study. Though each targets different authors and asks different questions, collectively they seek to understand how ascetics gained and exercised authority within the Church during late antiquity. The present study focuses more precisely on the multifaceted transformation of spiritual direction that accompanied this rise of ascetics to positions of authority. However, there is some overlap between these studies and my own, and at times I offer different interpretations. As a result, a brief overview of these texts and their conclusions is in order.

The first study to appear, in 2000, was Conrad Leyser's *Authority and Asceticism from Augustine to Gregory the Great*. Focusing on the West, Leyser maintains that Augustine and John Cassian offered competing theories about the role of moral purity in the acquisition of temporal authority in that Augustine refused to grant authority to monks, while Cassian defined authority in terms of moral rectitude.[90] Leyser devotes the majority of his study to subsequent authors who forged unique syntheses from these two models, culminating in Gregory, who, according to Leyser, "was able to harness the full force of ascetic detachment to the exercise of power in the world."[91] In many ways, the collective work of Robert Markus informs Leyser's historical perspective. According to Markus, Christianity in the West underwent an "ascetic invasion" between the careers of Augustine and Gregory that led, in part, to what he calls the end of ancient Christianity.[92] Leyser supplements that thesis through his use of discourse analysis and an examination of authority through discourse. For example, scholars traditionally interpret Pope Gregory I's many protestations about his own leadership as either the ritual gesture of a civic magistrate or the authentic expression of an ascetic reluctant to take office. Leyser, however, reads Gregory's declarations as a "rhetoric of vulnerability" central to his acquisition and continued exercise of authority.[93] In effect, Leyser's Gregory secured his position by calling attention to his inadequacies. Though the questions that Leyser puts to his texts are different from my own, the reader will find (in both studies) a Gregory who can effectively bridge the gulf between Augustine and Cassian.

Andrea Sterk's *Renouncing the World yet Leading the Church: The Monk-Bishop in Late Antiquity* grew out of a dissertation on Basil of Caesarea.[94] Though she offers a careful analysis of other authors, she maintains that the model of the monastic bishop that came to dominate the Byzantine Church was the brainchild of Basil. Sterk argues that Basil's monastic *Rules (Regulae)* and his ascetic *Morals (Moralia)* provided the keys not only for ascetic discipline but for leadership. She also notes that Basil raised at least three monks to the episcopate because he believed that only the "monk-bishop" could be trusted against the dual threats of heresy and the temptation of power. Interestingly, she also asserts that whether or not Basil was truly responsible for this integration, subsequent Byzantine hagiographers and canonists believed he was, and it was this received history that shaped later Byzantine notions of the episcopate.

Claudia Rapp's impressive monograph *Holy Bishops in Late Antiquity: The Nature of Christian Leadership in an Age of Transition* provides an excellent point of departure for my own study. She explores how three distinct types of authority (pragmatic, spiritual, and ascetic) coalesce in the episcopate in the late ancient Christian East. She argues that by the middle of the sixth century the episcopate in the East became more engaged with pragmatic (i.e., civic) authority than ascetic; consequently, she maintains, this led to both the increasing identification of Church with empire and the patronage of a bishop over his city.[95] Leading to that conclusion, however, she demonstrates that men of very different backgrounds were able to exercise authority in both the Church and the *polis*. And she cautions that we should not haphazardly oppose monks to bishops—not only did bishops have access to ascetic authority, but many monks became clerics. It is in this nebulous world of the monk-bishop that the present study explores the transformation of spiritual direction. In other words, it seeks to answer how ascetics who came to wield episcopal authority resolved the tension between their ascetic idealism and the realities they faced in ministering to the laity.

The chapters that follow explore the career and pastoral ideas of five influential Christian authorities of the early Church. Each chapter begins with a brief overview of the subject's life. Each chapter then examines the individual's criteria for spiritual authority and (where the evidence permits) his advice for subordinate ministers and his own methods of spiritual direction. As we will see, these authors drew differently from the ascetic and clerical traditions that they knew. They were not the only individuals to shape the pastoral traditions of the subsequent era; however, in selecting them, I strove to identify specific authors who not only cast a long shadow into the Middle Ages but also made an original contribution to the history of spiritual direction.[96]

To be sure, some readers will question my selection of authors. Why, for example, did I choose Nazianzen instead of Basil of Caesarea? Why did I not include John Chrysostom or Caesarius of Arles?[97] I hope that the reasons for selecting these five will become evident in the pages that follow. And like every scholar I hope that my work will, in some small way, inspire others to correct, complete, or improve upon my observations.

Athanasius of Alexandria and Ambivalence Regarding Spiritual Direction

The date of Athanasius's birth is in dispute. Although tradition puts it in 295, there is reason to believe that it was 299.[1] We know little about his life prior to his service in the clergy.[2] A popular account, first promoted by Gelasius of Caesarea, posits that Alexander (bishop of Alexandria from 313 to 328) stumbled across a boy on the beach playing bishop (he was baptizing a friend). Impressed, Alexander took the young Athanasius into his house and provided for his education. According to this tradition, Athanasius displayed considerable skill, and, when he was old enough, Alexander ordained him to the deaconate.[3] There is some circumstantial evidence to support this tale. For example, independent accounts recognize that Athanasius was not a man of wealth,[4] and some recent commentators have revised earlier, more generous, evaluations of his education.[5]

Upon his ordination, Athanasius became Alexander's trusted assistant. He took an active role in Alexander's administration and accompanied his bishop to the Council of Nicea in 325.[6] Among other things, the council addressed two Egyptian problems: the Melitian schism and the Arian heresy. With respect to the Melitians, the delegates adopted what many thought to be an adequate compromise.[7] The Arian deliberations were more complicated, but in the end the council denounced Arius and his supporters and affirmed the single essence (ὁμοιούσιος) of Father and Son. As a deacon, Athanasius would not have been part of the official deliberations. Nevertheless, he may well have been active, and, with time, many hagiographers extolled his contribution.

The council did not put an end to either the Melitian or the Arian questions. In fact, when Alexander died in April of 328, Athanasius was in Constantinople offering Alexander's objection to Constantine's order that Arius be readmitted to communion.[8] Athanasius returned to Alexandria and was shortly elevated to the see. The ancient sources, as well as the modern, differ in their descriptions of the election.[9] Athanasius was Alexander's chosen successor, but that does not seem to have prevented the Melitians or the Arians from trying to capitalize on his absence at the time of Alexander's death. The details of the controversy should not detain us here, but it is important to note that Athanasius's elevation was not without intrigue and lasting consequences.

The election was just the beginning of Athanasius's difficulties. At the outset of his episcopate, he faced a two-front war: against Arius's supporters throughout the empire and against the Melitians at home.[10] Unfortunately for Athanasius, Eusebius of Nicomedia forged an alliance between the two groups in the summer of 330, which led to Athanasius's first exile in 335.[11] Though Athanasius returned in 337, his stay was brief. His continued resistance to imperial policy concerning the Arians led to a second exile that lasted from 339 to 346.[12] Athanasius entered a self-imposed third exile in February of 356 when he fled imperial troops charged with his capture. By that time, the bishop had greater support in the city and the countryside. For several years, Athanasius moved secretly between the monastic settlements in Lower and Upper Egypt, appearing occasionally in Alexandria itself. Until the death of the Emperor Constantius in 362, however, Athanasius was very much a man with a price on his head.[13] The pagan Julian succeeded Constantius, and he too exiled Athanasius in 363.[14] But Julian's quick death a few months later guaranteed this to be a short interruption of Athanasius's activity. The aging bishop was forced into hiding a final time in the fall of 365. This too proved to be a brief hiatus, owing in large part to the vicissitudes of imperial politics.[15] Athanasius returned in February of 366 and spent his remaining years administering to his diocese. He died on May 2, 373.

The complicated details of Athanasius's tumultuous tenure as bishop have been effectively documented elsewhere. For our purposes, it is sufficient to note the tenuous circumstances in which Athanasius operated. It is little wonder that his corpus lacked a developed pastoral strategy—so little in Athanasius's life was static. What is certain, and of considerable importance to this study, is that Athanasius increasingly turned to the ascetic community for protection during his bouts with imperial and heretical foes. There his pastoral, theological, and political concerns converged.

Athanasius's own experience with asceticism was different from St. Antony's, whose eremitic life the bishop popularized in his famous *Life of Antony (Vita Antonii)*.[16] As a young man, Athanasius adopted an urban form of asceticism and, in all likelihood, knew little of the desert tradition before his elevation to the episcopate.[17] Thus Athanasius's ascetic experience would have been like that of many of the male solitaries living in and around Alexandria. He would have performed many of the renunciatory practices of Christian ascetics (e.g., prayer, fasting, chastity, almsgiving, and vigils), and he would have been active in parish life. When he became bishop, he probably came into increased contact with the female ascetics of the city. Like other fourth-century bishops, he had the responsibility of seeing to their spiritual and economic well-being.

By the middle of Athanasius's tenure in Alexandria, the ascetics in the desert outnumbered those in the cities. Whether they were in the cenobitic communities (like those of the Pachomian federation) or whether they preferred to practice their asceticism in relative isolation (like Antony or Ammonas), these renunciants were distinct from their urban counterparts in a number of ways. For example, they maintained their own churches, separate from married Christians. Though many of these monks (particularly the Pachomians) did have dealings with those "in the world," they generally did not worship with them. What is more, prior to Athanasius's tenure, the monks of the Egyptian desert were essentially free of episcopal oversight. According to David Brakke, Athanasius's survival depended upon his bringing these groups "into a formal relationship with his episcopal organization and hence at least somewhat under his control."[18]

There is little doubt that Athanasius directed a great amount of his attention to the ascetics (both urban and rural). There are, however, multiple ways to interpret this fact. Whereas Brakke reads political and theological maneuvering in Athanasius's activity, Kannengiesser finds devotion to the ascetic ideal. Indeed, Kannengiesser referred to the bishop of Alexandria as "the first authority in the Christian church who recognized the importance of monasticism for the Christian way of life."[19] This chapter will, in part, explore the extent to which Athanasius's various interactions with different ascetic groups informed his pastoral policies.

Before we begin that discussion, however, let us say a few words about Athanasius the theologian. Much has been made in recent years of Athanasius as politician and as ascetic. However, one might argue that his dramatic (and at times obstinate) behavior was, in many ways, a consequence of a determined and consistent theological vision. In perhaps his most important theological work, *On the Incarnation (De incarnatione),* Athanasius maintained that "God became man so that man might become God."[20] According to Athanasius, human nature, like creation itself, is good.[21] Through the Incarnation, the λόγος restores the possibility of the divine-human communion that was blocked by Adam's fall.[22] But concomitant with the grace afforded by the λόγος, it is necessary for humanity to participate in the process of salvation.[23] Thus, for Athanasius, free will contributes to the ongoing relationship between the individual and God.[24]

As he noted in his *Against the Gentiles (Contra gentiles),* Athanasius believed that Christians participate in their salvation by "holding on to the grace of the Giver."[25] Specifically, he thought that renunciation and ascetic discipline offered Christians (both married and monastic alike) the best opportunity to meet the responsibilities of their freedom. In fact, he held that an individual's salvation was, in part, dependent upon his or her adoption of ascetic practices.[26] Therefore, because humanity was required to participate in its salvation, it was incumbent upon the spiritual director (most especially the bishop) to assist his subordinates through instruction and example. As we will see, the bishop of Alexandria was one of the first to perceive his pastoral responsibilities to include inspiring (even demanding) ascetic behavior from those in his care.

CRITERIA FOR SPIRITUAL AUTHORITY

There is ambivalence in Athanasius's corpus with respect to the criteria for spiritual authority. On the one hand, his biography of Antony suggests that the saint's greatness (and therefore his authority in pastoral matters) derived from his ascetic accomplishments. On the other hand, the bishop of Alexandria often identifies the (Nicene) episcopacy as the lone source of biblical and doctrinal interpretation. In short, Athanasius presents two sets of criteria for spiritual authority: one ascetic, the other clerical.

Athanasius's biography of St. Antony reflects this ambivalence. At its core, the *vita* tells the story of a man who attempts to act upon the Gospel passage "If you wish to be perfect, go sell all that you have, and come follow me."[27] According to Athanasius, Antony sells his inheritance, provides for his sister, and then takes to the desert.[28] Antony begins his life of asceticism under the direction of a group of hermits living on the outskirts of his hometown. "He observed the graciousness of one, the unceasing prayer of another; was attentive of another's passivity and another's love for humanity."[29] Antony learns and cultivates a different aspect of the ascetic life from each of his teachers.[30] Notably, none of these spiritual gurus appears to have been a member of the clergy.

As Antony progresses in the ascetic life, the devil attempts to derail him.[31] And with the completion of his training (some twenty years in the making) Antony emerges as a triumphant ascetic, superior to the demons, and capable of leading disciples to similar spiritual heights. "As from a shrine, Antony came forth initiated in the mysteries and inspired [by the Holy Spirit]. . . . [T]hrough him the Lord healed the bodily suffering of many who came to him and [for others] he cast out demons. Moreover, he graced Antony's speech, so that he consoled many that were sorrowful and those at odds he made friends, exhorting all to prefer the love of Christ to the things of the world."[32] Antony's spiritual skill is comprehensive: he commands wild animals, scatters demons, and, most important, discerns the spiritual needs of his disciples.[33]

Antony's spiritual authority is shown to be derived from his ascetic accomplishments (both control of the body and victory over the demons). His chastity, poverty, and extreme fasting are, for the most part, taken for granted. Athanasius describes, in detail, the saint's ability to go without sleep, his physical battles with incorporeal demons, and his almost unbroken contemplation of God. And it is significant that Antony does not assume the role of spiritual father until he completes his twenty-year battle with the demons.

Yet despite Antony's spiritual greatness, or perhaps as an example of it, the saint ultimately submits to the authority of the bishop. Near the end of the *vita,* Athanasius articulates Antony's impression of the clergy: "[A]lthough this is who he was, Antony observed the canons of the Church rigorously and insisted that all of the clergy [κληρικόν] be honored before himself. For he was not ashamed to bow his head to bishops and presbyters, and if ever a deacon came to him for assistance, he spoke with him about what was useful but then took his place at the time of prayer, unashamed to learn himself."[34] In other words, we have the most famous of the eremitic saints, an obvious authority in spiritual matters, subordinating himself to the clergy.[35] It is, of course, possible to read into this account. Brakke, for example, has argued that the *vita* is not a historical witness but rather a literary construction designed to promote Athanasius's political and theological agendas.[36] According to Brakke, a significant purpose of the creation of this "alternate reality" was the depiction of Antony in a way that would garner the support of the monastic community.[37] It is also possible, however, that the *vita* accurately reflects Antony's humility—a virtue prized among the desert saints.

Further complicating our assessment of Antony is the extent to which Athanasius portrays him as a teacher—currently a question of some scholarly debate. Brakke maintains that he emphasizes Antony as an exemplar rather than as a teacher because the bishop of Alexandria remains suspicious of any type of academic teacher whose credentials are based upon learning (especially classical learning).[38] Rousseau has recently challenged that interpretation, suggesting that the author of the *vita* often portrays Antony as a type of ascetic teacher who imparts his knowledge of the faith to his disciples.[39] Rousseau appears to be correct when he concludes that Athanasius's authorship of the *vita* requires a reading of Athanasius that is more ambivalent about ascetic leadership as a source of authority. Indeed, the text is ultimately unclear about the extent of Antony's authority in the Church at large.[40]

Athanasius's ambivalence concerning the criteria for spiritual authority is telling. On the one hand, the bishop of Alexandria acknowledges Antony's ascetic experience to be a legitimate source of authority. The saint not only successfully leads his disciples to a higher spiritual plane but even serves as a teacher of the laity and clergy. At the same time, Athanasius seems to exploit the monastic virtue of humility in a way that subordinates Antony (and by extension all ascetics) to the clergy. To be certain, the competition between bishops and ascetics for authority was a very real issue at the time of Athanasius's writing. As a bishop who was predisposed to the ascetic life, Athanasius found himself tethered between two competing models. There simply were no easy answers—the many layers in the *Life of Antony* reveal an ambivalence that Athanasius personally felt.

Like the *Life of Antony,* Athanasius's correspondence reflects a tension between an ascetic and a nonascetic criterion for pastoral leadership. Though he typically respected the ascetic community's pastoral operations, on occasion Athanasius corrected the teaching of monastic leaders who he felt were ill informed about certain issues.[41] And he consistently defended the authority of the orthodox clergy. Interestingly, the correspondence also demonstrates the bishop's numerous attempts to recruit experienced ascetics for the Egyptian episcopacy.

Athanasius's epistle to Dracontius is particularly illuminating. Dracontius had been an abbot, most likely at Nitria, when he was elevated to the episcopacy in 353.[42] The election did not sit well with his former colleagues, who, in turn, warned Dracontius that as a bishop he would lose the many spiritual benefits of the ascetic life. Heeding their counsel, Dracontius refused his office and returned to his monks.[43] Athanasius's letter, written in 354, relates his disappointment: "[B]eloved Dracontius, you have brought us grief instead of joy, moaning instead of consolation; we expected to have you with us as a consolation, but now we see that you have fled."[44]

Of Athanasius's many arguments to persuade Dracontius, some of the most telling are those that detail the relationship between the clergy and the sacraments. "If everyone were of the same opinion as those advising you, how would you have become a Christian, since there would have been no bishops? Or if our successors share this opinion, how will the Church be able to sustain itself? Or do your advisers disdain [ordination] and think that you have received nothing? If so, such an opinion is fraudulent. Next they will think that the grace of baptism is nothing if they despise this."[45] Two issues are at stake. First, the sacrament of baptism unites all members of the Church. Because only the clergy can perform the sacraments, Athanasius reasons, the Church would disintegrate if every worthy candidate ignored his obligation. Second, Dracontius has received God's grace through ordination; if he turns back he risks not only his own salvation but also that of his flock. By binding the Church through the sacramental rites, Athanasius establishes the clergy as the principal agents of God's grace and authority on earth. Simply put, without the clergy there is no Church.

But at the same time, Athanasius appears determined to raise as many ascetics to the episcopacy as possible. He reminds Dracontius, "[Y]ou are not the only one who has been selected from the monastic rank, nor the only one to have presided over a monastery."[46] Ammonias, Serapion, Apollos, Agathon, Muitus, and Paul (all ascetics) dutifully accepted the responsibilities of the episcopate—Dracontius should be no different.[47] Eventually Dracontius conceded, and studies of the Egyptian episcopacy suggest that by the fifth century nearly every bishop in Egypt came from an ascetic background.[48] If this letter suggests any resolution to the ambivalence of Athanasius's position, it is that authority resides with the clergy (by virtue of their ordination) but that ascetics are the most qualified to assume the priesthood.

There are at least two reasons that the bishop of Alexandria would have selected ascetics to fill the pastoral void. As an ascetic, Athanasius probably believed that the life of renunciation well prepared a candidate for the ministry. In his twenty-fourth festal letter, the bishop declared: "[F]or a just father raises his children well when he carefully instructs others in accordance with his own virtuous conduct, so that when he encounters opposition, he may not be ashamed to hear, 'You who teach others can you not teach yourself [cf. Rom. 2.21],' but rather, like the good servant, may both save himself and gain others."[49] It is possible that by the 350s monasticism was the primary setting in which younger men were mentored by advanced Christians, and Athanasius may have believed that the "best and brightest" of Egyptian Christians no longer went to the catechetical schools of Alexandria but rather into the desert. In fact, it is unlikely that those schools even continued to exist. With all of their diversity, the monastic experiments that were thriving during Athanasius's tenure probably became (in his eyes) the logical place to recruit the Church's leaders. Though later authors (especially Gregory the Great) would be more explicit about their desire to recruit ascetics for the clergy, there is little reason to doubt Athanasius's faith in the value of ascetic experience.

A second explanation, the one that has found the most interest among scholars, is that of political and theological necessity. In the epistle to Dracontius, Athanasius remarks, "[E]ven if you are weak you should still accept the responsibility; otherwise enemies will use your flight as an opportunity to harm the Church, which would be left unprotected."[50] Though obscured by other more developed arguments, Athanasius's aside exposes the anxieties of the orthodox community in Alexandria.[51] Indeed, the See of Hermupolis Parva had a history of doctrinal infighting and was, for a time, occupied by the Melitians.[52] Athanasius complained that schismatic groups were appointing clergy in sees that were not their own.[53] And it is possible that his rivals were themselves recruiting candidates from local monasteries.[54] Regardless, the bishop of Alexandria struggled to rally the monastic community to his side against the Melitians and to place his allies in influential positions within the Egyptian hierarchy. When Dracontius did finally submit, he helped to establish a permanent link between the Alexandrian clergy and the monks of Nitria.[55]

Though seemingly innocuous, the Dracontius affair represents a profound shift in the history of Christian leadership. As other studies have documented, professional ascetics assumed clerical positions for the first time during the fourth century.[56] During subsequent centuries, the percentage of clerics who came from ascetic or monastic communities increased significantly.[57] Athanasius's recruitment of Dracontius and his colleagues does, in part, resolve the apparent inconsistencies in Athanasius's corpus with respect to the criteria for authority, but it created a serious pastoral problem for those who accepted his offer. How was Dracontius to administer his diocese? Did Athanasius expect him to impose a monastic regimen on everyone under his care? Did the laity accept him or spurn him? In many ways, Dracontius symbolizes the tenuous position of many ascetics who entered the clergy in the fourth, fifth, and sixth centuries. As we will see in the next chapter, Gregory Nazianzen imitated Dracontius's flight and return with remarkable exactness.

At this point we should say a little more about Athanasius's theological debates and the extent to which his confrontations with schismatic groups affected his policies with respect to spiritual leadership. There is little doubt that the most important criterion for authority in Athanasius's clergy was conformity to his version of orthodox Christianity. In Festal Letter 19, Athanasius suggests that the difference between saints and sinners is the knowledge of the true faith.[58] For Athanasius, one obtained this knowledge not through intellectual study but through obedience to the Lord and his appointed teachers.[59]

Despite his heightened concern about heresy, Athanasius was willing to allow some Arian clergy to retain their rank upon an orthodox confession of faith.[60] When Constantius died in 362, the pro-Nicene bishops in exile were allowed to return to their sees. Subsequently, Athanasius and his supporters convened a synod in Alexandria to determine what measures would be taken against Arian clerics. According to Athanasius, the provocateurs of heresy could be returned to communion, but only if they would forfeit their rank. Those who had fallen away "not deliberately but by violence and necessity" not only would receive pardon but could maintain their clerical standing.[61] Athanasius explained to Rufinianus the twofold logic of this decision. First, the situation required tolerance—in other words, a pastoral concession. Second, by employing otherwise perfectly acceptable candidates, the Church would not have to raise unqualified candidates to the ranks of the clergy.[62]

What was Athanasius's definition of a "qualified" candidate? Unlike Augustine, John Cassian, or Gregory the Great, Athanasius never defined in clear terms his criteria for pastoral leadership. The *Life of Antony* suggests that ascetic experience was the source of that saint's authority. But could that apply to anyone? When Athanasius extolled Antony's skills, he no doubt earned the respect of the ascetic community. But back in Alexandria, Athanasius argued that his own authority and that of his allies derived from the grace of the priesthood and that they preserved that grace through their continued support of Nicene Christianity. We know that Athanasius raised a number of monks to episcopal rank; yet we do not have sufficient evidence to determine whether Athanasius believed that the pool for episcopal candidates was to be drawn exclusively from the ascetic community. In fact, it is unlikely that Athanasius would have thought in terms of an ascetic versus nonascetic criterion for ordination. Unlike many Christian leaders of subsequent generations, he did not distinguish between ascetic and nonascetic Christians; indeed, theirs was a difference of degree, not kind. Athanasius did what he could to promote to the clergy those individuals who would contribute the most to his political, theological, and pastoral initiatives, including former Arian clerics. In many cases, this meant recruiting professional ascetics from the Egyptian desert.

IDEALS OF SPIRITUAL DIRECTION

Unlike some of the other authors surveyed in this study, Athanasius never produced a treatise on spiritual direction. Nevertheless, we are able to draw some general conclusions about his interest in the subject from his extensive corpus. Indeed, Athanasius reveals his pastoral agenda implicitly through his portrayal of Antony and his directives to those in positions of authority and explicitly through his own pastoral interaction with lay and ascetic subordinates.

The Example of Antony

Athanasius's rendering of Antony posits a man in complete control of the ascetic and spiritual formation of his disciples. In part, Antony instructs through example. He also speaks directly to his disciples, cautioning his followers about the temptations of demons and the deception of heretics. As an experienced mentor, Antony speaks of general themes when preaching to large audiences and specifically when advising an individual disciple with unique needs.

As noted, Antony spent approximately twenty years in ascetic solitude before he took on spiritual disciples.[63] According to Athanasius, Antony's pastoral skill derived from his many years of purgation. Thus Athanasius, through the example of Antony, relays that renunciation is a prerequisite for successful leadership.[64]

Although the *vita* reveals little of Antony's personal consultations with individual disciples, chapters 16 to 43 (nearly one-third of the entire text) contain a lengthy address by Antony to his followers. We might describe this oration as a how-to manual for the ascetic life. Through the voice of Antony, Athanasius presents an example of pastoral instruction. The purpose of the speech is to enable the spiritual growth of the audience. Antony encourages progress in renunciation,[65] cautions against the vices,[66] institutes mechanisms to avoid sin,[67] and offers several strategies for combating the devil and his demons.[68] According to Athanasius, the message has a dramatic effect on its audience:

> As Antony was saying these things, everyone rejoiced; for in some the love of virtue increased, for others contempt was rejected, for still others arrogance ended, and all were persuaded to despise demonic assaults. Moreover, everyone marveled at the grace given to Antony by the Lord for the discerning of spirits. And so their monastery was in the mountains, like a tabernacle filled with holy men who sang psalms, loved reading, fasted, prayed, rejoiced in the hope of things to come, labored for the benefit of the poor, and preserved love and harmony with one another.[69]

The importance of this passage is not its historical reliability but the spiritual potency that Athanasius attributes to Antony's sermon. Antony speaks with divine authority, and his words directly improve the spiritual condition of those in his audience — the τέλος of spiritual direction.[70] By detailing Antony's spiritual potency, the Alexandrian bishop simultaneously legitimizes the ascetic vocation and obligates other spiritual directors to follow Antony's ascetic example.

Athanasius's presentation of Antony in this excerpt may have been informed by Paul's reference in 1 Corinthians to his own willingness to become "all things to all people." As Clarence Glad has shown, Paul's adaptability not only was an important strategy for conversion but also was consistent with contemporary Greco-Roman models of teaching.[71] Similarly, Athanasius's Antony can address the needs of each of his individual disciples. But Antony's pastoral skill is, in a sense, superior to Paul's self-presentation in 1 Corinthians because Antony can actually administer a multitude of spiritual tonics in a single address. He doesn't have to offer individual guidance (though in a later passage it is suggested that he does): every listener is able to gain what he needs from Antony's sermon.

The text contains additional examples of Antony's pastoral prowess such as the inspired advice he gives to those who seek his counsel as well as the many miracles he performs for the benefit of individuals.[72] But Athanasius's Antony is also, perhaps surprisingly, concerned about doctrinal conformity: "And he was a wonder in his faith and piety, for he was never in communion with the Melitian schismatics, knowing, from the start, their wickedness and apostasy. And with the Manicheans and all other heretics he did not extend any friendship, or, if he did, only enough to tell them that they should return to piety. . . . Likewise, he hated the heresy of the Arians and instructed all to avoid them and their fraudulent faith."[73] Again, the importance of this passage is not its historical reliability but rather the image of spiritual leadership that Athanasius constructs through his account of Antony.[74] All good spiritual fathers, Athanasius implies, refuse communion with heretics and advise their disciples to do the same. In short, Athanasius's theological and ascetic vision is promoted by Antony's example of asceticism.[75]

The audience of the *Life of Antony* was ascetic. In the preface to the text, Athanasius declares that he has written the *vita* at the request of the ascetic community so that they may better emulate the great Antony. Therefore, it should come as little surprise that the bishop endorsed the ascetic character of Antony's pastoral activity.[76] But did he advocate the same vision of spiritual direction elsewhere? Is this ascetic model consistent with Athanasius's recommendations to other spiritual leaders, especially clerics?

The Example of Paul

In Festal Letter 11 (written in 339), Athanasius exhorts himself and his fellow ministers to follow the example of St. Paul. Describing the saint's character, he notes that the apostle possessed each of the virtues and was spotless before the Lord—whereupon he was taken to the third heaven (see 2 Cor. 12:4).[77] Yet Paul suffered mightily at the hands of his enemies and agonized over unrepentant members of his flock.[78] Emphasizing these points, Athanasius insists that it is not enough to practice virtue; the true minister is the one who suffers with his flock for their salvation.[79]

Using Paul as his model, Athanasius also shows that the successful minister is the one who responds to the precise needs of his followers.

> Some [Christians] he reproved angrily, as in the case of the Corinthians and Galatians. To others, he offered advice, such as the Colossians and Thessalonians. He approved of the Philippians and rejoiced in them. He instructed the Hebrews that the Law was a shadow. But as for his elect sons, Timothy and Titus, he trained them when they were near, and he prayed for them when they were far away. For he was all things to all people. And being himself perfect, he was able to adapt his teaching to the need of every one, so that by all means he might save some of them.[80]

In short, Athanasius indicates that spiritual direction should be modified to the needs of the individual. Though he did not invent this concept (it is pre-Christian) or develop it as fully as subsequent Christian authors, he seems to appreciate the intrinsic difficulty of spiritual supervision.[81] Not only does he acknowledge that one message will not suit all listeners, but he concedes that it is impossible to save everyone.

After recognizing the importance of individualized care, the bishop of Alexandria goes on to identify, in order, the chief responsibilities of the minister: "[St. Paul] believed that it was first necessary to instruct [the people] concerning Christ and his mystery and then later to show how one integrates

this teaching with one's way of life. This was done so that when they came
to know the Lord, they might desire to do those things that he ordered. For,
indeed, when the author of the law is unknown, none are able to accept it."[82]
The emphasis on theology is significant. The bishop of Alexandria declares
that doctrinal conformity is more important than virtuous behavior. Given the
context of the letter, it is not surprising that he focuses on doctrinal issues (he
was driven from his see by Arians). But by establishing theological instruction
as the most important of the pastoral responsibilities, the festal letter offers
a different emphasis from that of the *Life of Antony*.[83]

Additional Responsibilities of Spiritual Direction

Athanasius's more personal letters (to both ascetic leaders and the clergy)
contain other recommendations about the responsibilities of spiritual leadership. He exhorts Dracontius that the Lord's ministers must be willing to
sacrifice their own contemplation for the good of the flock.[84] Otherwise they
will be punished for withholding what they should have offered.

Scriptural instruction is equally important. Athanasius admonishes the
ascetic leader Ammoun: "[S]trengthen, father, the flocks under you, encouraging them with the apostolic [writings], leading them with the Gospels, counseling them with the Psalms."[85] The responsibility for scriptural instruction
was also a part of Athanasius's rebuke of Dracontius. When Dracontius
fled, he left his community with no one to interpret the Scriptures for them.
Athanasius warns, "[T]he laity expect you to bring them food, which is understood to mean the teaching of the Scriptures. As such, they expect to be
fed, but remain hungry because you feed only yourself. And then when our
Lord Jesus Christ comes and we stand before him, what excuse will you give
when he sees that his own sheep were starved for nourishment?"[86] Athanasius exhorts both Ammoun and Dracontius to interpret Scripture for their
flock. But elsewhere he insisted that Ammoun (and other ascetics) adopt his
own (i.e., Athanasius's) interpretation of key passages.[87]

Another pastoral technique present in the correspondence is οἰκονομία.[88]
As previously noted, Athanasius maintained that some less culpable Arian
clergy who came around to the Nicene position should retain their rank
upon a confession of faith.[89] This not only displayed the benevolence of the
Nicene Church but hastened the adoption of the true faith by preventing despair among the penitent. Though the exercise of economy would develop

considerably in the years to come, particularly in the spiritual father/spiritual disciple relationship, Athanasius happily employed its principles to heal the schisms that divided the Church, and he encouraged others to do the same.

SPIRITUAL MENTORING AND THE ASCETIC COMMUNITY

Bridging the gap between Athanasius's advice to other pastoral leaders and his own supervision of the laity, we turn to the vicissitudes of Athanasius's supervision of the ascetic community. As bishop of Alexandria, Athanasius understood himself to be the ultimate spiritual authority of Egyptian Christians, whether rural or urban, monastic or lay. For some ascetics, especially the Alexandrian virgins, Athanasius took an active role in their spiritual formation; for others, he relegated most pastoral responsibilities to the leaders of their community.

The ascetic community in Egypt experienced rapid growth during the fourth century. These men and women had much to offer the Church, but they were also a cause for concern. It was difficult for an urban bishop to exert any real authority over the majority of Egyptian ascetics who lived beyond the traditional, physical boundaries of the diocese. Moreover, monastic leaders, by virtue of their ascetic prestige, could establish themselves as spiritual rivals to bishops who were very much engaged in the world.

During Athanasius's tenure in Alexandria, the potential for discord became amplified by the threat of heresy. Because ascetics were generally more concerned with praxis than doctrine, Athanasius took it upon himself to make routine trips to the desert to ensure that the monks were free of Melitian and Arian errors. As Brakke aptly notes, "[T]he bishop's ultimate goal was to link ascetic Christians with the Orthodox episcopate and, when necessary, to detach them from competing Christian groups."[90] To be sure, Athanasius's pastoral involvement encompassed more than the teaching of orthodox doctrine, but, as we will see, that served as the core of his approach to both male and female ascetics.

Male Ascetics

When Athanasius wrote to Ammoun, the founder of the ascetic community at Nitria, he addressed him as "father" (πάτερ) and "elder beloved of God" (ὦ πρεσβῦτα θεοφιλέστατε).[91] In doing so, Athanasius employed the terminology of the ascetic community to recognize Ammoun's authority.[92] What is more, the bishop's enjoinder to "strengthen the flock under you" was an acknowledgment of Ammoun's position within his community.[93] We can assume from this and other evidence (e.g., the *Life of Antony*) that Athanasius respected the spiritual father/spiritual disciple model that was active in the ascetic community. Yet Athanasius's corpus is rather ambiguous concerning the supervision of the male ascetics. Though Athanasius acknowledged the spiritual authority of ascetic giants like Antony, Pachomius, and Ammoun, he also on occasion interrupted the instruction of spiritual disciples by their spiritual father—and when he did he brought to bear the full weight of his office. We might classify these "intrusions" in three categories: questions of doctrine, questions of practice, and questions of succession.

As noted, Athanasius's depiction of Antony as an ardent supporter of Nicene Christianity had political as well as theological implications. However, what some scholars of late antiquity have overlooked is the extent to which this portrayal of Antony also contains a pastoral element. To the extent that Athanasius believed that orthodoxy was a prerequisite for the Christian's salvation, his interest in doctrinal formation was pastoral. Indeed, by emphasizing Antony's orthodoxy, Athanasius informs the theological convictions of his readers. In other words, he plays a role in the spiritual development of the readers of Antony's *vita*. Athanasius did not limit his activity to subtle representations of Antony but actively promoted Nicene Christianity among the Egyptian ascetics.

Athanasius twice wrote open letters to the monks at Nitria who had protected him during his third exile (356–62).[94] In the first of these letters, he describes the Arians as "madmen" utterly deprived of the truth.[95] He goes on to promote the Nicene position using apophatic theology (a negative approach that describes only what God is not). The technique was well received in the ascetic community of the East because it rejected intellectualism and promoted mysticism.[96] Specifically, this approach to theology allowed Athanasius to distinguish the orthodox faithful from their rivals: Nicenes were careful and guarded; Arians were reckless and prideful. The bishop simultaneously disparaged his adversaries and encouraged his readers to forego intellectualism for the cultivation of piety.[97]

In his second letter to the monks, Athanasius warns his readers to avoid all contact with Arians.[98] It is not enough, he insists, to hold true to the Nicene faith; one must also avoid any contact with the enemies of Christ (i.e., the Arians).[99] This injunction is similar to the one put into the mouth of Antony in the *vita,* and it would have conflicted with the monastic virtue of hospitality.[100] Though hospitality was expected of all monks, the bishop of Alexandria worried that a monk, while entertaining a guest, would be likely to lower his guard. This relaxation, Athanasius maintained, could give rise to scandal, which could lead someone else into sin. "For when anyone sees you, the faithful in Christ, associate and communicate with such people, or worship beside them, they will think such interaction is acceptable and will fall into the trap of irreligion."[101] Athanasius sought to isolate the Arians; once they were isolated, he hoped to vanquish them.

In his letter to Ammoun, Athanasius's theological assertions blur the line between *orthodoxia* and *orthopraxia* (i.e., between doctrine and practice). Athanasius questions two monastic teachings in particular: that nocturnal emissions are a source of guilt and that marriage is sinful. The bishop of Alexandria presents his own answers to these questions and expects compliance from Ammoun and his disciples.

With respect to nocturnal emissions, Athanasius follows the medical authors of his day by understanding them to be a natural disposal of excess fluid.[102] Athanasius maintains that humans, as creatures of God, are innocent. Consequently, there is no sin associated with the natural activity of the body.[103] Members of Ammoun's community, and perhaps Ammoun himself, however, held otherwise. They believed that all ejaculations were sinful and reflected an impure soul. To counter such arguments, Athanasius defines sin as an act of will. Because nocturnal emissions occur contrary to will, he reasons, they are innocent.[104] To strengthen his case, Athanasius employs the Scriptures (whose correct interpretation remains in the possession of the episcopacy), especially Matthew 15:10–20: "[I]t is not what enters the mouth that defiles the man but what goes out."[105] Alternative interpretations, the bishop interjects, derive from ignorance and lack stability. According to Athanasius, the matter "is not open to question."[106]

We know from other sources that nocturnal emissions generated considerable anxiety for late antique ascetics. John Cassian, for example, alludes to them a number of times in his *Conferences* before offering a detailed analysis in the twenty-second conference.[107] Cassian's interpretation is more moderate. Without giving way to the antimaterialist tendency that may have prevailed at Nitria, Cassian nevertheless offers a more nuanced response than

Athanasius's somewhat offhand dismissal of the matter. In short, he believes that nocturnal emissions can have one of three causes: a natural secretion of the body; a guilty soul; or the devil's agitation. Indeed, Cassian shows a greater appreciation for the spiritual anxiety that this generated for ascetic communities. One recent commentator has suggested that Athanasius's response lacked a "pastoral" awareness.[108]

The second issue raised in the letter to Ammoun is that of marriage. As elsewhere in his corpus, Athanasius defines marriage as good, though less good than virginity.[109] Concomitantly, he maintains that sexual activity is not sinful so long as it used for the benefit of procreation.[110] Apparently, some in Ammoun's community believed that marriage, in and of itself, was unacceptable. This has led some scholars to believe that there was a Manichean presence in and around Nitria.[111] Either way, Athanasius responds that spiritual questions such as these depend upon circumstance. "The same act is at one time and under certain circumstances unlawful, while at the right time and under different circumstances it is both lawful and permissible."[112] Sexual contact is neutral: if adulterous, it is evil; if procreative, it is good.[113] On this question, unlike the first, Athanasius employs more of a pastoral touch. The monks of Ammoun's community should not judge married Christians in the world; they should simply appreciate the grace that has enabled their renunciation.

Elsewhere, Athanasius criticized those ascetics who sought a more rigorous existence by going entirely without sleep.[114] As with nocturnal emissions and marriage, the bishop of Alexandria maintained that ascetic practices had theological consequences. By linking praxis to doctrine, Athanasius brought ascetic discipline within the purview of episcopal control. Because the clergy alone could interpret Scripture and define orthodoxy, Athanasius exerted his authority over ascetic behavior when he believed his intervention was justified.[115] While some might interpret this as an extension of authority, Athanasius doubtless saw it as his pastoral obligation.

As bishop, Athanasius also asserted his authority among the desert ascetics at times when they were experiencing administrative chaos. When Pachomius died in 346, a succession crisis of sorts arose in his ever-growing monastic community. Just prior to his death, Pachomius had named an unlikely successor, a certain Petronius, whose family had made a considerable donation to the federation.[116] Petronius, in turn, appointed Horsisius to succeed him. Unlike Pachomius, Horsisius was not popular among the elders at Pbow, and in 350 one of the monasteries rebelled against him. Horsisius withdrew in disgrace, and another more respected monk, Theodore, essentially took control of the federation.[117] The joint rule of Theodore and Horsisius continued awkwardly until Athanasius's visit to the Thebaid in 363. At the bishop's instigation, the two leaders reconciled and Horsisius returned from his self-imposed exile. The details of this exchange are rather complex and tangential to our study; more pertinent is Athanasius's intervention in the matter.[118]

In resolving the dispute, Athanasius established himself (and the Alexandrian episcopacy) as the rightful arbiter of monastic conflicts occurring in the Egyptian desert.[119] What is more, his sanctioning of many of Theodore's disciplinary reforms further tied the federation to the Alexandrian episcopacy. Thus, when Theodore died in 368, Athanasius was in a position to choose the new successor.[120] As with many of Athanasius's activities there are multiple interpretations. Athanasius's intervention among the Pachomians was, to some extent, political—necessitated by doctrinal and economic need. At the same time, it was pastoral.[121] Indeed, the spiritual survival of the Pachomian community depended upon qualified and recognizable leadership. Though Athanasius left the spiritual formation of novices to the spiritual fathers of the ascetic community, he did what he could to provide stable leadership at the top of the federation.

The Alexandrian Virgins

Whereas Athanasius left the direction of male ascetics to their elders, he took an active role in the spiritual formation of female renunciants.[122] The female virgin, Athanasius declared, most exemplified the union of the λόγος and humanity.[123] As bishop, he had the responsibility to protect these women (many of them young girls) from physical and doctrinal harm. That task was more involved than we might assume. By the time of his tenure in office, virgins had become active participants in the theological and political disputes of the Alexandrian episcopacy. According to Athanasius, they sustained injuries from physical attacks by his theological and political rivals. It has been argued that Athanasius believed that his effectiveness as bishop was tied to his success among the virgins.[124]

Athanasius's first objective was to establish his authority. Though many of his interactions and conversations with female ascetics were not recorded, we do have portions of two letters that provide some information about their relationship. Near the end of the first letter, Athanasius self-deprecatingly refers to himself as "your bridegroom's servant" before issuing a command for conformity.[125] Elsewhere, Athanasius identifies himself as the legitimate successor to Bishop Alexander. He then presents his instructions as the words of their mutual "elder," "father," and bishop.[126] He goes on to expound to them a lengthy sermon that he purports Alexander to have delivered. Not coincidentally, the sermon reflects Athanasius's vision of female asceticism.

Athanasius showed little hesitation in regulating both the public and private behavior of his female ascetics. He prohibited them from going to the public baths or having any contact with lay men.[127] Ideally, they were to spend their time at home with their parents or in a communal environment under the instruction of elder women.[128] Moreover, they were to pursue silence and avoid laughter.[129] Here as elsewhere in the late ancient period, Christian virgins lacked the social mobility of their male counterparts.

Nevertheless, Athanasius encouraged female ascetics to worship alongside the laity in the city's churches.[130] He firmly believed that the *ecclesia* consisted of both married and celibate, whether in the city or the country—all who had been baptized in Christ belonged to the Church. His inclusion of female ascetics in the Alexandrian worship cycle had two practical pastoral advantages. For the ascetic, engaging the laity alleviated some of the strain of the life of seclusion; for the lay person, it provided a visible example of Christian piety.[131] It should be noted, however, that Athanasius had stringent requirements concerning the virgins' public conduct.[132]

Also, like other fourth-century episcopal officials, Athanasius vehemently denounced "spiritual marriages."[133] Typically, these so-called marriages consisted of male and female ascetics who lived together in continence. The male ascetic would protect and provide for the female, while the female would attend the domestic needs of the household. Athanasius acknowledged the economic benefit of such an arrangement, but he rejected it as a breeding ground for lust and scandal. Spiritual marriage was just one of the traps that could prevent the female ascetic from achieving true virginity (i.e., having Christ dwell within her).[134]

Though Athanasius instructed the virgins to adhere to the teachings and wisdom of their priests and eldresses, he was very much involved in their spiritual formation.[135] As noted elsewhere, the bishop of Alexandria understood doctrinal instruction to be a pastoral matter. In short, he sought to protect those in his care from what he believed were "wolves who could compromise their faith in God." In Alexandria at this time, there were a number of religious study groups led by well-educated men, many of whom were sympathetic to the Arian position.[136] Athanasius warns the virgins that they should not resort to male teachers but rather emulate the faith of the Virgin Mary, which he chronicled in his letters to them.[137] Moreover, he noted that the proper imitation of the Virgin's life required an accurate reading of Scripture, but scriptural interpretation remained the dominion of the episcopacy (i.e., Athanasius).[138]

Arius and his supporters were not the only deceivers from whom Athanasius sought to protect his virginal flock; there was also the rigorous ascetic Hieracas, who taught that marriage was evil and that ascetics should avoid anyone contaminated by it.[139] Athanasius's refutation of Hieracas resembled that of his letter to Ammoun—marriage was an acceptable form of Christianity that bore its own fruits.[140] To emphasize the respectability of marriage, the Alexandrian even refers to virginity as a type of marriage where a symbolic spiritual child is born of the bride (i.e., the virgin) and groom (i.e., Christ).[141] Athanasius's message is both pastoral and social. He tempers the pride that threatens the virgin who compares herself to the lay person. In turn, the spiritually secure virgin provides the laity an example from which to learn. Thus Athanasius creates a social environment in which married and celibate Christians assist one another and worship together.

A second pastoral device is that of the saintly exemplar. As he has done for the male audience of the *Life of Antony,* Athanasius influences the behavior of female readers by (1) providing an uncontested account of a saint's actions and (2) promising his readers that imitation of the saints is the best way to ensure one's salvation. In his letters to the virgins, Athanasius points to the Virgin Mary as the female ascetic par excellence:[142]

Mary was a holy virgin, having the disposition of her soul balanced and doubly increasing. For she desired good works, doing what is proper, having true thoughts in faith and purity. And she did not desire to be seen by people; rather, she prayed that God would be her judge. Nor did she have an eagerness to leave her house, nor was she at all acquainted with the streets; rather, she remained in her house being calm, imitating the fly in honey. She virtuously spent the excess of her manual labor on the poor. And she did not acquire eagerness to look out the window, but rather to look at the Scriptures. And she would pray to God privately, taking care about these two things: that she not let evil thoughts dwell in her heart, and also that she not acquire curiosity or learn hardness of heart. And she did not allow anyone near her body unless it was covered, and she controlled her anger and extinguished the wrath in her inmost thoughts.[143]

Athanasius defines his vision of female asceticism through his description of the Virgin's life. She was pure, meek, obedient, and pious. Elsewhere, he notes that she adopted a moderate asceticism—her levels of fasting and (lack of) sleep provided a reward but were not extreme.[144] However, his fondness for imitation is not restricted to the Virgin and the saints. Athanasius also encourages his female readers to follow the examples of the elders in their community. The Alexandrian virgins do not need male teachers to instruct them; they are better off following the pious examples of uneducated women.[145]

The letters to virgins evince other, commonsense pastoral techniques that Athanasius employed. For example, the first letter cautions its readers to exercise humility and avoid anything that might lead them to pass judgment on their colleagues.[146] The virgin is to remain focused on her individual goals and to ignore the success or failure of those around her. When necessary, the bishop also plays the role of the optimistic counselor who must revive the spirits of those who have become brokenhearted.[147] These final injunctions, and others like them, are so pastorally mundane that they reveal the familiarity with which Athanasius addressed this female audience.

SUPERVISING THE LAY COMMUNITY

The final way in which we will consider Athanasius's model of spiritual direction is by examining his interaction with and supervision of lay persons in his care. Unfortunately, we have few records of this type of contact.[148] What we do have are many of his festal letters, issued each year at the beginning of the Lenten season. These letters, like much of his writing to professional ascetics, were designed for general, not individual, readers. And given that he wrote many of them from exile, it should come as little surprise that he used them to explore doctrinal themes.[149]

As noted elsewhere, Athanasius's emphasis on doctrine had a pastoral dimension. In many cases, the festal letters were the bishop's lone opportunity to communicate broadly with the Christians of Alexandria. The letters address a number of theological points related to the paschal ceremonies. A recurring theme is that of the differences between the ancient Jewish customs and the Christian. For the most part, Athanasius praises the actions of the ancient Jews (particularly the Old Testament saints), but he rarely misses an opportunity to condemn contemporary Jews who fail to recognize Christ as the Messiah.[150] The letters also contain summaries of his teaching on the Incarnation and his doctrine of free will.[151] And he makes several connections between *orthodoxia* and *orthropraxia*.[152]

Athanasius's interest in the doctrinal formation of his readers is, in large part, shaped by his incessant trouble with the Melitians and Arians. In the twenty-fourth festal letter, he links all heretical views to the deception of the devil and instructs his readers to resist novel teaching. Citing St. Paul, Athanasius reminds his audience that the apostle "justly praised the Corinthians who maintained the faith that was in accordance with his traditions."[153] He then adds: "[T]he blessed Paul again gave directions to the Galatians who were in danger, writing to them, 'If anyone preach to you something different from what you have received, let him be anathema [cf. Gal. 1.9].' For there is no communion between the words of the saints and the fantasies of human invention."[154]

The rhetoric of religious conservatism is powerful. Athanasius was able to paint his opponents as newcomers, men who twisted the traditions of the apostles and betrayed the faith of the martyrs. As the Nicene bishop of Alexandria, Athanasius claimed to be the sole arbiter of apostolic teaching. Perhaps the most significant of the bishop's steps in this vein was his limiting the canon of Scripture to twenty-seven books.[155] "In these [books] alone is proclaimed the teaching of religion. Let no one add to them, nor retract from them. . . . [Apocryphal books] are the creation of heretics, who write them whenever they want, granting their own approval and assigning to them a date, so that using them as ancient writings they may have an opportunity to lead astray the simple."[156] Long recognized as an important development in the history of Christianity, Athanasius's thirty-ninth festal letter was a dramatic assault on the authority and teaching of his enemies. Not only did Athanasius claim, as bishop, the right of interpretation, he determined what qualified as Scripture.

In addition to doctrinal matters, the festal letters convey some of the earliest and most consistent enjoinders for married Christians to perform ascetic acts. Athanasius believed that the Incarnation provided all Christians with a measure of incorruption that could be maintained only through discipline.[157] Lent was an obvious time for Christians to "offer prolonged prayers, fasting, and vigils so that [they] may be enabled . . . to elude the devil."[158] Among other things, these letters describe a forty-day Lenten fast, which preceded Holy Week.[159] They also give considerable detail about the rationale for Christian fasting.[160] For example, the third festal letter refers to Lent as a period of purification required before the reception of the Eucharist on Pascha (i.e., Easter).[161] In another letter, Athanasius submits that fasting can and will perform miracles.[162] And in the sixth festal letter, Athanasius instructs married Christians in particular to take advantage of the season: "[L]et us fast like Daniel, let us pray without ceasing, as Paul commanded, all of us recognizing the season of prayer, but especially those who are in an honorable marriage, so that testifying to these things, appropriately celebrating the feast, we may be able to enter into the joy of our Lord in the kingdom of Heaven."[163]

Food abstinence was not the only form of renunciation Athanasius imposed upon his community during Lent. Christians were expected to attend prayer vigils, study the Scriptures, and forego any sexual activity.[164] Those living in the "world" were also to make peace with their neighbors and offer alms to the poor.[165] The fifth festal letter offers a mundane but typical example of Athanasius's Lenten admonition: "Let us purify our hands, let us cleanse the body. Let us keep our every thought free of deception; not relaxing into excess or giving into lust, but occupying ourselves entirely with our Lord, and with divine doctrines, so that being entirely pure, we may be able to partake of the λόγος."[166] In many ways, these pastoral instructions resemble those Athanasius issued in his letters to virgins. The difference is that the as-

cetic disciplines of married Christians were temporary and were not designated to separate them from the rest of society.[167]

Athanasius uses the tenth festal letter to make clear his view of marriage.
He writes: "[M]ercy is not confined to the perfect, but it is offered to others
also who occupy the middle and the third ranks, so that He might lead everyone to salvation."[168] Athanasius maintains the validity of marriage but grants
it a somewhat second-class status. Indeed, he continues, "[T]he [heavenly
kingdom] is various in proportion to the advance in moral attainment."[169]
In other words, although married Christians will attain the Kingdom, they
will not enjoy the same level of bliss as their monastic counterparts. The passage is important for another reason. The discussion is couched in terms of
God's ability to provide what each of his followers need individually. Athanasius writes: "[T]o those then who have not yet achieved perfection, He
becomes like a sheep giving milk. . . . [T]o those who have matured beyond
childhood, but still labor among the imperfect, He becomes their food,
according to their need. . . . But as soon as one begins to walk the road of
perfection, . . . he has the Word for bread and flesh for food."[170] Here the
bishop of Alexandria displays an appreciation for individualized and even
gradual correction, but he does not place the spiritual father in the equa-
tion. For Athanasius, it is Christ who discerns and provides for the Christian
athlete.[171]

While Athanasius was happy to encourage married persons to develop
their own ascetic spirituality, he was all the more willing to encourage the unmarried to embrace the monastic life. In his second festal letter, Athanasius
linked the practice of solitaries with the actions of the saints.

> You see, my beloved, how powerful are quietness and withdrawal from
> human beings in the troubles of life. You see how powerful is this
> kind of life and the pure conscience, for it makes the person a friend
> of God, like Abraham. . . . Moreover, the great Moses, likewise, when
> he withdrew from the land of Egypt, that is, from the deeds of the earth
> that are close to darkness, he spoke with God face to face and was saved
> from his enemies and passed through the desert. All these are shadows
> of the withdrawal from darkness to his marvelous light and the ascent
> to the city in heaven. They are patterns of the true joy and the eternal
> festival.[172]

In this letter, we find Athanasius, very early in his career, not simply encouraging asceticism but actively extolling the virtues of monasticism. Many have wondered at the explosion of Egyptian monasticism during the fourth century. One thing is certain—not only did that social phenomenon meet with Athanasius's approval, but the bishop of Alexandria actively endorsed it.

Beyond the generalized teachings of the festal homilies, there is a detailed example of personal pastoral instruction in his letter to Marcellinus. We know little about Marcellinus; it is possible that he was a "professional" ascetic, but there is nothing in the text to conclude as much. It is more likely that he was the type of lay correspondent that Athanasius treasured—a person who lived in the world but who had embraced an ascetic-like religious discipline, which included the reading of Scripture (an act Athanasius refers to as an ἄσκησις). The bishop of Alexandria commends Marcellinus for his devotion to the Bible, especially the Psalms, and admonishes him to allow the recitation of the Psalms to transform his entire religious discipline.

Early in the letter, Athanasius presents his ideas as the received "teaching of an old man."[173] Athanasius occasionally interrupts the story to make a point, but most of the text is presented in the third person. It is possible that Athanasius purposefully evokes the monastic guide/disciple relationship. If so, we might infer two things. First, although it is a modified form (he is not the elder, he conveys the teachings of an elder), Athanasius employs one of the most distinctive characteristics of spiritual direction in the ascetic community. Second, conceivably the recipient of the letter would also be familiar with the literary convention and Athanasius employed it because he knew that his message would be more powerful if it was styled as the teaching of an elder.

Athanasius's encouragement of reading the Psalms is deliberate because, he says, each of the genres of Scripture is incorporated into that single book.[174] Moreover, he argues, the Psalms have a pastoral function: they "represent and portray in all their multiplicity the various movements of the soul."[175] Therefore, one can find oneself, one's needs, and one's cures.[176] As a result, the Psalms, more than any other book of the Bible, teach how to improve oneself. The assistance provided by the Psalms is accentuated, Athanasius believes, by their verbal repetition. By singing them aloud, the Christian sees himself as if in a mirror and is able to amend his ways accordingly.[177] The lengthy letter provides a detailed analysis of the how different psalms carry unique pastoral benefits.

The development of the monastic psalter and Athanasius's encouragement of the recitation of the Psalms in this letter were neither directly related nor coincidental. The Psalms provided Christians with a body of hymns that were both edifying to the individual and functional for communal worship. Because they were generally thought to be safe from heretical interpretation, those in authority often encouraged their recitation. Athanasius's letter to Marcellinus was both an early example of the perceived functionality of the Psalms and an important witness to the bishop's formation of lay piety.

There is much in the Lenten prescriptions and the letter to Marcellinus to suggest that Athanasius was eager to incorporate asceticism into his instruction of the laity. Brakke argues (I believe rightly) that Athanasius shifted the focus of Christianity in Alexandria from intellectual speculation about God to the cultivation of ascetic virtue.[178] Lay Christians differed from their monastic counterparts only by degree. Though Athanasius may not have employed the techniques of the ascetic community in their advanced form, he certainly urged all (monastic and married alike) to ascetic renunciation. And in doing so, he facilitated the gradual asceticizing of spiritual direction in late ancient Christianity.

Why, we might ask, are the patterns of Athanasius's spiritual direction often so inconsistent? With respect to the criteria for spiritual authority, his corpus provides two very different, and in many ways competing, accounts: Antony the ascetic giant versus a doctrinally sound episcopacy. His directives to other spiritual leaders also oscillate between *orthopraxia* and *orthodoxia*. For example, the *Life of Antony* suggested to its monastic readers that the supervision of renunciation is a spiritual leader's most important responsibility, yet the injunctions in his personal correspondence and in his festal letters emphasized doctrinal conformity above all else. Furthermore, one could argue that his direct supervision of ascetics and lay persons drew inconsistently from ascetic and clerical patterns of leadership. Athanasius generally left the direction of male ascetics to the leaders of their communities, but that did not prevent him from dictating the proper interpretation of biblical passages or from intervening to appoint successors. With respect to the laity, Athanasius encouraged ascetic disciplines, if only temporarily. He expected fasting, chastity, vigils, and almsgiving. He also transformed other Christian practices into models of ascetic discipline (e.g., the recitation of the Psalms). But he never developed the spiritual father/spiritual disciple model of supervision (remember that in the letter to Marcellinus he does not present the teaching as his own; thus he does not present himself as the spiritual father).

Given Athanasius's continued absence from Alexandria, this final point is conspicuous. We know from his biography of Antony that Athanasius was familiar with the concept of the spiritual father. Therefore, why did he not encourage the laity in Alexandria to seek out trusted advisors in his absence? At least two possible answers emerge. First, the practice was by no means dispersed throughout the Church. Though Athanasius described Antony's pastoral skill and extolled his ability to discern the spiritual needs of all who visited him, it would not follow necessarily that the bishop of Alexandria would appropriate that model for himself or his diocese. The pastoral techniques of the ascetic communities were very much in development during Athanasius's tenure. Even though it is likely that he approved of the spiritual father model of supervision (in the context of an ascetic community), he may not have seen its need in an urban and lay environment.

The second and perhaps the more obvious reason for Athanasius's reluctance was the potential conflict it would create with one of his more important initiatives—discouraging his followers from attending the Arian study groups that operated in Alexandria.[179] The spiritual father/spiritual disciple model that operated in the ascetic communities paid little attention to ordination or theological orthodoxy. Athanasius spent much of his time trying to disrupt that practice in Alexandria. Though he may have looked favorably upon Antony's direction of a handful of hermits, Athanasius would not trust the care of his flock to the "spiritual guides" that roamed the streets of Alexandria.

Of course, this explains only part of the inconsistency in Athanasius's corpus. There is also the issue of the source of spiritual authority. I have argued that Athanasius's decision to raise ascetic leaders to the episcopacy resolves, in part, the conflict between the ascetic and clerical tendencies that we find in his writing. But that same decision put even more persons in his own difficult position of being trapped between an ascetic ideal and the responsibility of pastoral supervision. This tension was something that Athanasius never fully resolved.

In the *Life of Antony,* Athanasius praised the many skills of the recently deceased saint. If nothing else, the encomium of Antony earned Athanasius the support of the ascetic community for which he wrote. But back in Alexandria, he argued that his own authority and that of his allies derived from the grace of the priesthood and was preserved through their continued support of Nicene Christianity. As he moved forward, Athanasius elevated to the episcopal rank only those who conformed to his standards of orthodoxy. That many of them were experienced ascetics seems to have been an asset but perhaps not a requirement.

Finally, I would like to point to something of a paradox. I have argued that one explanation for Athanasius's ambivalence regarding spiritual direction was the increasing tension between the ascetic and nonascetic ideals of Christian leadership. Unlike many Christian leaders of subsequent generations, Athanasius did not differentiate between ascetic and nonascetic patterns of spiritual direction. Indeed, such a distinction might have been lost on him. Athanasius, perhaps better than anyone of his generation, took advantage of the monastic explosion that occurred in the Egyptian desert. He swayed the ascetic community to the Nicene cause and convinced its most capable leaders to serve the Church at large. Nevertheless, it is quite possible that he never realized just how much that same revolution in Christian piety had informed, perhaps even complicated, his own policies of spiritual direction.

T W O

Gregory Nazianzen's Struggle for Synthesis

Gregory Nazianzen was born in either 329 or 330 on a family estate near Nazianzus. Gregory's father, Gregory the elder, was the chief landholder and local patron of Nazianzus, a prosperous but rural section of Cappadocia located in modern-day central Turkey. Following his conversion to Christianity (he had belonged to a pagan sect known as the Hypsistarii), the elder Gregory moved quickly through the ranks of the clergy and was consecrated bishop of Nazianzus.[1] It should surprise few that he groomed his eldest son to succeed him in both roles (i.e., landowner and leader of the Christian community).[2]

Gregory Nazianzen was a late ancient aristocrat in many ways.[3] As a member of the Cappadocian *curiales,* Gregory benefited from the privileges of wealth and education. We know a good deal about his schooling. After a customary local education that would accompany his station, Gregory traveled first to Caesarea-Maritima to study at the school founded by the great Christian intellectual Origen. It was there that the young scholar probably came into contact with Basil, later bishop of Caesarea, a man who would become both his greatest friend and a source of intermittent hostility and despair.[4] From Caesarea-Maritima, Gregory went on to Alexandria before finally settling into Athens and Plato's academy in 348.[5]

Gregory remained in Athens for ten years, mastering the art of rhetoric and cultivating a distinctive form of Christianity that was at once ascetic and intellectually active. John McGuckin argues that Gregory, like Origen, was philosophically eclectic. He read Plato, Aristotle, the neo-Platonists, and the Stoics.[6] While at Athens, Gregory underwent baptism, an unusual step for someone of his age and position.[7] It was also during this period that the friendship of Gregory and Basil flourished.[8] An often repeated line of Gregory's funeral oration for Basil claims that while the two were in Athens they knew only two roads—the road to church and the road to school.[9] In what would become a recurring pattern, Basil disappointed his friend when he decided to leave school in 356 to pursue the life of monasticism.[10] Two years later, Gregory joined Basil, possibly turning down a position of rhetoric at the academy.[11]

Returning to Cappadocia, Gregory faced a dilemma. On the one hand, his father was advancing in age and expected Gregory to apply his talents to the family businesses. On the other hand, Basil hoped that Gregory would join him at his monastic settlement at Annesoi.[12] Neither alternative was ideal. Gregory felt compelled to serve his parents, but that life lacked appeal. He longed for the retirement of the ascetic community, but unlike Basil he was unwilling to seclude himself from the intellectual life and social environment to which he had been born.[13] Gregory was an anomaly—he wanted to combine social activity with ascetic contemplation.

In the winter of 361, Gregory the elder ordained his son to the priesthood. The younger Gregory felt a rush of resentment and fear. So he fled, traveling once again to Basil. Gregory remained at Annesoi for several months and might have remained there indefinitely had it not been for a crisis that forced his return. His father had done the unthinkable—he had signed a Homoian creed provoking a schism in the church at Nazianzus.[14] By Easter of 362, Gregory was back in Nazianzus, and with time he managed to heal the schism of his father's making.[15] In the years that followed, Gregory settled into a routine of ascetic retreat, living on a family estate in nearby Arianzum and preaching publicly in the Church of Nazianzus. But the initial crisis had been an omen of things come. Over and again, the people Gregory felt closest to would force him into situations of which he wanted no part.

Two episodes, in particular, require some attention: his elevation to the See of Sasima and his appointment to and ultimate resignation from the See of Constantinople. In 370, Gregory the elder helped ensure the election of Basil to the influential See of Caesarea.[16] The candidacy was an unlikely one in that Basil (a determined Nicene) was certain to garner opposition from the imperial court, which was, at that time, decidedly Homoian.[17] Imperial dissatisfaction manifested itself in 372 in the division of the traditional boundaries of Cappadocia that stood to undermine Basil's authority in the province. Hoping to maintain Nicene control, Basil established a new see in the small crossroads town of Sasima. Basil coerced Gregory to serve as the see's inaugural bishop. The move was a catastrophe in nearly every way.[18] Following an ordination that probably took place in Nazianzus, Basil, Gregory, and a group of pro-Nicene monks attempted to assert their authority among the lay community of Sasima during the festival of St. Orestes (a local martyr). However, in the end, Anthimos, Basil's Homoian rival, secured the tithes from the festival, and the Nicene party was rebuffed by a Homoian mob.[19] Worse still, Gregory deeply resented playing the role of pawn in Basil's ecclesiastical politics.[20] In a series of letters to Basil and his autobiographical poem *On His Own Life (De vita sua),* Gregory bemoaned the treachery of his "friend," who had secured for him what, in Gregory's eyes, was no more than an isolated dust bowl.[21] He added the stinging comment, "[T]he pretext was souls; but in reality, of course, it was the desire for authority, authority, if I dare to state it, of taxes and tithes, which have the entire world in terrible confusion."[22]

A reconciliation of sorts followed. Gregory retained his episcopal dignity but essentially abandoned Sasima, remaining instead with his father in Nazianzus.[23] But this unusual (and essentially uncanonical) solution later caused additional problems when he became bishop of Constantinople.[24] Gregory returned to his pattern of intermittent ascetic retreat and clerical service in Nazianzus until 375, when he moved into a more permanent retirement in Seleukia.[25] In 379, however, he reentered public service when he accepted an invitation to go to Constantinople to defend the Nicene minority in the city.[26]

This "mission" of Gregory's coincided with the rise of a new emperor, Theodosius, who had committed himself to the Nicene faith. However, Gregory's success in the city was by no means guaranteed. For one, the emperor was embroiled in a dangerous conflict with the Goths and had not yet made his way to Constantinople. Moreover, the Arians controlled all of the city's churches, and Gregory's services were, on occasion, interrupted by Arian agitators.[27] Nevertheless, it was in this context that Gregory offered his famous "five theological orations" (Orations 27–31), which anticipated the Chalcedonian formulas of the Trinity, Christ, and the Holy Spirit.

While Gregory may have been a master orator, as a politician he was a failure. Soon after the emperor's arrival in Constantinople in 380, Theodosius's agents laid the foundations for a new council that would ultimately settle the

Arian question. Now the recognized bishop of the capital, Gregory assumed control of the synod when its initial leader, Meletius of Antioch, died at the beginning of the proceedings. This was a perilous development, and it soon became obvious to everyone, even Gregory, that he was the wrong man for the job.[28] As McGuckin notes, "[W]hat began as a wonderful gathering to celebrate the Nicene ascendancy had developed into a nightmare."[29] Gregory resigned from both the council and the See of Constantinople in the summer of 381. He delivered a farewell oration (Oration 42) in which he reminded those gathered that it was he who had rescued the city from the Arians and that it was up to them, the delegates, to ratify the doctrine of the Trinity.[30]

From Constantinople, Gregory went into a self-imposed exile. He spent his remaining years in relative seclusion editing his orations, writing poetry (some of it theological, much of it caustic), and reproving those whose theology he found inadequate.[31] Undoubtedly, the vicissitudes of Gregory's public career influenced his view of Christian leadership. Moreover, even the orations that he delivered early in life bear, through the editorial process, the residue of his bitter experiences in Sasima and Constantinople. Gregory died on his family estate in either 390 or 391.

CRITERIA FOR SPIRITUAL AUTHORITY

What made Nazianzen's approach to spiritual direction innovative is that he blended the ascetic and clerical traditions.[32] This is most clearly expressed by his criteria for spiritual authority. Ostensibly, Gregory upheld the authority of the episcopate.[33] However, it was his standards for clerical election that marked Gregory's synthesis of the two pastoral traditions. In short, Gregory believed that the Church should be run by well-educated aristocrats (the common practice of the post-Constantinian institutional Church), but only by those aristocrats who had achieved purification through renunciation and contemplation.

In the first of his theological orations, Oration 27, Gregory attacks those who enter upon theological discussions and assert themselves as teachers but lack the proper qualities for leadership. Gregory begins his diatribe, "[N]ot everyone is suited to discuss theology, no, not everyone. The subject is not so cheap or so common."[34] While his chief aim in the oration is to dismiss the

Arian leadership as intellectually irresponsible, there is an undercurrent of high-born arrogance to his rhetoric. Gregory claims that to know God one must be truly at leisure (σχολάσαι).[35] At this time, many Romans believed that philosophical contemplation was the unique privilege of the aristocratic class because they alone enjoyed the necessary *otium,* or life of leisure.[36] By establishing this life of leisure as a requirement for theological leadership, Gregory equates philosophical speculation with theological understanding. More important, he effectively confines spiritual authority to the aristocracy.

In his poem *On Himself and the Bishops (De seipso et de episcopis),* Gregory critiques the ignobility of those "new" bishops who forced his resignation in Constantinople: "[S]ome of them are the offspring of tribute-mongers, who think only about falsifying accounts. Others come straight from the tax booth and the honor you get there; others from the plough, with a fresh sunburn; some also from among laborers with the ax and hoe; others still have just left the navy or army. They still smell of the ocean or exhibit the brand of the army."[37] Nazianzen implies that these men are unqualified because of their common beginnings, in effect linking the potential for Christian leadership to social class.[38]

Gregory anticipates that his opponents will argue that the apostles were poor fishermen who lacked education, and his response is twofold. First, the apostles were men of great faith and great asceticism; those qualities trump the limitations of a common birth. However, the men who orchestrated his removal from Constantinople do not possess the faith or the asceticism of the apostles. "Answer one thing," Gregory demands of his opponents, "can you exorcise demons, free a man from leprosy, or the dead from their tomb?"[39] Without those spiritual gifts, a leader must rely his dignity. Second, Nazianzen challenges the notion that the apostles were uneducated. "If these authors were not skilled with words, as you accuse, how did they succeed in converting kings, cities, and assemblies?"[40] Nazianzen confesses that he has spent his entire life in books but struggles to understand the intricate meaning of the Scriptures. They are complex, he argues, and require a level of attention that only a man of learning can provide.

Nearly twenty years earlier, when he first identified his criteria for spiritual authority in his second oration, Gregory maintained that too many who held the position of preacher lacked the intellectual capacity for leadership. "If anyone boldly assumes it and supposes it within the power of everyone's intellect [διανοίας], I am amazed at his intelligence, not to mention his folly."[41] Gregory opened his twentieth oration with an equally damning comment that he lives in an age of "instant experts and ordained theologians, who believe that they only have to wish it and they are wise."[42] Not surprisingly, Gregory dismissed the opinions of those who lacked the spiritual purity necessary to understand the faith, but he also implied that many were unable to comprehend, intellectually, the finer points of orthodox doctrine—a disqualification for instructing others.[43] For Nazianzen, theology was a complicated science that required training and dedication; the mentally lax or ill prepared were certain to fall into one heresy or another.[44]

Gregory did not seem to differentiate between intelligence and education. In his encomium for Athanasius, Gregory claimed that the saint briefly studied literature and philosophy so that he would not be unskilled in those subjects or ignorant of the things that he chose to renounce.[45] He also noted that the same Athanasius "surpassed in intellect all men known for their intelligence."[46] In the funeral oration for St. Basil, Nazianzen pushed this point further still by criticizing those Christians who did not think that education was an important prerequisite for episcopal leadership:

> I take it all rational men agree that the first of our benefits is education. I refer not only to its most developed sense [i.e., Christian learning], which dismisses the ambitious fineries of logic and holds only to salvation and the beauty of spiritual contemplation; but also to education in general, which many Christians foolishly scorn as hostile and dangerous and as something that turns us away from God. The heavens, earth, air, and all such things should not be condemned because some have falsely interpreted them. . . . Instead, we select from [pagan authors] what is useful both for life and enjoyment [ἀπόλαυσιν] and we avoid what is dangerous.[47]

Gregory probably offered this eulogy on the third anniversary of Basil's death, shortly after he left Constantinople—roughly the same time as the autobiographical poems. Whereas he identifies Basil as a paragon of learning and nobility, Gregory caricatures his opponents as incompetent buffoons of low birth and inadequate education.[48] Such a censure was circular—in Christian antiquity, only the curial class would have had access to the level of education that Gregory seems to require of the episcopate.

And Gregory was by no means a social revolutionary.[49] Though all may have been equal in Christ (cf. Gal. 3:28), for Gregory that did not justify the dissolution of the social structures of the Roman world. On more than one occasion, Nazianzen exhorted his audience to be satisfied with their rank and not to seek advancement. In his nineteenth oration, Gregory states, "[M]y brothers, everyone should remain in the rank [τάξει] to which he was called, even if he deserves a better one. A man is held in higher esteem if he accepts his position rather than desiring one that he has not been given."[50]

One could interpret Gregory's position as a pastoral maneuver designed to urge the laity to adopt a more ascetic view of world—one that encouraged them to be satisfied with what they had rather than to lust for what was unnecessary. Another, more political interpretation might emphasize Gregory's endorsement of the social parameters that governed Roman society.[51] Gregory benefited from the privileges of a noble birth, and though he rejected many of its advantages, he did not seem to be in any rush to dissolve class barriers.[52]

While we may read a fair amount of self-presentation into Gregory's criteria for authority, the call for an educated clergy was quite practical. As we will see, one of the cleric's chief responsibilities in Gregory's eyes was the dissemination of orthodox doctrine. To the extent that a priest or bishop failed to proclaim the Gospel clearly, he failed as a spiritual director.[53] To be sure, Gregory argued, orthodoxy was more important than rhetorical flourish, but one needed to be able to defend orthodox teaching with clarity.[54] And while Gregory did not believe that education or rhetorical skill would enhance an individual's opportunity for salvation, he insisted that both were required of the clergy.[55]

By identifying rhetorical skill and intelligence as two of the characteristics of authority (and by portraying a lack of either as a failure in leadership), Gregory confirmed the importance of education as a prerequisite for leadership. Given the state of education in the Greco-Roman world at that time, Gregory was, in effect, confining pastoral leadership to the *curiales* and the aristocracy. Though this perspective may run counter to modern sensibilities, such assumptions about leadership were commonplace in antiquity and prevalent among the Christian hierarchy in the post-Constantinian Church.[56] What distinguished Gregory's vision of authority from those of a previous generation was his insistence upon a second component—asceticism.

For all of his eccentricities, Gregory was typical of a growing number of bishops in the late fourth century—a well-born *curialis* who shied away from many of the privileges and symbols of wealth that the Greco-Roman world valued. The turn to asceticism, curiously enough, may have afforded Gregory, and many like him, with even greater access to power and authority than pagans of equal financial means could have enjoyed.[57] Indeed, it was precisely because Gregory had possessed (but ostensibly abandoned) the aristocratic life that he understood himself to be worthy of leadership.

To be sure, Gregory's ascetic experience was not as physically demanding as that of some others. He neither lived in the desert nor perched upon a pillar; he subjected himself to neither the rigorous fasting nor the poverty of other famous ascetics. Some have characterized his practice as intellectually rather than physically ascetic (perhaps in continuity with the classical tradition).[58] Supporting such a thesis is Oration 26, in which Nazianzen reflects that "nothing is more invincible, nothing more incomprehensible than philosophy. All things will yield before a philosopher does. . . . The philosopher is immaterial, yet material; uncircumscribed by a body, yet in one; heavenly, yet earthen; impassible in the midst of passions, submissive in every respect but wisdom, triumphant in his victory over those who think they are better."[59] Gregory strove for philosophical meditation that could be achieved only in retreat. The opening lines of his second oration, known as the "Apology for His Flight," well describe his desire for retreat (ἀναχώρησις) and stillness (ἡσυχία).[60] According to Nazianzen, the escape from the distractions of the world enabled the contemplation of God—what he called "true philosophy." For him, understanding the Scriptures depended upon isolation and stillness—prerequisites for clearing the mind and spirit.[61] "[O]nly the pure can understand He who is pure."[62]

Nevertheless, there was more to Gregory's pursuit of purity than the Hellenistic conception of *askesis,* which focused almost entirely on an intellectual purification of mind/soul.[63] Although Gregory's physical renunciations might not have rivaled those of the desert fathers, his autobiographical poems offer some details about them, such as fasting, vigils, humble clothes, and austere bedding.[64] Consequently, education and clerical rank without purification (both intellectual and physical) and contemplation did not guarantee orthodox doctrine or a successful ministry; a precise understanding of Christian truth required asceticism.

The importance of asceticism is prevalent in Gregory's earliest orations concerning Christian leadership. In the "Apology for His Flight," he distinguishes between those who lead and those who are led. "For the perfection of the Church, [the leaders should be those] who surpass the majority in virtue and nearness to God, performing the functions of the soul in the body and of the *nous* of the soul."[65] The spiritual director is distinguished from his community by his virtue and his nearness to God—in other words, by his ascetic accomplishment. Later in the same oration, Gregory notes, "[O]ne must be cleansed before cleansing others; wise to make others wise; enlightened to give light; near to God to lead others; sanctified to sanctify; possessing the hands of leadership to lead; instructed to give instruction."[66]

Such an overt bridging of the ascetic and clerical traditions required justification. And so Gregory turns to the Scriptures. He begins with St. Paul and emphasizes his renunciation. "I say little of his labor, his watchfulness, his suffering in hunger and thirst, in cold and nakedness, those who assailed his body from the outside and the demons within. I pass over completely the persecutions, synods, jailing, shackles, accusers, tribunals, the daily and hourly deaths, the basket, the stoning, and the whipping."[67] We could interpret any of these hardships as ascetic sacrifice. But Gregory continues: "[H]e supercedes carnal things; he rejoices in the things of the spirit; he is not ignorant of knowledge but claims to see through a mirror darkly. He is bold in the spirit and attacks his body, as though it were an opponent. What is the lesson? . . . Not to be proud of earthly things, or arrogant from knowledge or excite the flesh against the spirit."[68] Paul had knowledge, but, equally important, he had purged himself of the carnality of the world. Gregory offers dozens of similar examples to show how the saints of the Old and New Testaments provided successful leadership to their communities.[69]

Oration 6, known as the "First Oration on Peace," is an interesting complement to the "Apology for His Flight." Both stem from the schism in Nazianzus circa 362. By the time of the sixth oration, Gregory had managed to mollify the monks who had broken away, and the homily marked the reunion of the community. The oration illustrates Nazianzen's skill as an orator trained in subtlety.[70] He begins by explaining his delay to respond to the schism as the consequence of his cultivation of the ascetic life. "This is why I was silent and humble, retiring far away from every comfort, and a cloud, in a sense, covered my heart and cast a shadow over the sunlight of my words."[71] By stressing his own renunciation, Gregory achieves two things: he assuages the monastic party by adopting their ideals as his own but at the same time

cleverly critiques them for stepping beyond the boundaries of their own sup-
posed practice. In other words, if Gregory, as a cleric, was unwilling to enter
into the fray of a theological dispute because he was too engrossed in the
life of contemplation, the monks should have been all the more reluctant to
do so.[72]

Susanna Elm has recently shown that when Gregory presented his virtual
succession to his father's see in his sixth oration, he described it as a logical
progression from a simplistic to a more sophisticated form of leadership. Indeed, in the "First Oration on Peace," Gregory dismisses his father's doctrinal failures (i.e., the signing of the Homoian creed) as the naive mistake of a
pious old man.[73] He offers similar explanations in the funeral oration for his
father (Oration 18.8) and in his *On His Own Life* (vv. 53). According to Elm,
the challenges of the post-Constantinian Church required a more refined form
of leadership. For Gregory, the missing element was ascetic fulfillment. His
retreat enabled him to cultivate the mastery of self and text that his father
(both a married man and landowner) had been unable to achieve.[74] Not only
did asceticism provide Nazianzen with credibility among the monastic party,
but the particular form of his *askesis* (intellectual and contemplative) enabled
him to develop his theological positions.

Gregory played the asceticism card to the greatest effect in his contests
with the Eunomians in Constantinople and then later against those from his
own party who forced his resignation from the capital.[75] In the first of his theological orations (Oration 27), he argued that one must be a master of medita-
tion ($\theta\epsilon\omega\rho\iota\alpha$) and purified in body and soul before one could listen to a theological discourse.[76] Naturally, the one who offered such a discourse should
be all the more accomplished. The implication was that the neo-Arians who
controlled the churches in Constantinople (and elsewhere) were incapable of
offering an accurate account of the doctrines of the Trinity, Christ, and Holy
Spirit precisely because they lacked the most fundamental of the prerequisites
for Christian leadership. It was no wonder that their teaching was flawed,
Gregory reasoned; their leaders had no basis for authority.

In later years, Gregory became increasingly vocal about the failings of the
episcopacy in his era. Each of the autobiographical poems (*On His Own Life,
On His Own Affairs [De rebus suis]*, and *On Himself and the Bishops*) decries the
worldliness of bishops, especially Nektarios—the man who replaced him in
Constantinople. In *On Himself and the Bishops,* Gregory identifies six episcopal

officials, including Nektarios, whom he believes to be unfit for the office.[77] According to Gregory, these men are politicians, insufficiently ascetic, and incapable of theological discourse.[78]

The autobiographical poems were also designed to rehabilitate Gregory's reputation in the capital.[79] The attributes of spiritual authority that he espouses in the poems are precisely the attributes that he possesses; the ignoble characteristics that he mocks belong to Nektarios and other newcomers.[80] Thus, when Gregory rebukes Nektarios's instability and lack of asceticism, the aging Cappadocian is, in part, drawing attention to his own virtues.[81] Gregory was a man of dignity. He depicted his resignation from Constantinople as an honorable withdrawal from unworthy enemies.[82] Nektarios and those like him were incompetent because they were unable to transcend the material and social world around them. In all ways theirs was the path of failure.

We must be careful, however, not to overcontextualize Gregory's comments concerning leadership that stem from the poems and orations related to his time in Constantinople. A trend in recent scholarship on Gregory is to caricature this material as the bitter comments of a spurned leader, designed almost entirely to construct an honorable reputation for posterity.[83] Such a reading, however, does not fully account for the consistency with which Gregory endorsed both ascetic and aristocratic qualities as the measuring stick for spiritual authority. That Gregory probably exaggerated Nektarios's failings is not enough for us to conclude that he championed only those qualities that he believed could distinguish him from his opponents in Constantinople. From his earliest orations, Gregory identified asceticism and nobility as prerequisites for leadership—qualities that he claimed (albeit rhetorically) to lack.

We find further confirmation of Gregory's criteria for spiritual authority in his funeral orations, especially those for his father, St. Basil, and St. Athanasius. While the content of these eulogies is historically unreliable, they offer a clear view of Gregory's ideas and ideals with respect to spiritual leadership, unfettered by the politics of Constantinople.[84] Whether the orations accurately convey the truth about Basil's or Athanasius's life is unimportant; they no doubt reflect the excesses typical of public eulogy.[85] For our purposes, it is more important that they also reveal what Gregory wants his audience to think about the proper supervision of the Church.

The oration for Gregory the elder is, perhaps, the most interesting because the younger Gregory must extol his father's effectiveness as bishop, all the while knowing that he failed the most important test—that of orthodoxy. Gregory achieves this by carefully subordinating his father's role as Christian teacher and emphasizing his asceticism, faith, and pastoral success among a group of rustic farmers.[86] The emphasis on asceticism is a particularly interesting turn given that he continued to live with his wife. The eulogy does not ignore doctrine altogether. Gregory notes that while his father may not have been an articulate spokesman for the faith like "some of our modern wise men," he was, nonetheless, a "father and teacher of Orthodoxy."[87] And although he may have taken the "second place as orator, he surpassed all in piety."[88] In short, the elder Gregory is to be remembered for his renunciation, pastoral leadership, and piety.

In the orations for Athanasius and Basil, however, we find Nazianzen's most pronounced statements on Christian leadership. He begins the oration for the Alexandrian bishop with a subtle distinction between the vast majority of Christians and those rare individuals, like Athanasius, who are able to transcend the world and attain θέωσις (deification): "[W]hoever has been permitted to escape by reason and contemplation from matter and this fleshly cloud or veil . . . and to hold communion with God, and be associated, as far as human nature can attain, with the purest light, blessed is he, both for his ascent from hence and for his deification there."[89] This acknowledgment, more than anything else, establishes Athanasius's pastoral authority in Gregory's eyes. Much of the remainder of the oration is Gregory's explanation of how the late bishop of Alexandria was able to attain such a high state of spiritual excellence.

In part, Athanasius's success derived from his meditating on the Scriptures. Gregory writes that with the twin supports of Scripture and contemplation, God entrusted Athanasius with the care of a spiritual flock. Athanasius was a worthy leader because he was at once doctrinally sound (identified by his foundation in Scripture) and ascetically advanced (demonstrated by his attainment of pure contemplation). Gregory explains that Athanasius was the perfect model of the contemplative priest.[90] He combined the active life of ministry with the contemplative life of the ascetic.

The same was true of Basil.[91] Nazianzen portrays both Athanasius and Basil as successful or, more specifically, as saintly bishops precisely because they found the proper balance between the active and contemplative life. In his oration for St. Basil, Gregory recounts the late bishop's many confrontations with the Arians. Noting Basil's responsibility as bishop to articulate orthodox doctrine in the face of heresy, Gregory provides an interesting detail about his friend's action: "After as long a period of contemplation and private spiritual meditation as was possible, in which he considered all human arguments and mined the depths of the Scriptures, [Basil] authored a faithful treatise."[92] For Gregory, it was not Basil's Athenian education or his authority as bishop but his successful life of contemplation that enabled him to refute heresy so successfully. What is more, Basil's asceticism was not a means to an end; he transformed his contemplation into action: "[H]e added to his reasoning the assistance that comes from service; he visited, corresponded, consulted, instructed, censured, rebuked, threatened, reproached, . . . he cultivated every type of assistance and procured from every source the specifics of the [spiritual] illness."[93] Basil, like Athanasius, was a model bishop because he combined ascetic meditation with priestly responsibility. I believe that Nazianzen was the first bishop to emphasize a combination of these ideals.

In many ways, the bridging of administrative and ascetic qualities made good pastoral sense. As an ascetic, Gregory's idealized priest was above suspicion and attracted the admiration of the laity; as a well-educated nobleman, he was also able to articulate Christian truths and lead with authority. But other factors may have led Gregory in this direction. For one, we should not discount the fact that this was a characterization of his own experience. Gregory, like each of the authors of this study, attached his criteria for authority to an idealized conception of his own preparation for leadership. Gregory's assertion that spiritual authority was both institutionally and charismatically based also allowed him to ease the rising tension between monks and the episcopate. In the post-Constantinian era, ascetics (and especially monks) increasingly presented themselves as modern-day martyrs, an image that was, no doubt, designed to promote their spiritual authority over an episcopate that had, in their eyes, been compromised. By retaining the authority of the institutional Church while insisting upon ascetic renunciation as a prerequisite for clerical candidacy, Gregory introduced a compromise between clerical authority and asceticism that would characterize leadership for the medieval Church, both East and West.

THE ACTIVE CONTEMPLATIVE

> My mind was in the midst of a noble conundrum because I was searching for the
> most excellent among excellent pursuits. I had long ago decided to cast aside com-
> pletely all fleshly things, and now the resolution pleased me more. But as I considered
> the possible ways to holiness it was not easy to find the better or more serene. . . .
> Finally, after much wandering between the two [life of action and life of contem-
> plation], I came to this solution because it brought a calmness to my soul. I had
> observed that those who enjoy the active life do good to some of the people they
> encounter but to themselves they do no good because they are twisted about by
> the anxieties that disorder their serenity. On the other hand, those that remain
> detached are somehow more stable and in noetic stillness see God. But being
> alone, their charity is lamentable since their lives are anti-social and harsh. I chose
> a middle way between [a life that was] unfettered and one that was integrated, one
> that combined the contemplation of the former with the service of the latter.
>
> Gregory Nazianzen, *On His Own Life* vv. 279–312

For Gregory, it was not enough that a man satisfied the ascetic and intellectual requirements for leadership; he had to cultivate the φρόνημα (mind-set)
of each tradition. Here too, Gregory broke new ground in concepts of spiritual direction. Ideally, Christian authorities were to combine the contemplation of the ascetic life with the activity of the well-trained administrator. We
have seen this concern expressed in the orations for Basil and Athanasius,
but the synthesis of the active and contemplative life was also present in
Gregory's earliest orations on leadership.[94]

When the elder Gregory ordained his son to the priesthood in 361, clerical service and monastic *otium* were thought to be mutually exclusive.[95] The
younger Gregory wrote about his ordination as an act of coercion, and he
worried that as a cleric he would be forced to abandon learning and contemplation. Torn between anxiety and duty, he fled to Basil for refuge. In his
"Apology for His Flight," which was written upon his return, Gregory explained his ambivalence: on the one hand he thought he was unqualified for
the priesthood, while on the other hand, he felt that life in isolation was
selfish. Gregory came back to Nazianzus, he tells us, because the good of the
Church outweighed his own suffering and feelings of inadequacy. "I know,"

he writes, "that direction and order are better than anarchy and disorder."[96] This polarity between unworthiness and duty provided the basis for Gregory's solution.

To be sure, the rhetoric of refusing office had long been a topos of political behavior, something with which Gregory was familiar. The idea goes back to Plato, who argued that the most qualified leader was the one who refused the dignity of office; only the power-hungry sought to lead.[97] Likewise, the concept of *otium* or retirement had also been a part of Greco-Roman political theory because it provided the opportunity to immerse oneself in philosophy and education.[98] As Peter Brown notes, it was the philosopher who could bridge the two ideals—someone who privately cultivated his trade in retreat but then spoke with authority to the most important political and social questions of his age.[99]

Susanna Elm argues, I believe rightly, that in the process of defending his behavior Gregory not only adds a twist to these classical topoi but produces a new paradigm for Christian leadership—that of the active contemplative.[100] According to Gregory, the ideal leader is the one who balances the needs of the community with his own spiritual advancement, or, more precisely, between the turbulence of the world and the stillness of retreat.[101]

In the second oration, Gregory notes that ascetic experience, though a prerequisite for leadership, is not sufficient in and of itself.[102] Those who are qualified must sacrifice themselves for the good of the community. Likewise, a successful ministry requires striking the proper balance. On the one hand, though a priest must be virtuous he must not be so concerned with his renunciation as to neglect his study of Scripture or comprehension of doctrine. On the other hand, the priest must not become so occupied with the affairs of men that he neglects his own life of retreat.[103]

It is with Moses, the Jewish patriarch, that Gregory locates the ideal connection between renunciation and leadership.[104] After a lengthy examination of the ascetic and pastoral skills of biblical heroes (both Jewish and Christian), Gregory identifies Moses as the paradigm.[105] For Nazianzen, the connection is a logical one. Moses was raised as an aristocrat and received the best secular education of his era. He combined that training, however, with a rigorous ascetic life before he assumed a role of leadership among the ancient Jews. Like Gregory, Moses initially also refused office but then assumed his rightful position.

Moses's authority, Nazianzen writes, is revealed by the fact that he was the only one of his people holy enough to encounter God. Even Aaron and his priestly sons were forbidden.[106] Moses's piety, which was an ascetic piety, combined with his successful leadership to enable him to converse with God. Elsewhere, Gregory speaks of Moses's encounter with God as a moment of theosis, or divinization.[107] However, in the second oration, Nazianzen employs the example of Moses to justify his own previous flight—Gregory rejected the idea that he was Moses's equal, and therefore he resisted leadership. Nevertheless, the reference to Moses does as much to establish Nazianzen's credibility as to dismiss it. Through this comparison, Gregory links himself to the ancient patriarch in the minds of his audience. In effect, Gregory notes that most prelates neither take the priestly office seriously nor understand its prerequisites. In contrast, Gregory emphasizes that Christian authorities must strive to be like Moses, a man who perfectly balanced contemplation and action.

The irony, of course, is that many criticize Gregory for his inability to strike that elusive balance.[108] As both a priest and bishop in Nazianzus, Gregory may have shied away from the daily administrative responsibilities associated with clerical service.[109] He seems to have preferred to spend his time in the comfortable confines of his parents' estate or with Basil in Annesoi, interacting with the broader Christian community only through public preaching. Following the death of his father, Gregory went into a more permanent retreat in Seleukia, where he shied away from leadership altogether.[110] Even in Constantinople, where Gregory was more actively involved in the administration of the Church, he often absented himself when the toil of clerical service became too much for his temperament or health.[111]

Much of Gregory's reflection on leadership (including the need to balance action with contemplation) was provoked by conflict, in either Nazianzus or Constantinople. In his *On Himself and the Bishops,* the most aggressive of his autobiographical poems, his defense of his behavior combines with his critique of his opponents to reinforce his vision of the parameters of leadership. To be sure, Gregory equates the qualities of leadership with those that he possesses; he paints his rivals' actions as failures. But there is more to Gregory's presentation of the active/contemplative than self-preservation. Throughout his corpus, Nazianzen identifies a harmonious balance between ministry and action as the only means to provide successful spiritual direction. A few years into his retirement, Gregory became more at peace with what had happened in Constantinople, and he admitted that he had not been up to the challenge that the capital presented.[112] Gregory recognized that he could not maintain a contemplative life in an environment torn by politics and vanity, so he chose a safer course, a life in retreat.[113]

Despite Gregory's personal struggles in Nazianzus, Sasima, and Constantinople, his conceptualization of spiritual direction as a balance between the active and contemplative life is of great significance.[114] In Byzantium, Gregory's corpus became a central component of the educational system. His grammar, style, and ideas formed the basis of the Byzantine curriculum. His was the authoritative voice in theology, and his pastoral model became the paradigm for Christian leadership.

IDEALIZING SPIRITUAL DIRECTION

In the introduction I argued that doctrinal formation was one of the hallmarks of spiritual direction in the clerical tradition. For Gregory, much like Augustine, it was the defining quality of a leader. Gregory lived in an age of great doctrinal turmoil, and he became the most influential spokesperson for the Nicene cause after Athanasius. Today he is probably best known as the author of the five theological orations, which helped to shape the Orthodox doctrine of the Trinity. But his concern for quality doctrinal instruction pervades most of his corpus, not just the "theological" orations.[115] For example, in the "Apology for His Flight," Gregory identifies preaching as the most important responsibility of the clergy.[116] He notes that the questions are many and the stakes are high, so that the priest must be prepared to discuss any subject of theology. For example, the laity will want to know what humanity was like before Adam's lapse, what will become of it at the Second Coming, and what the Trinity is composed of.[117] Nazianzen remarks that such questions require not only doctrinal competence but also the ability to discern how, with whom, and to what extent such matters should be discussed. A misstep in any direction is sure to lead to an incorrect interpretation of orthodox truth, resulting in damnation not only for the cleric but also for the laity.[118] To illustrate the complexity of teaching the doctrine of the Trinity, Gregory notes: "It is necessary to not be so in love with the Father that you surrender his fatherhood, for whose father would he be if the nature of the Son was separated from him and ranked as a creature. . . . Nor can one be so in love with Christ as to not preserve his filial standing (for whose son would he be, if the Father was not his beginning) and the honor of the Father as beginning [ἀρχῆς], in as much as he is Father and begetter."[119] Communicating this to the laity required more than academic learning; it required discernment and oratorical skill.

As noted, Nazianzen extolled both Basil's and Athanasius's rhetorical talents. Not only did they live virtuous lives and understand the higher truths of the Christian message, they nourished the faithful with the nectar of the Gospels.[120] Conversely, Gregory characterizes poor episcopal leadership with insufficient preaching. In *On Himself and the Bishops,* Gregory decries that just about anyone can become a bishop regardless of training and credentials.[121] He demands of his opponents:

> Teach me what the Trinity is. How is God one but separate; one in majesty and nature, a unity, and at the same time three? What about the nature of angels? Of the twofold world? How is omniscience righteous when so many things seem unjust? What is the rationale of the soul or of body? Of the Old and New Testaments? What about the Incarnation, which so transcends comprehension? Or what is this combination of disparate elements for a single glory—dying for the purpose of a reawakening, the return to heaven, or even the resurrection itself?[122]

To be sure, both Gregory's praise of his allies and his critique of his enemies are informed by his sense of self. Gregory believes that he, through God's assistance, saved the capital from the Arians and that he did it through preaching.[123] Perhaps the most painful part of Gregory's humiliation is that he has been replaced by men who, in his eyes, do not take preaching seriously.

In his correspondence with other clerical leaders, Gregory called upon his colleagues to uphold the Nicene faith and to root out all forms of heresy.[124] Nazianzen wrote two letters to Cledonius that attacked the teachings of the Apollinarians.[125] He also sent a letter to Nektarios near the end of 383 mildly critiquing the bishop's inaction against the "the most grievous of all the woes facing the Church—the boldness of the Apollinarians."[126]

There are additional pastoral responsibilities that Gregory admonishes his clerical readers to cultivate. And it is Nazianzen who makes the first decisive step to incorporate ascetic techniques of spiritual direction into a plan for clerical leadership. Specifically, Gregory acknowledges and encourages the spiritual director to adopt an individualized and gradual system of supervision that takes advantage of the monastic concept of οἰκονομία.

In the second oration, Gregory states that it is not enough for the Christian leader to understand orthodox doctrines—he must be able to overcome all the obstacles that prevent him from passing that knowledge on to the laity. He observes that there is great diversity within the Christian community and that consequently the spiritual father must tailor his message accordingly:

> The same medicine and the same food are not administered identically to dissimilar bodies, but differently according to the degree of sickness or health. Likewise, individual souls are treated with discerning words and therapeutic instruction. Those who are experienced [with spiritual healing] are a witness to this. Some are led by doctrine, others are brought to bear by example; some need incentives, others need restraint; some are sluggish and hard to rouse to the good . . . others are immoderately fervent in spirit, and it is difficult for them to control their impulses.[127]

In what will become a pastoral convention among later Church fathers, Gregory speaks of the necessity for a spiritual advisor to differentiate between men and women, rich and poor, old and young, and monks and lay people.[128] The accomplished spiritual father is the one who molds his advice to the unique strengths and weaknesses of his disciples.[129]

As noted in the previous chapter, the idea of adaptability and versatility in the process of psychagogy (i.e., spiritual direction) was a common principle in many of the ancient philosophical schools and was extolled by Aristotle, Cicero, Plutarch, and others.[130] In fact, many of the specific distinctions that Gregory and subsequent Christians came to identify as important circumstances for the individualization of spiritual direction had been identified by the ancients.[131] As part of his education, Gregory was no doubt familiar with this concept; his use of these pedagogical maxims was, in part, the fruit of that education. But what made Gregory's appropriation of these classical conventions not only distinctively Christian but notably ascetic (in the Christian sense) was his prescriptions for spiritual healing.

Borrowing the distinction between ἀκρίβεια and οἰκονομία (or between strictness and condescension) from the monastic community, Gregory notes that the shepherd must be willing to bend the rules of normal behavior if he is to heal those under his care: "[I]n some cases we must appear angry even if we are not, disdainful even though we do not disdain them, or show despair even though we do not despair, according to their nature. Others still, in fairness, we must offer healing and humility so that they may hope for better things."[132] The priest is to be harsh with the harsh and gentle with the meek. Essentially, Gregory's spiritual director is something of a chameleon, able to alter his demeanor whenever his pastoral circumstances change. Elsewhere, Gregory extols St. Paul's ability to combine strictness and "loving kindness" as necessary.[133]

The concept of οἰκονομία is not as developed in Gregory's writing as it is in Basil's monastic literature and John Chrysostom's *On the Priesthood*. However, the fact that the concept is present at all demonstrates Nazianzen's interest in ascetic conceptions of spiritual direction. The appeal of flexible rules, as far as Gregory is concerned, is that they enable the spiritual director to advance gradually those under his care.[134]

In the funeral oration for his father (Oration 18) Nazianzen provides an example of gradual correction successfully applied. According to Gregory, when his father assumed the episcopate in Nazianzus the flock was undisciplined and poorly instructed. Exercising great economy, the elder Gregory slowly improved the situation through gentle, pastoral speech and by setting an example.[135] He was not rash or conceited. He taught with simplicity and avoided rhetorical excess. In short, the elder Gregory was a model bishop because he improved the spiritual condition of his flock through gradual ascetic advancement.[136]

Underpinning each characterization of pastoral care is the notion that the person in authority (presumably a cleric) will direct the spiritual formation of those in his care. The terms *shepherd* (ποιμήν) and *flock* (ποίμνιον) are everywhere in Gregory's corpus.[137] Nazianzen does not consistently employ the phrase for "spiritual fatherhood" (πνευματικὸς πατήρ) that monastic writers were beginning to use in his age.[138] But he certainly conceives of a similar relationship in which the laity turn to their clerical leaders for continuous pastoral encouragement and direction. In his "Apology for His Flight," Nazianzen disqualifies himself from leadership (albeit rhetorically) by noting that he has not sufficiently submitted himself to a spiritual master: "[O]ne part of philosophy is too lofty for me—the responsibility to direct and govern souls, in other words the charge of caring for a flock—until I have rightly learned to submit myself to a shepherd and have my soul purged."[139] In a subsequent oration, Gregory takes for granted that disciples (μαθητάς) obey their pastors and teachers (ποιμέσι καὶ διδασκάλοις).[140]

Instead of using the term *spiritual father,* Gregory more frequently writes of the spiritual physician. In a passage that Pope Gregory I borrowed for his own pastoral treatise, Nazianzen writes: "[D]irecting a man, the most variable and diverse of creatures, seems to me, indeed, to be the art of arts and science of sciences. Anyone may recognize this by comparing the work of the physician of souls [ψυχῶν ἰατρείαν] to the treatment of the body."[141] He goes on to show that this spiritual physician has both the greater responsibility and the more difficult task.[142] Nevertheless, the comparison is an apt one for Gregory. "The physician [of the body] will prescribe medicines and diet and guard against things that cause injuries. . . . Sometimes, he will make use of the scalpel or even more severe remedies; but none of these things, extreme as they may appear, is as difficult as the diagnosis and cure of our habits, passions, lives, and wills."[143] The analogy between spiritual director and physician continues for much of the text and appears elsewhere in his corpus.[144] For her part, Susanna Elm identifies the analogy of the philosopher-physician as a logical one for Gregory because physicians "were the only 'aristocrats' who derived their status not only from their 'noble birth,' but because they had undergone a period or rigorous training."[145]

DIRECTING THE LAY COMMUNITY

There is a difference between the ideals that Nazianzen espoused when he was writing a treatise on spiritual direction or mocking his contemporaries and the actual pastoral direction that he provided to those under his care. We are, unfortunately, limited in our knowledge of Gregory's daily interaction with the laity. The recorded evidence derives from public orations, which he initially presented to generally mixed audiences in Nazianzus and Constantinople and then later revised, and his letters, which were often more professional than pastoral.[146] Nevertheless, two themes do run consistently through these records—the salvific benefit of ascetic renunciation and the need for doctrinal conformity.

For all his preference for the educated elite, Gregory's pastoral advice was remarkably pedestrian. He taught everyone (rich, poor, married, and celibate) to cultivate ascetic detachment. His congregations were encouraged to fast, remain sober, eschew comfortable living (luxurious clothing, furniture, etc.), and give generously to the poor. In short, Gregory instructed his followers that the path to God was paved with temperance and simplicity—the cultivation of reason or theological sophistication had little to do with one's salvation.[147]

The ascetic life, according to Gregory, was not confined to the professional monastic; lay persons also were expected to limit physical pleasure and direct their attention to God. Gregory cautioned those who had assembled for a martyr's festival:

> If we are here to serve the delights of the stomach and to indulge fleeting pleasures and ingest what is of no value, and if we think this a proper place for drunkenness rather than sobriety, an opportunity for the buying and selling of goods rather than ascent, or (if I dare to say it) of θέωσις, of which the martyrs are the intercessors, I do not accept the event at all. For what has the chaff to do with the wheat, debauchery of the flesh to do with a martyr's passion? The one is of the theater, the other in my congregation; the one among the intemperate, the other among people of moderation; the one among those who love the flesh, the other among those who release themselves from the body.[148]

All Christians were to practice moderate renunciation—Church holidays were no occasion for impropriety, regardless of how festive they were.[149]

Gregory extended his directives beyond the realm of public behavior. Christians were to observe relative austerity in all aspects of their daily lives (e.g., food, clothing, home decorations). At the opening of a hospital complex in Caesarea, Gregory scolded those who enjoyed the comforts of luxurious clothes while others went cold and hungry: "We lavish ourselves with

soft, flowing, and translucent clothes, which are made of linen and silk—
clothing that is, in fact, conspicuous (for this is my impression of everything
that is superfluous), and we are careful to store away vain and useless provisions that will be enjoyed by moths and the decay of time. [The poor], on
the other hand, lack enough food for survival. Woe to my insolence and woe
to their suffering!"[150] A few lines later, Gregory continues the critique:

> As for us, we gloriously enshrine ourselves on a high and lofty bed
> amid extraordinary and delicate tapestries, yet we are unable to endure
> even the sound of their cry. Sweet-smelling flowers are placed upon
> our floors . . . and our table is drizzled with perfume . . . in order that
> we may be all the more pampered. . . . Our tables are crammed with the
> deceptions of many cooks, all assembled in a contest to see who will
> most excessively flatter our indecent and ungracious stomach—that
> grievous burden and instigation of evil.[151]

Gregory demands asceticism but (one could argue) in moderation. The Christian family need not live like paupers, but it should abandon that which is
unnecessary. He maintains that unlike physical ailments the pampering of
the body is the result of a misdirected will. According to Gregory, Christians
who wish to escape the snares of luxurious living are able to freely choose
the life of renunciation. As such, asceticism provides a vehicle for spiritual
ascent, even for the married.[152]

Throughout his orations, Gregory consistently extolled the benefits of
charity and suffering.[153] Though neither is distinctively ascetic, in Gregory's
hands these virtues complement his more forceful requirements for renunciation.[154] In his fourteenth oration, Gregory calls on his listeners to reject
the trappings and allure of wealth and to embrace almsgiving and acts of
charity.[155] In the fifth chapter of the oration, Nazianzen argues that everyone is blessed with a unique set of virtues and challenged by his or her own
passions. Despite that multiplicity, charity serves as the lone mechanism by
which everyone can perform good.[156] "[F]ollowing Paul and Christ himself,
we must consider love to be the first and greatest of the commandments because it is the culmination of the Law and the Prophets. I find its most essential component to be the love of the poor. . . . [O]f all things, nothing serves
God as well as mercy because no other thing is more proper to God."[157] By

the end of the sermon, Gregory's oratory reaches such a pitch of excitement that he promises the remission of sin through almsgiving.[158]

Similarly, Gregory extols the benefit of suffering, both physical and emotional. As early as the apostle Paul, Christians had written about the value of suffering. Gregory appropriates this maxim in a variety of contexts. In his first oration on peace, he compares the suffering of the ancient Jews to the plight of those who endured the schism in the church at Nazianzus. "For sometimes, this very thing—suffering—has a therapeutic value for salvation."[159] Consoling the same community in the wake of excessive taxation, Gregory draws a similar conclusion, though this time it is directed at the suffering associated with material loss and not community discord.[160]

In his sixteenth oration, Gregory offers his most complete theological assessment of the value of suffering. In 373, Nazianzus experienced a series of disasters that left the region economically destitute.[161] Gregory scrambles to explain to his bewildered congregation how God could allow such devastation. He explains that natural disasters are God's way of reminding the world of the terrors of eternal damnation. The inhabitants of Nazianzus, therefore, should be thankful that God has graced them with a warning and provided them with time to repent of their sins. In Gregory's retelling, the events that struck the region were acts of divine mercy and not punishment. Ultimately, God tests those He loves, and His rebukes are the signs of His fatherly affection.[162] "For every soul that is not chastised is not healed," Gregory offers.[163] The response to suffering should be thanksgiving, fasting, and repentance, not despair.[164] Almsgiving and suffering are not distinctively ascetic qualities. However, through an asceticizing hermeneutic, Gregory aligns almsgiving and suffering with the more obvious ascetic enjoinders of fasting, temperance, and chastity.

The ascetic quality of Gregory's pastoral strategy is more forcefully confirmed by a few examples from his correspondence, where he pushes his agenda a step further. In 368, Gregory's brother, Caesarius, narrowly survived an earthquake in Bithynia. Caesarius's home had been destroyed, and Gregory interpreted his brother's miraculous escape as a fitting opportunity for him to finally abandon his secular career and devote himself to the religious life. Gregory begins the letter, "Fearful events are not without use to the wise . . . for although we pray that they may not occur, when they do they instruct us."[165] He goes on to note that Caesarius should now commit himself fully to God—something that, by Gregory's reasoning, is impossible as long as Caesarius remains in a secular profession.[166] The letter is instructive in that it reveals the extent of Gregory's commitment to the ascetic life and his difficulty in persuading those closest to him to do likewise. In the same letter, Gregory must apologize for having to make the appeal (i.e., for Caesarius to abandon his secular career) so often, but Gregory believes that the circumstances warrant this final petition.[167]

Nazianzen similarly admonished Gregory of Nyssa, Basil's younger brother. At a rather young age, Nyssa had been ordained to the minor rank of reader. However, he was unfulfilled and took a position in rhetoric, giving scandal to the Church and especially to Basil. Gregory writes the future bishop of Nyssa to reprimand him for his conduct. According to Nazianzen, Nyssa has turned his back on the Church, preferring the title of professor to Christian.[168] Anticipating Nyssa's response that he, Nazianzen, had been both a Christian and a professional rhetorician, Gregory notes that he was not ordained when he taught rhetoric and upon his ordination abandoned his secular ambitions to pursue a life in the Church. In short, Nazianzen accuses Nyssa of descending back into the world. A Christian, especially a cleric, should always move toward detachment, not engagement with the secular.

Further evidence of Gregory's commitment to lay asceticism stems from his funeral oration for his sister Gorgonia, who died in 369 or 370. The panegyric includes many of the conventions of classical eulogy as they were appropriated by Christian orators. Throughout the oration, Gregory attests to her faith, virtue, and acts of piety (especially her generosity for the poor). Tucked neatly into these various biographical details and hagiographic conventions, however, is a series of statements regarding her ascetic disposition that were, no doubt, designed to encourage imitation among Gregory's listeners (especially his female listeners).[169] He comments more than once on her disregard for physical beauty or material comfort.[170] He frequently notes the tears, vigils, and prostrations that were the hallmarks of her rigorous asceticism. But it is in his discussion of Gorgonia as a woman who was both wife and ascetic that Gregory becomes especially eloquent. He claims that the married and the celibate life each have their individual strengths and weaknesses—neither absolutely binds one to God nor restricts one from God.[171] According to Gregory, Gorgonia, more completely than anyone else, cultivated the best of each life while carefully avoiding related limitations.[172]

Gregory's message is that holiness is available to all Christians, even those in the throes of raising a family. Married Christians, including women with children, can attain the blessed life, but they must, like Gorgonia, cultivate ascetic detachment.[173]

According to John McGuckin, Nazianzen's feelings for his older sister were mixed—although he respected her ascetic discipline, theirs was a rather distant relationship.[174] It may be that he did not know what to make of his sister's austerities. As noted, Gregory's was a refined, gentlemanly form of asceticism. Gorgonia, however, seems to have embraced many of the pious disciplines of the desert ascetics even though she was a wife and mother and even though she remained a catechumen until just before death.[175] Not only did she convince her husband to live in celibacy during the later years of their marriage, but she also entered the altar of a church and committed an act of "pious impudence."[176] Had she not been his sister, or, perhaps, had she not been a member of the elite, Nazianzen's attitude might have been different.[177]

Nevertheless, Gregory's portrayal of Gorgonia is of a perfect woman, a model for both virgins and mothers. What is more, he, like other male authors of the period, occasionally characterizes his heroine's achievements as masculine. Not only does he speak of her becoming more holy than the men around her, but he describes her as possessing characteristics often associated at that time with manly holiness (e.g., contemplation and the cultivation of reason and virtue).[178] Gregory of Nyssa would later characterize his own sister, Macrina the Younger, in a similar way.[179]

Gregory also addressed to female ascetics a pair of poems that encouraged them to cultivate ascetic disciplines but to do so cautiously. In one of these poems, *Prescriptions for Virgins (Praecepta ad virgines),* he warned that women committed to virginity should not cohabit with men who were not their blood relatives.[180] As we saw in the previous chapter, the cohabitation of male and female ascetics became increasingly popular as the ascetic movement spread. For Gregory, the practice was scandalous not only because it was an overt source of temptation but because it gradually led to what he called a poisoning of the soul.[181] Instead, Gregory encouraged women inclined to the monastic life to enter an established community or to remain at home with parents or possibly their siblings.[182] Corroborating this position is a collection of letters to virgins who lived at home or under the protection of their bishop.[183] Although Gregory does not seem to have taken as active a role as Athanasius with respect to the continuous spiritual direction of virgins (at least there is less evidence for it), his opinions about their lives and their role in the community are consistent with those of many of the ascetically inclined bishops of his era.

In addition to ascetic detachment, Gregory's pastoral concerns frequently involved doctrinal formation. We should recall that Gregory delivered the five theological orations to his congregation at the Church of the Anastasia in Constantinople. These orations served Gregory on many levels, but we should note that one of his concerns was to shape the theological beliefs of the people to whom he was ministering. Yet despite his willingness to push the theological debate in new directions and to support with great stubbornness what was at the time a controversial position (the divinity of the Holy Spirit), Nazianzen's pastoral practice was one of doctrinal toleration.

As early as the 360s, we see Gregory subordinating theological precision to Christian unity.[184] The first confrontation in which he participated was the schism in Nazianzus. As noted, it had been Gregory's father who had been theologically clumsy, not the monks who broke from his authority. The controversy pushed Gregory to his rhetorical limits as he tried simultaneously to appease the rigorous faction and retain his father's dignity. He welcomed back the monastic party by appropriating their ideas and congratulating them for their steadfastness. But Gregory also chastened the monks for rejecting the authority of their bishop. In the end, this was an effective policy.

When Gregory went on the theological offensive, whether in Nazianzus or in Constantinople, he always enabled his opponents to return to the fold without retribution. Ironically, this policy of moderation led (in part) to his own dismissal from Constantinople in the summer of 381.[185] When the Nicenes returned to power with the support of Theodosius, there was a growing sense among many of them that they should punish the Eunomians (and Homoians), who had been their persecutors.[186] But Nazianzen was not persuaded. Instead, he addressed his own party with his twenty-second and twenty-third orations, arguing that Christians should always forgive those who had wronged them.[187] Gregory reasoned that heretics and schismatics should be the objects of pity and not hatred.[188] As long as they pledged to amend their ways, Gregory was willing to recognize both the baptisms and the ordinations of most of the Homoians.[189]

The policy of toleration was pastoral and generous. Gregory believed that the most effective way to bring healing (both to the former offenders and to the Church at large) was to grant this blanket οἰκονομία. In the auto-biographical poem *On His Own Life,* Gregory asks: "Tell me, you assembly of struggling boys who are now in command; do you think that gentleness is weakness or that courage must be frantic and reproachful? Was this an opportunity for an insatiable desire for power to push, drive, steal, and destroy? Or was it an opportunity to heal with the medicine of salvation? The second option offered two advantages: people are made moderate by the use of moderation, and I was in a position to gain their praise and support."[190]

Gregory's reasoning is explicit. He had extended the olive branch of οἰκονομία because he had believed it would allow for reconciliation.[191] His willingness to recognize Homoian baptisms (which he might not have considered to have been Trinitarian) demonstrates the extent of his willingness to bend the rules to bring peace to the Church. Many of the Nicenes were not as conciliatory.[192]

In addition to pursuing a policy of moderation with his former opponents, Gregory actively discouraged theological speculation and discussion among the laity. We might characterize Nazianzen's ideal as one in which the laity were doctrinally informed but submissive. In several orations, Gregory made the point that theology is not for everyone.[193] In the twenty-seventh oration, he remarked, "[I]t is not the continual remembrance of God that I would hinder, but only the conversing about it."[194] As noted, Gregory developed that thesis in an attempt to discredit his Eunomian competitors as intellectually and ascetically incompetent. At the same time, the proscriptions against speculation and idle conversation that he naturally extended to the laity well characterize Gregory's approach to pastoral care.

For Gregory, anyone who lacked the ascetic and intellectual credentials for theological investigation was sure to bring harm to himself and others.[195] By definition, lay persons living in the world were unable to uncover the truth about God's mysteries for themselves. While we may view this as an elitist proposition, it made good pastoral sense to Gregory. One's salvation was not determined by one's ability to articulate the doctrine of the Trinity; rather, it depended upon simpler things. Do you give to the poor?[196] Do you fast? Do you pray? Are you obedient to your instructors?[197] These are the questions that Gregory put to his congregations. While many will credit Gregory with articulating the orthodox doctrine of the Trinity, he discouraged those under his care from pursuing such questions by themselves.

Gregory's corpus demonstrates a rough familiarity with many of the pastoral techniques of the ascetic community (e.g., the spiritual father, οἰκονομία, and gradual correction). However, much of the evidence for this derives from the homilies on leadership (e.g., "Apology for His Flight"), which he may not have delivered in public. And there is much less evidence for his application of ascetic standards from the correspondence.[198] The one ascetic pastoral technique that does occur with some regularity in Gregory's preaching is that of the saintly exemplar.

We have already explored the orations for Gregory's father, St. Athanasius, and St. Basil. Though they do not conform precisely to the genre of the *Vitae Patrum* or Pope Gregory I's *Dialogues (Dialogorum Libri IV)*, they do extol certain attributes that Gregory undoubtedly wished to pass on to his audience. For example, in describing the life of his parents, Gregory establishes a paradigm for marriage that he hoped to promote among the laity of Nazianzus.[199] Likewise, Nazianzen champions Athanasius's and Basil's ascetic austerities, their contemplation, and their willingness to undergo suffering and hardship for the sake of orthodox truth.[200] He also notes their patience in the face of opposition and the compassion they showed to their enemies.[201]

In some ways, the fifteenth oration (more than the encomiums already listed) fits closely with the model of the spiritual exemplar that was gaining momentum in the monastic community. In December of 362, Gregory preached a homily on the occasion of the newly established feast of the Maccabean martyrs.[202] Nazianzen submits that these men deserve recognition and honor even though their suffering antedates Christ's crucifixion.[203] In fact, he compels his audience not only to recognize the piety of the Maccabeans but to "emulate their valor" and to move from "commemoration to imitation."[204] By imitation, Gregory does not mean martyrdom; rather, he leads his audience to those aspects of the story that he hopes will resonate. In the last section of the homily, he summarizes what he expects his congregation will take from their Hebrew predecessors: "Priests, mothers, children, let us imitate them: priests, in honor of the spiritual father Eleazar, who well demonstrates what is best by both his words and deeds; mothers, in honor of that noble woman, by showing true love to your children and commending them to Christ—this type of sacrifice brings sanctity to the married life;

children, by respecting the holy ones and spending your youth not in the ful-fillment of shameful passions but by fighting against the passions and war-ring mightily against the modern-day Antiochus."[205] Gregory uses the Mac-cabean martyrs to advance his ideas about Christian behavior. The festival does not so much serve as a call to martyrdom as provide an opportunity to encourage real commitment to the faith—the type of commitment that leads a mother to sacrifice her son(s) in the name of God.

Gregory's use of the saintly exemplar was limited, and one might argue that it was confined to the martyrs.[206] It was during Gregory's lifetime that members of the ascetic community began to expand the cult of martyrs to include the post-Constantinian martyrs (i.e., the ascetic saints of the desert). By the fifth century, the lives and sayings of the ascetic fathers had become an important vehicle for disseminating patterns of piety and for reinforcing the parameters of authority within the spiritual father/spiritual disciple model. But here too Gregory's orations provided a foretaste of things to come. He commended the seven Maccabean youths for their obedience to their "father" Eleazar. Eleazar, of course, was not their biological father but their spiritual leader (their priest). Nazianzen extolled Eleazar's ability to offer to God the seven young men, "the fruit of his guidance."[207] Thus Gregory in his retelling of the story incorporated several topoi of ascetic literature (e.g., the spiritual father/spiritual disciple and the emphasis on obedience) to weave together not only the pre-Christian and Christian martyrs but also the monastic and secular Christian communities.

Unlike Athanasius, who made little distinction between ascetic and non-ascetic Christianity, Gregory Nazianzen was very much aware of the grow-ing divide in the Church. One might even argue that by insisting upon asce-tic qualifications for leadership Gregory helped to define that separation. But ultimately Gregory's was a policy of incorporation, not division; he worked to connect the ascetic and secular strands within the Christian community.

This is most clearly demonstrated by his criteria for leadership. By insisting upon an intelligent and elite clergy, Gregory conformed to the general practice of the post-Constantinian Church; by requiring those same men to demon-strate and maintain ascetic renunciation, Gregory evinced the penetration of the ascetic community into the broader Church. The most qualified leader was the one who had the dignity and education of the privileged class while being, at the same time, someone who had rejected the advantages of nobility.

On a theoretical level, Gregory did more than anyone before him to describe the duties of spiritual direction. His "Apology for His Flight" virtually initiated a new genre of Christian literature. I have suggested that one of the inspirations for this creation was the rising tension between institutional and charismatic traditions of leadership. Through this oration, Gregory hoped to strike a compromise between these competing traditions. As we will see by way of comparison in subsequent chapters, Gregory's was not the most complete synthesis of the ascetic and clerical models because in some respects the two traditions were not yet fully developed. However, he was the most creative in his attempt to bridge the two traditions. He bestowed upon later generations the very notion that such a bridging was not only possible but also necessary.

THREE

Augustine of Hippo and Resistance to the Ascetic Model of Spiritual Direction

Augustine, like Nazianzen, brought an analytic mind and a gift for rhetoric to the priesthood—traits that Augustine came to expect from every priest. Born in 356 in Thagaste, he received a quality classical education. As a boy, he learned rhetoric by reading Virgil, Cicero, Sallust, and Terrence. He did not study Greek authors and never developed an aptitude for the language.[1] He completed his education in Carthage, where he began a career as a teacher of rhetoric. From Carthage, Augustine spent a brief period in Rome before achieving professional success in 384, when he was selected as the professor of rhetoric in Milan (a favorite Western residence of emperors).[2]

In these early years, Augustine underwent several religious conversions.[3] Though enrolled as a catechumen in his youth, he had not found fulfillment in Christianity.[4] He commented in his *Confessions (Confessiones)* that he had thought the Bible to be a philosophical embarrassment.[5] On the other hand, Cicero's *Hortensius* and the Platonic philosophy therein awakened his religious feeling.[6] Following that initial encounter with Platonism, Augustine drifted toward Manicheanism and spent nine years as reader of the sect.[7] Among other things, the Manichean claim to place reason before faith had been an appealing concept to the inquisitive Augustine.[8] But when he arrived in Milan, Augustine had already grown dissatisfied with the Manichean version of wisdom.[9] His discontent coincided with a chance meeting with that city's Nicene bishop, Ambrose. Ambrose gave Augustine a new appreciation for the biblical texts through allegorical interpretation.[10] As a result, Christianity began to appear more sophisticated and compelling to Augustine.

Through the influence of Ambrose, Augustine gradually came to acknowledge the foundational precepts of orthodox Christianity, but he remained unable to embrace chastity of body or spirit. "The time passed and I was slow to turn to the Lord. Day by day, I deferred to live in him but did not defer to die in myself. Desiring a pleasant life, I still feared it, and fleeing from it, I sought it. I told myself that I would be miserable if I deprived myself of the caresses of a woman; and I resisted, without trying, the [spiritual] medicine that heals such an infirmity."[11] In his *Confessions,* Augustine presented sexual activity and Christianity as mutually exclusive endeavors. For him, marriage and Christianity could not coexist.[12] His philosophical colleague Alypius insisted that the celibate life was a necessary step on the path to true philosophy.[13] In many ways, Augustine's conversion was an ascetic one.[14]

Between his reenlistment as a catechumen in Milan (September, 386) and his eventual baptism at the hands of Ambrose (Easter, 387), Augustine retired to Cassiciacum. There he adopted the way of life so cherished by Gregory Nazianzen and other members of the late antique Roman elite—*vitae otium.*[15] As the guest of the wealthy Verecundus, Augustine enjoyed the leisure of the philosopher's life. Like Nazianzen's, what distinguished Augustine's *otium* from a typical Roman's was the commitment to chastity and his belief that he and his colleagues were pursuing a distinctly *Christianae vitae otium.*[16] Augustine maintained that philosophy held the mysteries of God.[17] He and his interlocutors pursued the theological conundrums of evil, the soul, and the Trinity.[18] For Augustine, rational investigation led to truth.

Augustine's biographer and trusted disciple Possidius reported that the future bishop returned to North Africa shortly after his baptism. Upon his arrival, he settled on the family estate (in Thagaste) with a small community of friends who sought the ascetic life.[19] There "they committed themselves to God through a life of fasting, prayer, and good works."[20] Augustine and his community were identified as *servi dei*—servants of God. They were baptized laymen dedicated to chastity.[21] They displayed a fascination for the practitioners of a more rigorous renunciation, but their focus was intellectual.[22]

Two years after his return to Thagaste, Augustine's life changed once more. Traveling to Hippo to scout a recruit for his community, Augustine was "seized" by the local congregation and ordained to the priesthood.[23] Undaunted by his ordination, he established the religious commune he sought, although it consisted of the city's clergy rather than lay ascetics.[24] Whether

Augustine authored a *regula* for this monastery is a matter of scholarly debate. Nevertheless, it is certain that he continued to supervise his house of
clerics after he became bishop of Hippo in 395.[25] Moreover, he established
a house for female ascetics and when necessary rebuked those who resisted
the authority of the abbess.[26]

Like Gregory Nazianzen, Augustine was well positioned to fuse the ascetic and pastoral traditions. He described his conversion to Christianity as an
ascetic awakening.[27] In Cassiciacum and Thagaste, he had lived as an ascetic: celibate, moderate, and contemplative. Augustine went to Hippo in the
process of building a monastery but instead soon found himself placed into
a position of priestly authority. Early in his clerical career, Augustine wrote
that the monastic life was the ideal Christian existence.[28] Once ordained, he
continued his austerities, yet he perceived a disconnect between his former
idealism and public pastoral service. He believed that his years of contemplation had not prepared him for his new role. Thus, as he began his ministry, Augustine requested a sabbatical in order to learn the skills of pastoral
leadership: "but the [practice of pastoral care] I did not learn as a boy or in
adolescence; instead, I was at that time just beginning to learn to counter my
own sin (for, at that time, I knew no other purpose), when I was the assistant
captain, when as yet I could not even handle the oar."[29] Through analysis of
the specifics of Augustine's pastoral career, it will become apparent that the
famed bishop of Hippo rarely utilized his ascetic training with respect to the
priesthood.

THE CRITERIA FOR ORDINATION

Like many bishops of his era, Augustine noted the paucity of qualified
priests.[30] However, unlike many of his colleagues, he centered his criteria
for ordination on education and social class. In his *On Christian Teaching (De
doctrina Christiana),* a treatise composed for preachers, Augustine identified
rhetorical expertise as the single most important skill possessed by a Christian *doctor* (i.e., teacher) because the preacher communicated doctrinal information through public speaking.[31] Augustine posited two additional theses:
(1) rhetorical sophistication was a craft developed by only the most intelligent
candidates, and (2) only those who mastered it could achieve a successful

ministry.[32] We might note that Augustine's prescription for clerical success closely resembled his own preparation for the priesthood.

To be sure, Augustine required his clergy to remain celibate, and we know that he organized the clergy in Hippo into a community.[33] Concerning celibacy, Augustine followed the position of Ambrose and Siricius (bishop of Rome, 384–99), which prohibited a married clergy.[34] This opinion was not universal (e.g., Basil of Caesarea and Gregory Nazianzen had opposed it), but it was increasingly popular in the West.[35] Augustine also expected his clergy to dispose of their possessions before they entered the community.[36]

The correspondence, particularly the recently discovered letters, provides ample insight into Augustine's screening for candidates. In Epistle 18*, the bishop identified moral impurity and a lack of zeal among potential candidates as obstacles to ordination.[37] Elsewhere, he argued that the scarcity of priests *(inopiam clericorum)* stemmed from a reluctance among *curiales* to accept ordination.[38] As observed in previous chapters, the *curiales* initially swarmed into the clerical ranks in the wake of Constantine's conversion. However, that influx began to wane by the fifth century.[39] For his part, Augustine believed that the failure of the *curiales* to accept ordination derived from the fact that they would continue to be subject to the taxes of the curial rank even if they abandoned secular life and joined the priesthood.[40]

Further statements suggest that Augustine thought that only the *decuriones* possessed the dignity and skill necessary for pastoral leadership. He wrote, "[A]nd what is more, people do not notice the fact that at this time men of [curial] rank are lacking. . . . When there are no such men in the cities or in the rural areas around the cities, we groan in vain for the weak and miserable whom we are unable to help."[41] Unlike Nazianzen, who had sought candidates who possessed both nobility and ascetic experience, Augustine focused especially on social class as the principal prerequisite for clerical office.[42] As we will see, Augustine's priest was not a spiritual father in the monastic mold—he was an administrator and disseminator of Christian doctrines. The bishop's use of the *curiales* was quite practical.

The case of Pinianus is an interesting lacuna in Augustine's policy to recruit well-educated men of means. Pinianus was the wealthy son-in-law of Albania and the husband of Melania the younger. After the birth of his second son, Pinianus acquiesced to his wife's desire to adopt the ascetic life. Sometime thereafter, he traveled with her and his mother-in-law to their estates in Africa. During a sojourn to Hippo in 411, Pinianus was pressed by the laity (perhaps even in the form of a mob) to accept ordination. He declined with little objection from Augustine. Epistle 126 is Augustine's carefully crafted reconstruction of the events designed to free himself from any involvement in the case that might attract the ill will of the highly influential Albania, who apparently did not want her son-in-law (or her property) to fall into the possession of the Church at Hippo. Maureen Tilley suggests that the pressure to ordain Pinianus must have been immense, yet Augustine deferred to the man's wishes.[43] His excuse was that he could not ordain anyone against his wishes. But if we take him at his word, he even helped Pinianus articulate his public rejection of ordination.

The case of Pinianus aside, we can look to the development of the ecclesiastical court system and the burden it placed upon the late antique episcopacy as one explanation for the need of curial administrators. For Augustine, the episcopal courtroom was a constant source of irritation.[44] Even Possidius recognized the extent to which it burdened his hero.[45] Therefore, it is likely that judicial responsibility informed his selection of new priests and that Augustine required his candidates to be legally astute.[46]

Given Augustine's background and his preference for a celibate clergy, we might have expected the bishop of Hippo to have turned to the monasteries to fill pastoral vacancies, yet he did not recognize monasticism as a legitimate preparation. In some instances, he even suggested that monasticism presented an obstacle. Epistle 60, which was written to Bishop Aurelius and dated 401, is particularly illuminating. According to this letter, two men abandoned their monastery in Hippo and moved to Aurelius's diocese. Aurelius ordained one of them to the deaconate and held similar plans for the second. Augustine was incensed. Not only had the monks forsaken their cloister, clearly indicating that they were unfit to rule, but also Aurelius had not consulted with Augustine before elevating a monk from his diocese to the ranks of the clergy. Augustine added a stinging comment about the pastoral potential of monastics: "Even a good monk rarely becomes a good cleric, for even if he endures celibacy he may lack the necessary education or the requisite integrity of character."[47] Augustine's prejudice is explicit. Monks often lack education and integrity (i.e., social stature)—their renunciation does not merit the privilege of pastoral authority.

Similar expressions of hostility exist elsewhere in Augustine's correspondence. While attending a council in 404, he wrote to the clergy in Hippo (in part) to console them about the scandalous activities of a few monks. He concluded by noting, "[W]hile it is difficult to find more accomplished men than those living in monasteries, so also I have not found worse than those taken with sin in monasteries."[48] Later Augustine informed the congregation at Suppa that he would not consent to their request for one of his monks to be ordained in their church.[49] Augustine did not think the man was sufficiently qualified for clerical office. In that case, a life of asceticism under Augustine's supervision had not adequately prepared the monk for the pastoral responsibility of the deaconate. In another letter (Epistle 48), Augustine instructed an abbot that he should be thankful that God had not made him a cleric because he would have had to deal with numerous responsibilities. Clearly, Augustine did not equate the direction of monks with the direction of the laity.

In 423, Augustine wrote to Pope Celestine to report the unfortunate circumstances of a monk, Antoninus, whom Augustine had raised to the episcopacy.[50] The Diocese of Fussala was in need of a bishop, and the young priest whom Augustine had selected withdrew himself at the last minute. Rather than ask the elderly bishops to make the long journey once more, Augustine hastily advanced a *lector,* Antoninus, from his monastery.[51] Following dozens of complaints in the months that followed, Augustine was forced to take punitive action against Antoninus.[52] The letter to Pope Celestine is significant because it details the North African's remorse for hastily granting episcopal authority to an untrained monk.[53]

Augustine's reception of Donatist clerics is equally enlightening. Perhaps nothing induced his ire more completely than the Donatist practice of (re)-baptizing Christians who joined them. In contrast, Augustine eagerly recognized the baptism of Donatists and extended that accommodation to the rite of ordination.[54] According to canon law, any cleric who sinned seriously (and apostasy was no doubt serious) forfeited his authority and had to return to the laity. But Augustine had several reasons to shift the Church's policy, and he willingly acknowledged the pastoral authority of Donatist clergy who returned.[55] For one, the controversy had originated during a disputed election, and a key issue had been the efficacy of an ordination by "polluted" hands. Augustine, who consistently scrutinized the rigorous practices of the Donatists, adopted a policy of accommodation with respect to ordination. In doing so, he offered a subtle critique of Donatist elitism and accentuated orthodox benevolence.[56]

There is a second, equally pragmatic explanation. Augustine, shrewd as he was, probably believed that Donatist clerics would be more willing to convert (and encourage their congregations to do likewise) if they were able to retain their rank and authority. On a number of occasions, he wrote directly to Donatist clerics gently urging them to return to orthodox Christianity.[57] By recognizing the ordination of Donatists, Augustine not only hastened their return but addressed another sticky problem—the shortage of priests in North Africa.[58]

Why was Augustine willing to ease ecclesiastic restrictions for the purpose of filling clerical positions but at the same time unwilling to employ monastics for the same purpose—even those whom he knew well? Three mutually reinforcing factors seem to have been at play: he believed that education and social class determined one's competency; he privileged administrative competence over spiritual purity; and (as we will see) his polemical confrontations drove a wedge between himself and the ascetic community.

MENTORING SUBORDINATE CLERGY

Augustine's *On Catechizing the Ignorant (De catechizandis rudibus)* and *On Christian Teaching* provide some insight into his mentoring of subordinate clergy. In both texts, Augustine attended to the mechanics of oral delivery and emphasized the importance of doctrinal instruction. Written in 405, Augustine's *On Catechizing the Ignorant* served as a manual for the pastoral role of catechist.[59] At that time, a convert to orthodox Christianity went through four stages in the catechetical process. The text addresses those who belonged to the first of the four stages, the *accedentes*. The *accedentes* were a collection of potential converts, typically pagans, heretics, and the children of Christians. These candidates were also known as the *rudes*, and they included both rustic and educated people. Augustine identifies two responsibilities for the minister: to discern the genuine motivations for conversion and to provide a comprehensive lecture to prepare potential converts for their catechumenate. Throughout the text, the bishop of Hippo emphasizes the importance of an effective delivery, following, in most ways, the teaching of Cicero.[60]

With respect to content, Augustine encourages the catechist to differentiate between the educated and the uneducated.[61] He indicates that while the catechist can assume an educated man's knowledge of the Christian tradition and expect a legitimate desire for conversion, the motives of the illiterate are more open to doubt.[62] By making this distinction, Augustine endorses a common pastoral strategy of his era, whereby situation dictates action.[63] As an example of this principle, Augustine tells us that his own catechetical template (i.e., chapters 16–25) is most appropriate for city dwellers who possess little or no education.[64]

Some of the challenges of public speaking are addressed in chapters 10 through 15. For example, Augustine describes the inadequacy of language to express one's thought.[65] Additionally, he submits that the catechist should not assume that a listless audience indicates a flawed presentation.[66] On the contrary, it is impossible to know whether silence stems from religious awe, shyness, a lack of comprehension, or boredom. Therefore, the instructor should probe his audience to ascertain the level of comprehension and then alter his presentation accordingly.[67]

Certain elements of *On Catechizing the Ignorant* were innovative. It was the first Latin catechetical treatise to supplement the biblical narrative with Church history.[68] It was also the first to point to the Decalogue of Moses as the foundation of Christian morality.[69] Before Augustine, moralists had contrasted the "way of life" to the "way of death."[70] But Augustine traced the Christian moral ethic to the customs of the ancient Jews. Yet the emphasis of Augustine's sample address was clearly doctrinal. Augustine understood that the catechist's most important role was the dissemination of elementary dogmas through a survey of biblical events. He did not stress models of Christian living or piety.[71]

In his *On Christian Teaching*, Augustine further developed his pastoral model. In book 4, he defined the responsibilities of the "interpreter and teacher of Holy Scripture." Those duties included the defense of the faith, instruction in doctrine, the refutation of heresy, and the conciliation of the hostile.[72] Thus the *doctor* (Augustine most likely had in mind senior clerics) had to reproach, entreat, or rouse his audience as necessary. Characteristically, Augustine's interests in education and mental capacity eclipsed concerns for spiritual or ascetic readiness. Once again, he stressed the need for clerics to possess a powerful intellect.[73] As he had in *On Catechizing the Ignorant*, Augustine devoted considerable attention to the development of rhetorical skill.[74] A Christian preacher had to remember that clarity was uniquely important.[75]

Also encouraged were eloquence, diction, and attentiveness to punctuation.[76] It is worth noting that Augustine made more references to Cicero in book 4 than to Scripture. This underscores Augustine's emphasis on education and rhetorical development as critical skills for successful leadership.[77]

From his correspondence, we find further evidence of his instructions for the clergy, especially the importance of the liturgy and the dispensation of the Church's charity.[78] In one letter, Augustine chastised a fellow bishop, Possidius, who had insisted that his congregation abandon jewelry, cosmetics, and fine clothes.[79] Augustine argued that such rigor was reserved for ascetics; though not virtuous, the worldly practices of the laity required toleration.[80] Such evidence gives credence to Robert Markus's contention that Augustine responded to Donatist and Pelagian perfectionism with a "vindication of Christian mediocrity."[81]

Another letter dating to 418 is equally informative.[82] Augustine wrote to the future Pope Sixtus to communicate his appreciation for their mutual campaign against the Pelagians. Of pastoral significance is a brief remark near the end of the letter in which Augustine encouraged careful consideration in the instruction of the ignorant. He noted: "[O]n behalf of the weaker and more simple sheep of the Lord, pastoral vigilance and extreme care must be employed against those who secretly and fearfully (but perseveringly and quietly) teach this error. . . . Moreover, we should not neglect those who through fear hide their opinions under a profound silence."[83] Augustine warned that Pelagians had spread their "disease" among those lay persons who were unable to protect themselves. As a shepherd, Sixtus had to protect his flock. He had to interrogate his subordinates and purge them of false teachings. The expectation of Sixtus's involvement in the religious life of his subordinates might draw comparisons to that of an abbot and his disciples.[84] The difference was that Augustine (and therefore Sixtus) was concerned with doctrinal conformity—there was no discussion of spiritual progress such as one would find in the ascetic community.[85]

Augustine's mentoring of subordinate clergy focused on three pastoral responsibilities: instruction in rudimentary elements of doctrine, celebration of the sacraments, and the distribution of charity. Unlike many of his contemporaries who brought ascetic patterns of spiritual direction to the episcopacy (e.g., Nazianzen, Basil, Chrysostom, and Ambrose), the bishop of Hippo did not repeatedly advocate the continuous supervision of subordinates. Instead, he handled spiritual direction as though it were an administrative matter. Perhaps Augustine's relative neglect of his subordinate clergy related to his own meager pastoral instruction both before and after his ordination.[86]

AUGUSTINE'S DIRECTION OF THE LAY AND MONASTIC COMMUNITIES

Despite his casual interest in the mentoring of clergy, Augustine devoted considerable attention to his own pastoral responsibilities. Access to the bishop's pastoral side is most easily attained through an examination of his incidental or occasional communications (i.e., letters and sermons). Not surprisingly, these too advanced Augustine's doctrinal agenda.

In the year 412, Augustine encouraged Volusian, the uncle of the "younger" Melania, to compose a list of theological questions that troubled him.[87] Unlike many of his correspondents, Volusian possessed a "gifted mind" and a "lucid power of speaking," and the bishop enjoyed nothing more than providing authoritative answers for such capable disciples.[88] In turn, the nobleman presented Augustine with a series of questions related to the Christological debate.[89] Augustine began his response by noting the incapacity of humans to comprehend all there was to know about God and his creation. Yet despite that disclaimer the letter was exhaustive, offering a carefully articulated statement of orthodox teaching.[90]

Interestingly, this epistle offered several theological axioms but little moral or "practical" advice. In other words, Augustine encouraged and stimulated Volusian intellectually. He did not issue guidelines for praxis such as fasting, vigils, or almsgiving. Even the injunctions to love God and one's neighbor were explained in philosophical terms: "[B]y these means perverse minds are amended, weak minds are nourished, and strong minds are delighted. This doctrine has no enemy but the one who persists in error, not knowing its healing power, or, though suffering, remains averse to its cure."[91] Augustine distinguished between those who could comprehend this message and those who could not: "[I]t is necessary to defend [proper teaching] against those with insufficient minds who despise [the truth] with their arrogance, boasting that they can do great things, while in fact they can do nothing to heal or even restrain their own vices."[92] The bishop of Hippo responded similarly in other letters to well-educated correspondents.[93]

Even those whom Augustine understood to be less sophisticated received letters that emphasized doctrinal conformity. In 408, Augustine responded to Italica, a Roman noblewoman, about her naive questions concerning the ability to "see" God.[94] The bishop distinguished the physical world, which is seen, from God, who is invisible. Augustine reasoned that to see God was to become like God. And how did one become like God? According to the bishop, "[W]e shall become more like him, the more we advance in knowledge of him and love."[95] Once again, the bishop of Hippo stressed knowledge— he did not exhort specific practices, ascetic or otherwise. This is especially noteworthy because Italica was a recent widow. It is curious that he did not encourage her to remain a widow or adopt some form of prayer regimen, as he did other widows.

The letter to Italica is also significant in that she was a woman. In a recent article, Maureen Tilley surveys each of Augustine's missives to women and offers some provocative conclusions.[96] Briefly, Tilley maintains that Augustine's few pastoral letters to women (always women of rank) serve mostly as an outlet for his theological positions. Moreover, they show little pastoral sensitivity and do not treat their recipients as equals. The letter to Italica, for example, is drafted to offer solace to a woman who has recently suffered the loss of her husband, but it quickly devolves into a sophisticated analysis of why she will not behold her husband until the next life. As Tilley aptly put it, "[I]t is difficult to see how this letter might have been any consolation to a recently bereaved widow."[97]

For our purposes, what is most interesting is that although Augustine's letters to women lacked a sensitive touch they actually offered more practical advice than those he addressed to his many male correspondents. For example, Epistles 130 and 131, which were written to Proba (Italica's mother-in-law), offered instruction on prayer, fasting, and almsgiving. Proba was also a widow, and Augustine gave her every encouragement to maintain her spiritual nobility by exercising well the rank of widow. She also was to give her wealth to the poor because retaining it would bring her no consolation in this life or the next. With respect to prayer, the main theme of Epistle 130, Augustine admonished Proba to imitate the brief, frequently repeated prayers of the Egyptian monks who offered them like arrows darting toward heaven.[98]

Epistles 130, 131, and 150 (which were written also to Proba and to another daughter-in-law, Juliana) praised widowhood and virginity. It was to this same Juliana that Augustine dedicated *On the Good of Widowhood (De bono viduitatis)* in 414. Taken collectively, these texts represent Augustine's most extensive pastoral encouragement of the ascetic life (e.g., chastity, fasting, and almsgiving) and some of the most detailed, practical pastoral instructions. While the other letters to women did not offer the same measure of ascetic or spiritual encouragement, taken as a whole Augustine's correspondence to women was unique within his corpus. Let us examine why.

Tilley maintains that Augustine never saw women as equals, either socially or intellectually. She provides ample evidence that his pastoral advice was gendered (i.e., given similar circumstances he would instruct a man to do one thing and a woman to do another).[99] A gendered bifurcation may also explain his eagerness to encourage ascetic detachment among virgins and widows while offering so little ascetic encouragement to his male correspondents.[100]

Among modern scholars of religion, a fashionable way to read this type of gendering is through the lens of power and authority. It is quite possible that male religious authorities could more easily control ascetic women than nonascetic women.[101] By encouraging Proba, Juliana, and Demetria (Juliana's daughter) to divest themselves of their property and by establishing himself as their doctrinal and ascetic advisor, Augustine, at the very least, increased his standing among these wealthy women. In contrast, the legitimate threat that men of ascetic renown posed to Augustine's authority might explain his reluctance to encourage ascetic activism among his male correspondents. Given that Augustine's correspondence with women was atypical in many ways, in the final analysis it is not surprising that his proclivity to endorse asceticism also was gendered.

Pastorally speaking, two additional themes emerged from Augustine's correspondence. The most significant was his penchant for instructing his readers in orthodox doctrine. Augustine, busy as he was, responded to the theological questions of the laity, especially those of the aristocratic and educated classes (both male and female alike). Like many other Christian authorities, he also recognized the importance of individual circumstances.

However, what distinguished Augustine from some of his contemporaries was that he measured the capacity of his listeners in terms of their intellectual acumen rather than their spiritual standing. To be fair, the bishop of Hippo did not differentiate between mental and spiritual enlightenment. In fact, he evaluated spiritual development in a register of intellectual capacity.

But many of his contemporaries worked from a different perspective. As we will see, intellectual ability and spiritual health were often unrelated for John Cassian and Gregory I.

Moreover, Augustine rarely established spiritual regimens for his male correspondents. Generally, only the letters to women offered advice with respect to social interaction or guidelines for worship, and he never encouraged a rigorous ascetic discipline.[102] On this point we could trace a connection to Cicero.[103] Unlike the desert fathers, Cicero believed that the cure for an ailing soul was philosophy. Augustine's preoccupation with the intellectual suggests that he, like Cicero, believed that spiritual illness required cerebral medicine and not physical *askesis*.[104] One implication is that participation in the Christian community was an intellectual affiliation, one that did not require physical displays of piety (e.g., fasting or the reception of the Eucharist).[105] An alternative interpretation might stress the overriding importance of grace in Augustine's theological perspective. Either way, the bishop of Hippo, unlike many of his contemporaries, rarely established ascetic regimens for his correspondents despite his own pursuit of renunciation.[106]

An important exception to this pattern occurs in Augustine's seven extant Lenten sermons.[107] These homilies include all of the components that we might expect from a late antique Christian bishop speaking to his diocese. He explains the purpose of the upcoming Paschal events and encourages both mental and physical preparation for those events. Specifically, the sermons encourage fasting and almsgiving. On the first point, Augustine suggests that Christians are to fast not only during Lent but throughout the entire year. Sermon 206 begins: "[T]he season of Lent has come, so it is time that I encourage you because we owe good works to the Lord consistent with the spirit of the season, works that are beneficial to us, not the Lord."[108] Six of the seven Lenten sermons similarly encourage ascetic rigor. In one of them (Sermon 207), the bishop notes, "[I]t is not that certain foods are to be reviled but that physical pleasure is to be prevented."[109] The value of Sermons 205 to 210 is all the more apparent when we contrast them to Sermon 211, the last of the Lenten sermons. This final homily is the second longest ascribed to the Lenten period, but it provides no endorsement of ascetic piety.[110] Instead, the focus is on forgiveness. Perhaps this is because it stems from a time after 410 and at the beginning of Augustine's concern with the Pelagians.

What do these sermons reveal about Augustine's pastoral practice? They suggest that he was concerned with more than the intellectual comprehension of doctrine. But given their context (after all, they were delivered during Lent) they do little to alter the thrust of the bishop's pastoral strategy. In short, Augustine pursued two pastoral objectives—instruction in orthodox doctrine and the tailoring of his message to the intellectual capacity of his audience.

A Casualty of Orthodox Rhetoric?

When Augustine entered the clergy in 391, he left much of his ascetic past behind him. Though he remained chaste and organized his clergy into a communal house, he made little attempt to wed the ascetic tradition to pastoral leadership. I believe that Augustine's vigorous polemical career limited both his affiliation with and his endorsement of the ascetic enterprise. Many of Augustine's enemies (both heterodox and orthodox) ascribed more to the ascetic endeavor than he was willing to concede. As a result, his own polemic impeded any desire he may have had to combine ascetic discipline and spiritual direction.

Manicheans and Antimaterialism

It is well known that Augustine spent time as a Manichean before his conversion to Christianity.[111] By the late fourth century, Manicheanism had spread into the many regions of the Roman Empire and competed actively for converts from Christianity and paganism. Essentially a dualistic religion, Manicheanism distinguished between a good principle and an evil principle that were in eternal conflict with each other.[112] Because humans contained both an element of goodness (an immaterial soul) and an element of evil (a physical body), some Manicheans adopted a rigorous asceticism.[113]

Following his Christian baptism and return to North Africa, Augustine unleashed a barrage of literary attacks against his former co-religionists. Of his many polemical moves, Augustine distinguished between Manichean antimaterialism and the virtuous abstinence of orthodox Christians.[114] Manicheans, he charged, abstained from flesh and wine, but their abstinence was incomplete because they gorged themselves on exotic foods.[115] More dangerous still, the Manichean fast originated, not from a love of God or a desire to subdue the passions, but from an ill-conceived hatred of material things.[116]

While it was easy to identify the Manicheans' antimaterialism (after all, it was a claim they accepted), it was considerably more difficult to criticize Manichean renunciation without simultaneously discrediting orthodox ascetics. Augustine tried to resolve this problem by distinguishing motivations. In his *On the Morals of the Manicheans (De moribus Manichaeorum),* he stated: "[A] story of Catiline is put forth that he could endure cold, thirst, and hunger. Indeed, this wretched sinner did have these things in common with our Apostles. What, then, distinguished the parricide from our Apostles if not different motivations? He tolerated these things to gratify his most immoderate passions; they, on the other hand, endured them in order to restrain the passions and subdue them to reason."[117] A few years later, he noted in his *Against Faustus the Manichean (Contra Faustum Manichaeum)*: "Christians (not heretics, but Catholics), in order to subdue the body so that the soul may be more humbled when praying, abstain not only from meat but also from certain vegetables, without believing them to be unclean. . . . You, on the other hand, do not believe that any creature is good and call it unclean, saying that all bodies are made by the devil."[118] Augustine was claiming that orthodox asceticism was virtuous because it had control of the passions as its goal. By contrast, Manichean abstinence derived from a flawed theology that did not respect the dignity of God's creation. Logically speaking, this was a slippery slope. It would not be difficult to extend this criticism to any form of ascetic practice, either orthodox or otherwise.

Resting on the shaky foundation of intent, Augustine's defense of orthodox asceticism remained unsteady. His attack on Manichean antimaterialism and its subsequent misguided asceticism made difficult any endorsement of ascetic behavior. It is not surprising that little in Augustine's corpus from this period encouraged the ascetic life. In fact, just a few short months after he composed his *Against Faustus the Manichean,* Augustine offered his strongest statements in favor of marriage.

It is well known among scholars of the late fourth century that Augustine sparred with Jerome over marriage just as the bishop's attacks on Manicheanism were drawing to a close. At issue was Jerome's aggressive assertion that virginity was superior to marriage.[119] In 401, the bishop of Hippo issued two treatises, *On the Good of Marriage (De bono coniugali)* and *On Holy Virginity*

(De sancta virginitate). Together with *On the Good of Widowhood* (written in 413), Augustine established three "goods" of marriage: procreation, fidelity, and the sacramental bond.[120] He carefully identified the orthodox position as being one of moderation, in contrast to the polarized extremes of Jovinian (who saw no virtue in chastity) and the Manicheans (who rejected marriage altogether). For Augustine, Jerome's denigration of marriage strayed too close to the Manichean position.

The opening lines of *On the Good of Marriage* distinguished between marriage, which Augustine called "the first of the natural bonds of human society," and sexual intercourse, which had as its only fruit the procreation of children.[121] Marriage, in and of itself, Augustine reasoned, was a positive expression of Christian sacrifice and love. It was sexuality, not marriage, that needed tempering. This important distinction provided Augustine with a middle road between the unnecessarily rigid view of Jerome (or worse still the Manicheans) and the family-oriented social world in which Augustine lived.[122] Augustine reinforced this moderate position by identifying marriage as a good and honorable condition that was nonetheless inferior to celibacy.[123]

Despite his acknowledgment of celibacy as the greater good, it is easy to read in Augustine ca. 401 a concern with the trajectory of orthodox asceticism. Eventually, he would go so far as to insist that Adam and Eve would have generated offspring through the sexual process even if they had not fallen from grace.[124] That position directly countered other, more ascetic, interpretations of Adam, Eve, the Fall, and sexuality.[125]

Donatists and Perfection

Theologically speaking, the Donatists resembled Orthodox Christians in most ways; the difference lay in their discipline and ecclesiology.[126] They saw themselves as a purer, more authentic Church than that filled by their rival Caecilianists (Orthodox). The Donatists maintained a rigorous penitential code and denied the validity of sacraments conferred outside what they considered to be the Church.

Soon after his election to the episcopacy, Augustine turned his attention to the Donatists, whose numbers probably equaled or even exceeded those of the Orthodox in many parts of North Africa. Lacking a decisive theological platform, the high-minded Augustine often resorted to petty assaults on his opponents. For example, note Augustine's response to the charge that the Caecilians were guilty of *traditio:* "[I]f I were to say that this [slander] is said of men of your character, you would reply, 'Prove it.' Indeed, how have you proven it [against us]? If you think that it is demonstrated simply because it is said, there is no need to repeat the words. Pronounce the same judgment against yourselves as though coming from us. Do you not see that I have proven it if a mere statement amounts to evidence?"[127] While this argument lacked a theological basis, it was rhetorically effective. Augustine implied that the perfectionist strain in Donatist ideas and initiatives was overly rigorous, uncharitable, and un-Christian. Moreover, the Donatists were simply not as pure as they claimed. Augustine gleefully noted that many of the Donatist leaders were no better than convicted felons. He pointed to Rusticianus, a former priest who had been accepted by the Donatists despite his "reprehensible conduct" and considerable debts.[128] Augustine accused Primus, another Donatist cleric, of defiling nuns in Spain.[129] And then there was the case of Optatus, the Donatist bishop of Thamugadi. Optatus belonged to a militant wing of the Donatist community (the Circumcellions). Some scholars believe that this group was more interested in divesting North Africa of wealthy Roman landlords than it was in promoting the Christian faith.[130] To Augustine's alarm, some within the Donatist community revered Optatus as a martyr.

For Augustine, even the claim of perfection was theologically suspect. According to the bishop of Hippo, the Church was a "school for sinners," not a "society of saints."[131] The Church brought healing to all who had need, and it could not exclude those who had sinned. Augustine pounced on Donatists who claimed that the validity of the sacraments depended on the purity of the celebrant. He countered that it was God who saved and not clerics. In his *Against the Letters of Petilian (Contra litteras Petiliani),* Augustine argued: "[N]o one, even if he is free of sin, can make his neighbor innocent because he is not God. Otherwise, if we were to expect that the innocence of the baptized were manifested by the innocence of the baptizer, then each would be the more innocent in proportion to having found a more innocent person by whom to be baptized."[132] In a later text, he added that the minister (whether pious or sinful) was only the instrument by which the grace of Christ was distributed—the salvific power remained in God's hands.[133] The purported sanctity of the Donatist clergy was irrelevant.

Peter Kaufman has rightly drawn our attention to the possible discrepancy between the holiness that the Donatists professed and the perfectionism Augustine claimed for them.[134] But whether the assertions were authentic or fabricated, Augustine presented his rebuke of Donatist perfectionism with a rhetorical flurry that not only impeded his ability to employ the resources of the ascetic community but actually suppressed spiritual mentoring.

One of the most popular themes in ascetic literature of the late antique period was its call to perfection. Christ had commanded those who wished to be perfect to sell what they had and distribute it to the poor.[135] Many embraced the ascetic life in an attempt to achieve this elusive perfection. Numerous ascetic authors addressed the topic.[136] For example, John Cassian's eleventh conference was entitled *On Perfection*. However, Augustine's interests remained elsewhere. He spent much of his career criticizing heterodox groups who competed for the religious allegiance of the laity. If exposing the error of Donatist doctrine meant forgoing the use of ascetic ideals and categories, Augustine eagerly closed the deal. He strove to restrain arrogant schismatics, not forge connections between pastoral traditions. However, what many readers of Augustine may not realize is the extent to which the Donatist affair shaped his vision of pastoral authority.

Quite unlike the ascetics of his day who privileged the spiritual leader of a community, Augustine actually diminished clerical authority. Ministers were needed to perform the sacraments and instruct the faithful, but their personal sanctity had little if any impact on the salvation of the community. Clerics served functional and administrative roles; theirs was not the job of sanctifying. We are well served to contrast this attitude with John Cassian's. Just a few short years after Augustine's anti-Donatist treatises, Cassian detailed the larger-than-life accounts of the spiritual giants of the Egyptian desert. Cassian vested considerable authority in those saintly figures—authority that derived almost exclusively from their ascetic perfection.[137] For Augustine, that approach was too dangerous. Christ was the only spiritual leader who could be accounted perfect.

Pelagians and Ascetic Optimism

For our purposes, the Pelagian controversy was the most significant of Augustine's theological contests. On this point the bishop's rhetoric and theology most completely clashed with ascetic models of spiritual direction. Of the many doctrinal questions raised by Pelagius and his partisans, the most fundamental concerned human nature and the power of free will. According to Pelagius's detractors, the most egregious of his assertions was that humans could merit their own salvation without divine assistance.[138] While some monastic authors (e.g., Cassian) maintained that Pelagius had gone too far, an element of his message must have resonated with ascetic audiences.[139] They probably reasoned that God would acknowledge their sacrifices. After all, it was reasonable to think that their *askesis* would be beneficial.

Between 411 and his death in 430, Augustine aggressively fought what he believed to be an overly optimistic view of the postlapsarian human condition. He countered Pelagius's claims by emphasizing Adam's lapse and its effect on his descendants. Specifically, Augustine taught that the Fall initiated mortality, corruption, and a depraved will. Without God's assistance, all were destitute, mired in concupiscence and greed. Even infants that nursed at their mothers' breasts displayed this depravity.[140] For Augustine, the consequence of this original sin *(peccatum originale)* was damnation.[141] Not even the souls of miscarried children were free from this punishment.[142]

God's grace and grace alone rescued men and women from a dire fate. While Pelagius had maintained that individuals could effect their own salvation, Augustine countered that such a doctrine replaced the need for Christ. "If righteousness stems from nature, then Christ died in vain [Gal. 2.21]. If, however, Christ did not die in vain, then human nature cannot be justified and redeemed from God's most righteous wrath (in other words, his punishment) except by faith and the sacrament of the blood of Christ."[143] In addition, Augustine maintained that the grace of Christ was entirely free and unrelated to merit.[144]

Regarding free will, Augustine held that only Adam possessed a truly free will. Following him, the will had become an agent of disobedience, being unable to perform well.[145] Merit, according to Augustine, required divine intervention (i.e., grace). Clarifying his position in *On Correction and Grace (De correptione et gratia),* he argued: "[B]ut this grace is so complete that it is impossible for a man to apprehend the good itself or to continue in the good through his own will, unless he is made to will."[146] At issue, of course, was the notion that free will led Christians to trust in themselves, rather than in God: "[I]t is to be feared that the advocacy of free will be understood in such a way as to not account for God's assistance and grace in leading a pious life and a good manner of life, to which the eternal reward is due. Otherwise, when [Christians] lead good lives and perform good works (or rather think that they have led good lives and performed good works), they should dare to glory in themselves and not in the Lord."[147] By removing both initiative and soteriological participation from the individual, Augustine rejected the efficacy of asceticism.[148] In his *On Grace and Free Will (De gratia et libero arbitrio),* the bishop of Hippo struck at the most visible badge of ascetic achievement—celibacy. "God's gift [i.e., grace] is indispensable for the observance of the precepts of chastity."[149] Even the ascetic's prayer for chastity was initiated by grace.[150] Summarizing his critique of ascetic optimism, he wrote: "[T]hus no one can say that God's grace is conferred upon him because of the merit of his work, or because of the merit of his prayers, or because of the merit of his faith. Nor should anyone believe that the doctrine [of the Pelagians] is true who holds that the grace of God is given to us in proportion to our own merit."[151] Even more disturbing to many of Augustine's readers was his conclusion that those who would be saved, the "elect," had been selected from the beginning of time.

Not surprisingly, many ascetics found Augustine's anti-Pelagian campaign unsettling.[152] The most famous of his critics was John Cassian.[153] But even some of Augustine's loyal supporters found his position puzzling. In 426, the abbot of a monastery in Adrumentum, a city in the province of Byzacium on the North African coast, sent a delegation to Hippo requesting that Augustine explain his apparent rejection of free will. The bishop backpedaled. He delayed the emissaries long enough to compose two treatises, *On Grace and Free Will* and *On Correction and Grace,* wherein he sought to balance grace and free will.[154] However, what he produced was a convoluted doctrine that acknowledged human cooperation but at the same time restricted the initiative for that cooperation to preexistent grace. Again, he explained his position in the context of chastity: "It is concerning conjugal chastity itself that the apostle speaks when he says, 'Let him do what he will, he does not sin if he marries [1 Cor. 7.37]'; and yet this too is God's gift."[155]

Throughout the controversy, Pelagius's supporters responded vigorously. Julian of Eclanum focused on Augustine's contention that original sin passed from parents to offspring through the procreative process.[156] Indeed, the linchpin in Augustine's counterargument to Pelagian optimism had been the belief that Adam's sin spread through the concupiscence associated with procreation. According to Julian, Augustine had simply refashioned Manicheanism.[157]

Augustine scrambled to defend himself. In the bishop's treatise known as the *Unfinished Work against Julian (Contra Iuliani opus imperfectum),* we learn that Julian had not only accused Augustine of promoting a Manichean hatred of the body but had drawn passages from Augustine's own treatises to support his argument.[158] Augustine responded by arguing that the preeminence of Adam's unvitiated nature made his fall more disastrous than the sins of average people. Thus Adam's fall affected everyone.[159]

More than any other, this controversy exposes the quagmire in which Augustine's theology had placed him. The end result of Augustine's critique of Pelagius's optimism was a further distancing from the ascetic community. During the latter days of the controversy, Augustine publicly chastened local monasteries.[160] It is not at all surprising that episcopal authorities and ascetic communities rejected his soteriology and his doctrine of predestination.[161]

Elizabeth Clark argues that throughout the Pelagian controversy Augustine's view of the Fall and sexuality remained more ascetic than certain scholars have been willing to admit.[162] As accurate as that position may be, Augustine's theology of original sin did little to mollify monastic concerns and also did not alter his approach to pastoral direction. Simply put, the Pelagian controversy expanded the chasm between Augustine's clergy and the ascetic tradition because the bishop of Hippo rejected the opinion that an ascetic vocation engendered spiritual benefits.

Monastic Vagabonds and Other Issues

Augustine's rhetoric was by no means restricted to schismatic and heretical foes. On a number of occasions, he exposed individual Christians who (according to Augustine) had exploited the monastic vocation. He criticized ascetics who refused to work, scolded men and women who forced their spouses to embrace chastity, and publicly humiliated the men of local monasteries. Coming from a bishop, such attacks were permissible, if not expected. But the public manner in which they were presented and the bravado with which they were expressed suggests more than simple episcopal governance.

On the Work of Monks (De opere monachorum) records the most famous of these episodes. Around the year 400, a community of vagabond monks from the East took up residence near Carthage. These foreigners scandalized the local clergy in many ways. They wore their hair long, did not bathe, begged for their food, and refused to work. Aurelius, who was the bishop of Carthage, asked his friend to issue a treatise against the monks.[163] Accepting the invitation, Augustine ridiculed the itinerants' laziness and poked holes in their theology. They had justified their leisure with the Gospel passage "[C]onsider the birds of the air who neither reap nor sow."[164] Augustine countered that they were opportunists who manipulated the Scriptures.[165] Somewhat comically, he stated that he wished his life were as easy as a monk's, for even an honest monk only worked a few hours a day (in contrast to peasants, who toiled long hours in the fields, and to bishops, who were consumed with numerous responsibilities). If for no other reason, Augustine ordered them back to work as an act of obedience.

Though a brief treatise, it crystallized Augustine's view of an ascetic vocation within the Church. In and of itself, the ascetic life was nothing special. Monks needed to work just like everyone else. Surely, the continent had a unique calling, but that did not privilege them in this world or the next. Moreover, an ascetic lifestyle did not erase one's respect for decorum. Wild-haired anchorites had no place in Augustine's church. Furthermore, the bishop joked that they were imposing their own unemployment on the local barbers.[166] I dare say that Symeon Stylites would have received a rather cool reception had he ascended a pillar in Hippo Regius rather than Syria.[167]

On the Work of Monks was not the only incident. Augustine censured many ascetics who did not meet his standards. We learn from his correspondence that he reproached a certain Ecdicia for her husband's lapse into sin.[168] Apparently, she and her husband had agreed upon a life of continence, but the latter (being unable to persist) sank into adultery. Augustine accused Ecdicia of forcing celibacy on an unwilling (and incapable) husband. He also reprimanded her for relinquishing her husband's property without his permission and for donning the widow's garb before his death.[169] In short, Augustine chastened this woman for her adoption of a monastic discipline while she was still married.

In a letter to Eudoxius, who was the abbot of a monastery in Capraria, Augustine sneered that Eudoxius should be thankful that God had placed him in a monastery rather than in the world.[170] The responsibilities of an abbot were fewer and less burdensome than those of a cleric. To repay God's good favor, Eudoxius should appreciate his position and be especially guarded in his supervision of the monastery.[171]

Additional evidence suggests that Augustine had turned his back on or, at the very least, had mixed feelings about the ascetic movement. Take, for example, the case presented in Epistle 83. A priest had died leaving behind modest possessions but no will. Both the parish that he served and the monastery in which he had previously resided made a claim on the inheritance. Alypius, the bishop of Thagaste, suggested that the money be split between the two communities. Augustine, however, determined that the parish should receive the entire sum because monks were expected to abandon their wealth before entering a monastery. In this case, Augustine reasoned, to rule (even partially) on behalf of the monks might encourage future monks to act inappropriately. Though nothing about this episode was particularly suspect, we can contrast this approach to the one taken by Pope Gregory I. In nearly all of Gregory's judicial rulings concerning money, he found in favor of monastic communities.[172]

There is much about Augustine's career and thought to suggest that he advocated asceticism. He spent the years between his baptism and ordination in a form of monastic retreat. Once ordained, he organized members of the local clergy into a communal house. On occasion, he even endorsed ascetic disciplines, especially fasting. But Augustine also distinguished between acceptable and unacceptable Christian behavior. More often than not, ideologies and practices identified with the ascetic life stood outside what Augustine defined as orthodox. Whether it was the antimaterialism associated with Manicheanism, the perfectionism ascribed to the Donatists, or the optimistic views of the Pelagians, Augustine's rhetoric limited the extent to which he could freely embrace ascetic principles. These controversies introduced a theoretical wedge between Augustine and his past. As a result, Augustine's pastoral model was distinctively nonascetic. While Conrad Leyser has effectively demonstrated that Augustine was not trying to discourage spiritual striving among his community (he was instead discouraging spiritual elitism), the bishop's policies were noticeably distinct from those of some famous contemporaries such as Gregory Nazianzen, Basil of Caesarea, and John Chrysostom.[173] Given his polemical career, it is understandable that Augustine did not endorse the pastoral strategies of the ascetic community.

John Cassian and the Spiritual Direction
of the Ascetic Community

John Cassian's life remains shrouded in mystery. The prevailing opinion is that he was born in Scythia Minor (modern-day Romania) circa 360.[1] Whatever his actual place and date of birth, Cassian's proficiency in Greek and Latin enabled him to converse easily with ascetic and episcopal authorities around the Mediterranean.[2] In his late twenties/early thirties, Cassian left his homeland and extensive property and with a trusted comrade, Germanus, settled in a monastery in Bethlehem.[3] From there, he and Germanus twice sojourned into Egypt, where they spent a total of up to ten years sitting at the feet of some of the most famous ascetics of the era.[4] Near the beginning of the fifth century, they permanently departed Egypt and went to Constantinople, where John was ordained to the deaconate by John Chrysostom. Cassian's stay in the Eastern capital, however, was short-lived. When the emperor ordered Chrysostom into exile in 404, Cassian and Germanus became part of the delegation that went to Rome to plead Chrysostom's case before Pope Innocent.[5] Cassian remained in Rome (at least temporarily), where he was ordained to the priesthood. It is uncertain where or in what capacity he served before moving several years later to Massalia (Marseilles) in southern Gaul.[6] Once in Marseilles, however, Cassian organized two monasteries (one male and one female) and composed three treatises: *On the Institutes of the Cenobium and on the Remedies for the Eight Principal Vices* (hereafter referred to as *Institutes [Institutiones]*), *Conferences [Conlationes],* and *On the Incarnation of the Lord against Nestorius (De incarnatione Domini contra Nestorium,* hereafter referred to as *On the Incarnation*).[7] The dating of these treatises is also problematic.

Most likely, Cassian composed the *Institutes* around 425 and the first install-ment of the *Conferences* shortly thereafter. He probably published the second set of conferences around 427 and the last group in the following year. Be-tween 429 and 430, John authored *On the Incarnation* at the request of Leo of Rome (the future pope by that name). It is believed that he died in Marseilles in the 430s.[8]

Although he was not the first Easterner to shape Gallic Christianity (Ire-naeus of Lyon, d. ca. 200, had come from Asia Minor), scholars credit John with transferring Eastern monastic traditions to the West.[9] That claim rests on the material presented in the *Institutes* and the *Conferences*. Books 1–4 of the *Institutes* dictate the customs of Egyptian ascetics such as a monk's dress, his diet, and the rituals of his communal prayer. The *Conferences* offer thor-ough exegetical and theological justifications for each of those practices. Cas-sian dedicated entire books to subjects such as the aim of the ascetic life (book 1), the eight vices (book 5), and the balance between free will and grace (book 13).

Although he is never identified by name, Evagrius of Pontus lies behind much of Cassian's corpus.[10] It was Evagrius who first identified and listed the eight passions, which Cassian transformed into the eight principal vices.[11] Like-wise, Cassian's description of the monk's dress was probably derived from Evagrius's letter to Anatolius, which came to serve as the prologue to the *Prak-tikos*.[12] More generally, Cassian's interiorization of the spiritual contest, strate-gies to confront vice, and pursuit of passionlessness (ἀπάθεια) all resonate with Evagrian ideas. It is important to note that Cassian did not adopt Evag-rius's theology uncritically. John resisted Evagrius's speculative ideas, par-ticularly those that smacked of Origenism or did not promote the cenobitic ideal.[13] For example, he replaced Evagrius's monastic goal of *gnosis* with purity of heart.[14]

Cassian's devotion to the Eastern ascetic tradition is evident throughout his works, even in the introductions. John dedicated the *Institutes* to Castor, who was bishop of Julia Apta (a town near Marseilles). According to Cas-sian, Castor sought advice for the construction of a *cenobium* in his diocese. John's response was simple: adopt the monastic traditions of the East (par-ticularly those of Egypt) and all will be well.[15] Later in the same preface he acknowledged other monasteries in Gaul, but he dismissed them as mis-guided and soft.[16] For Cassian, nothing in Gaul could compare to the apostolic foundations of the East.[17] And with the *Institutes,* Cassian established himself as the lone spokesperson for the Eastern tradition.

Even more than the *Institutes,* the *Conferences* solidified Cassian's authority in Gaul. Written in three installments, Cassian's *Conferences* imparted the ascetic wisdom of legendary anchorites from the Egyptian desert. Though presented as authentic conversations among Germanus, Cassian, and the hermits, these texts emphasized the theological concerns of southern Gaul at the time. The dedications were particularly significant. Cassian offered the first set of conferences (1–10) to Leontius, bishop of Fréjus, and to his brother Helladius, an anchorite. Cassian would have known that the island monastic center of Lérins lay within Leontius's diocese.[18] In fact, he dedicated the second collection of conferences (11–17) to Honoratus, who was the abbot of Lérins, and to one of his monks, Eucherius, whom Cassian knew to be fascinated with the Eastern tradition.[19] Cassian presented the final group of conferences (18–24) to four monks, one of whom (Theodore) eventually succeeded Leontius as bishop of Fréjus in 432 or 433. Cassian knowingly identified and honored those men who were most capable of promoting his distinctively Eastern ascetic program.

Cassian is, of course, also known for his rejection of Augustine's *sola gratia* soteriology, which serves as another reminder of Cassian's Eastern perspective.[20] Contrary to Augustine, and like most of his contemporaries (especially in the East), Cassian believed that Adam's sin subjected humanity to spiritual and physical death but only partially corrupted the "image and likeness of God" in which Adam had been created.[21] For John, one could participate in one's salvation through ascetic discipline and a refocusing of one's soul toward God. This concept is most explicit in the thirteenth conference, where Cassian insisted that salvation required both divine grace and human cooperation.[22] This placed him well within the Eastern theological tradition but in opposition to Augustine.

For years, historians have mistakenly labeled Cassian as a "semi-Pelagian"— an anachronistic and prejudicial label.[23] In doing so, they have allowed a single author (Augustine) to serve as the measuring stick of orthodoxy. Not only is that approach theologically biased, it is historically unsound.[24] John and his co-religionists conformed to a well-developed and widespread view when they advocated the combination of grace and human initiative.[25] It was Augustine's anti-Pelagian excessiveness that was theologically novel, but

the approval of the late bishop's ideas at the Second Council of Orange in
529 might have suggested otherwise.[26]

Notwithstanding the black eye that Cassian and his colleagues received for
challenging Augustine, both the *Institutes* and *Conferences* enjoyed wide circulation throughout the medieval era in the Latin West and in the Greek East.
Both the *Rule of the Master (Regula magistri)* and the *Rule of Benedict (Regula Benedicti)* advocate disciplines found in the *Institutes* and share the philosophical approach to leadership and spiritual direction outlined in the *Conferences.*[27] Benedict twice acknowledged Cassian's influence, and he recommended Cassian's
works as the archetype of monastic teaching.[28] Yet Cassian's ascetic instructions (like those of his mentor, Evagrius of Pontus) rarely received direct acknowledgment, especially in the West. Even Gregory the Great, who so clearly
absorbed Cassian's ideas, never openly acknowledged his debt to the ascetic author.[29] The East, however, treated Cassian's texts more favorably. Abbreviated
versions of the *Conferences* and the *Institutes* circulated in Greek translations—
a rare honor for a Latin author. Perhaps the greatest testimony to Cassian's
approval in the East is his presence in the *Apophthegmata Patrum.* Cassian was
the only Latin author included in that collection.

In the following pages, I argue that John Cassian embraced the spiritual
father/spiritual disciple method of pastoral supervision. In his recent monograph, *Authority and Asceticism from Augustine to Gregory the Great,* Conrad Leyser
suggested that there were certain limits to Cassian's satisfaction with a community that included persons of different spiritual levels.[30] It is true that in his
sixteenth conference Cassian offered a narrow understanding of friendship,
in which lasting friendship could exist only among those who maintained an
equal level of virtuous perfection.[31] However, it is possible that Leyser over-
estimates the link between Cassian's comments with respect to friendship and
the community in general. To be sure, Cassian (like many late ancient writers)
believed that friendship existed only between persons of equal virtue, but
that did not preclude the possibility of a harmonious and even an idealized
monastic community composed of persons at different spiritual stages. The
very premise of the *Conferences* is that novices can advance through the instruction of their elders. Moreover, the prescriptions for this interaction are
provided in detail in the first four books of the *Institutes.* While perhaps only
a slight modification of Leyser's position, my belief is that Cassian embraced
and spread the spiritual father/spiritual disciple method of pastoral direction
as the most effective means for cultivating a Christian society.

SPIRITUAL AUTHORITY IN CASSIAN'S ASCETIC COMMUNITY

For John Cassian, not all ascetics were capable of taking on disciples.[32] Generally speaking, he identified progress in the monastic life as the most important criterion for spiritual leadership. Naturally, this entailed a cultivation of the ascetic life, including fasting, chastity, poverty, vigils, and the abandoning of family and friends. The *abba*s to whom he attributes the words of his lengthy *Conferences* no doubt achieved renunciatory perfection, and their ascetic achievements are, in many ways, taken for granted. Instead, Cassian details their sage advice for the ascetic advancement of others.

It is important to note, however, that Cassian's criteria for spiritual leadership encompassed more than renunciation. Cassian remarks in the first of his conferences, "[F]asts, vigils, meditation on Scripture, and being deprived of all possessions are not perfection; they are the tools for perfection."[33] Likewise, in the eleventh conference, Cassian describes perfection not as an achievement of *askesis* but as "love for the divine."[34] Thus one does not attain the status of elder by asceticism alone. For Cassian, authority is granted only to those who have previously achieved perfect love by coupling renunciation with obedience and discernment.

In a less than subtle critique of the indigenous monastic leadership of Gaul, Cassian rebukes those who assume pastoral authority before they have themselves displayed obedience: "[W]e see that there are a variety of rules and regulations in use in foreign areas because we often have the audacity to preside over a monastery without first having learnt the system of the elders. Instead, we appoint ourselves abbots before we have, as we should, been ourselves disciples, and skip hastily to ask others to observe our fancies rather than to preserve the well-tried experience of our predecessors."[35] In Egypt, Cassian counters, monks dutifully obey their superiors and never presume the obedience of disciples before they have first learned humility as a disciple. He claims that "no one is elected to supervise a community of brothers before he has himself learnt through obedience what he ought to teach to those who will submit to him."[36] Even the elder relies on the instructions of the fathers who preceded him.[37]

The virtue of obedience is closely linked to humility, which Cassian, like most late ancient ascetics, identifies as the most lofty of the virtues (it is the antidote to pride, the most dangerous of the vices).[38] According to Cassian, humility is present only in those persons who have cultivated it through experience. Those who have attained purity of heart, the *scopos* of the ascetic life, always acknowledge that their spiritual advancement is the result of God's mercy, not their own efforts.

> Thus [the elders] stated that they hoped for the reward of the life to come not because of their good works but on account of the Lord's mercy. They took no pride in their vigilance of heart that was greater than others, which they attributed to divine grace, not their own effort. Moreover, they did not flatter themselves because they were better than the careless who were lukewarm and inferior. Rather, they achieved a permanent humility by thinking of those [previous fathers] whom they knew truly to lack sin.[39]

Humility, learned through obedience, separates the elder from the novice.[40]

In addition to *askesis* and obedience, spiritual discernment (*discretio*) signifies authentic spiritual leadership.[41] In fact, it is one of the prerequisites for spiritual advancement. "No virtue can either be perfectly attained or sustained without the grace of discernment."[42] Abba Moses, the elder to whom Cassian attributes an entire conference on discernment, warns that a monk who does not possess discernment will be like a person wandering in the dark of night—he will not only fall into dangerous ditches but frequently go astray on level ground.[43] So Moses argues that *askesis* without discernment is of little use.[44] *Discretio* sees a person's thoughts and actions and perceives everything that must be done for improvement.[45] Without *discretio,* the clarity of the mind and the actions of the body are obscured, "wrapping them in the blindness of vice and the darkness of confusion."[46]

Despite his tendency to emphasize the role of human cooperation, Cassian insists that discernment is granted by the Holy Spirit. "You see, then, that the gift of discernment is not a worldly or trifling matter but a generous gift of divine grace."[47] Though Cassian instructs his readers that the cultivation of discernment begins with obedience and humility, ultimately it is a gift and as such operates as a marker that distinguishes authentic from inauthentic leadership.[48] In effect, it is discernment that links the eighteen *abba*s of the *Conferences* because each is able to impart knowledge of God's mystery (*discretio* in action) to his disciples.

Beginning with St. Paul (see 1 Cor. 12.10), several early Christian writers explored the "discernment of spirits" (διάκρισις πνευμάτων), but few developed a pastoral application for the term.[49] In Athanasius's *Life of Antony (Vita Antonii),* for example, discernment of spirits referred principally to the recognition of demonic activity.[50] For Evagrius, it was the linking of demonic activity to a monk's temptations.[51] But for Cassian, discernment has a broader application. Through discernment, an elder can deliver inspired messages and perceive the difference between vice and virtue.[52] In a subtle but significant shift, Cassian transforms the "discernment of spirits" into a discernment of the passions, which has a broader pastoral application. Indeed, Cassian's discernment is multidimensional: like Antony's, it identifies demons, but it also serves a wider range of pastoral needs.

For example, in the fourth book of the *Institutes,* Cassian details the ascetic formation of novices joining the community. Among other things, Cassian notes that the elder who supervises the initiates must discern whether they possess a real or an imagined humility.[53] As part of the process, they are instructed concerning the dangers of hiding their thoughts or desires from their elder. They are also encouraged to dismiss their own appraisal of their condition and to rely entirely upon their spiritual father's assessment.[54] The presumption is that *discretio* provides the elder with a form of supernatural grace that enables him to discern what is best for his disciples and counsel them accordingly (i.e., relaxing or invigorating an ascetic regimen).[55]

If a monk lacks discernment, he can rely on the insight and teaching of his elder.[56] Moses warns that a monk should follow the teaching of an "elder" not on the basis of the number of gray hairs on his head but on the basis of his commitment to the traditions of the fathers—a sign that he possesses not only integrity but discernment.[57] Here Cassian implies that a monk should choose his elder carefully, although in the *Institutes* Cassian had suggested that the novice did not select his spiritual mentor.[58]

One additional element of Cassian's understanding of authority is the preeminence of Egyptian traditions. By acting as the lone arbiter of what constituted "Egyptian monasticism," Cassian was able to include or exclude practices as he deemed necessary. Much as Athanasius was able to regulate who was acceptable and who was not on the basis of Nicene Christianity, so Cassian was able to create for his Gallic audience not only a pattern of ascetic living but the criteria by which ascetic authority was bestowed.

Rhetorically, Cassian achieved this with the claim of antiquity. As he explains near the outset of the *Institutes,* there are nearly as many forms of monastic life as there are monasteries—a clear sign of their impropriety.[59] To correct that problem, Cassian promises to expound the "ancient teaching of the fathers, which has been maintained to the present day among the servants of God throughout Egypt."[60] In Egypt, Cassian boasts, monasteries are not established at the whim of a single renunciant; rather, they continue unbroken through a succession of elders and their traditions.[61] In fact, he claims that the earliest Christians were regarded as monks and learned their discipline from St. Mark the Evangelist.[62] That these customs are different from those of Gaul demonstrates, for John, how far the Gallic Church has slipped from the original Christian practice. In short, the multiplicity of Gallic ascetic practices and their lack of cohesion with John's construction of an idealized Egyptian asceticism gave Cassian a platform to assert his own authority and to establish a criterion for spiritual leadership that not only shaped the ascetic communities in Marseilles and Lérins but went on to inform episcopal authority in the Gallic Church for generations.[63]

Throughout the *Institutes* and *Conferences* Cassian emphasizes the role of the spiritual father as the bridge between a novice monk and spiritual enlightenment. Within his system, authorities are known by their ascetic achievements, humility, discernment, and conformity to the Egyptian tradition. His identification of these requirements comes as little surprise; they derive from his pastoral techniques.

METHODS OF SPIRITUAL DIRECTION

Though there are dozens of pastoral techniques at work in Cassian's corpus, five stand out because of their impact on subsequent Latin ascetic and pastoral literature: the process of gradual correction, the use of *condescensio,* the internalization of the spiritual battle, the balance between action and contemplation, and the communication of ascetic and moral ideals through idealized accounts of past heroes.[64] These pastoral mechanisms not only constitute the heart of Cassian's model of leadership but provide the foundation on which Pope Gregory I based his own pastoral theology.

Gradual Correction

In Cassian's ideal spiritual father/spiritual disciple relationship, an elder knew the intimate secrets of his subordinate's heart and was thus able to set him on the road to spiritual perfection.[65] The combination of the disciple's obedience and his elder's *discretio* made that goal possible. Once the elder assessed his disciple's condition, he established a long-term path to spiritual recovery that necessitated an individualized and specific strategy. For example, with respect to fasting, Cassian did not believe that regulations should be uniform; instead, the spiritual father should take into account a person's age and health as well as his spiritual status.[66] Because the road to spiritual enlightenment could take years to complete, it was necessary for the elder and disciple to remain in frequent communication so that any new development could be treated appropriately (whether by reproach, encouragement, or a new prescription).[67] While Cassian did not invent the model, he did more to define its practice and spread its application in the West than any previous Christian author.[68]

In book 4 of the *Institutes,* Cassian outlines the gradual steps that a man takes upon entering monastic life. In Egypt, Cassian maintains, all new candidates spend a period of ten days lying prostrate outside the monastery.[69] Following that public humiliation, the abbot strip-searches the candidate for money and then assigns him to the guest master.[70] The initiate remains one year under the tutelage of the guest master, assisting him with the care of strangers and visitors.[71] Assuming he survives the year, the initiate then enters the wider community as a novice under the direction of a newly assigned elder.[72] This elder instructs the novice in humility, obedience, labor, meditation, and poverty.[73] To encourage the discipline of obedience, Cassian relates the story of a monk who, under the direction of his spiritual father, watered a dry stick twice a day for a year without questioning the order.[74]

Throughout the *Institutes,* Cassian praises Egyptian ascetics who respect their elders and progress through their wisdom. In the *Conferences,* however, we find a more concerted effort to anchor the gradual instruction of disciples in theological principles. Commenting on the eight principal vices, Cassian notes that the spiritual battles waged by individual monks are necessarily unique. "Although the eight vices upset all of humanity, they do not attack everyone the same way. For one, the passion of lust is dominant, to another wrath is uncontrolled, in a third vainglory rules, and in yet another pride exists, and although it is clear that we are all subject to each of the vices, we suffer from them in different ways and proportions."[75] But, he argues, one can devise a strategy for every spiritual contest. For example, a monk who suffers from physical passions (e.g., gluttony or lust) requires a physical remedy (such as fasting and vigils). Likewise, spiritual passions (e.g., vainglory or pride) demand spiritual solutions (such as love and humility).[76] It is the responsibility of the spiritual father to determine an appropriate course of action.

To ensure advancement, Cassian emphasizes the difference between the *scopos* and the *telos* of the monastic life.[77] In his first conference, Abba Moses teaches Cassian and Germanus that a monk must concentrate on his intermediate goal *(scopos)*, which is purity of heart. From purity of heart, the kingdom of God (the *telos* or end) follows. A monk who focuses on his end, the kingdom of God, will be lost.[78] But the monk who concentrates solely on the immediate necessity, purity of heart, maintains the prospect of success.[79] The various ascetic disciplines (e.g., fasting, vigils, and the abandoning of family) assist the monk in search of his goal, but they do not in themselves provide that goal.[80] Without purity of heart, John argues, a monk's renunciation is pointless.[81]

Condescensio

One of the most important spiritual tools possessed by a spiritual father is *condescensio.* As noted in previous chapters, *condescensio* (οἰκονομία) refers to a spiritual father's temporary relaxation of a prescribed reprimand. According to Cassian, one effective application of *condescensio* is the temporary indulgence of a minor vice for the purpose of rooting out a more dangerous passion. Note, for example, his willingness to permit vainglory (one of the eight vices) in an attempt to conquer lust: "In at least one way, vainglory is beneficial for novices who remain tempted by carnal vices. If a novice, otherwise harassed by the spirit of fornication, should hear a spoken word, he may think of the dignity of the priestly office or of the opinion of those who might think that he is holy and innocent, and if because of this consideration he rejects the unholy temptation of desire . . . he restrains the greater evil through a lesser one."[82] It is notable that in the case of a novice Cassian identifies lust as a greater evil than vanity. In his schema of the vices in the *Institutes,* Cassian lists vanity as the seventh of the eight vices (i.e., one of the most dangerous) because it has both carnal and spiritual origins.[83] For the novice, however, the temporary application of *condescensio* by his spiritual advisor can assist in the battle against lust and prepare him for the more dangerous spiritual contests in the future.

John's most deliberate justification of *condescensio,* however, occurs in the seventeenth conference. Here Cassian recalls that he and Germanus had failed to keep their promise to return to Palestine—they opted instead to remain in Egypt.[84] When they confessed this sin to Abba Joseph, the elder responded that the two had acted appropriately because, in the end, the spiritual benefit outweighed the fault of a broken vow. "Out of necessity one forgives the evil of a lie when the damage of speaking the truth and the benefit granted by the truth do not offset the harm caused [by the truth]."[85] Drawing from the example of St. Paul, Abba Joseph added: "He became weak to the weak when, by way of concession and not by way of command, he permitted intercourse for those who could not control themselves; just as he fed the Corinthians with milk rather than solid food."[86]

Not surprisingly, Cassian maintained that the use of *condescensio* was the exclusive privilege of the elder; a monk was not permitted to administer it to himself.[87] Cassian also warned that an excessive use of *condescensio* would cause great damage.[88] If unchecked, it could lead to lukewarm religion. To demonstrate his point, he submitted that too many Christians had adopted a watered-down faith. In particular, Cassian pointed to the Gentile converts of whom less was required upon their entry to the faith.[89] "But this liberty, which was conceded to the pagans because of the weakness of their new faith, gradually began to spoil the perfection of the Church." Eventually, he argued, even the leaders relaxed their strictness.[90] What Cassian probably did not realize was that it was not the initial incorporation of Gentiles into Christianity but the influx of converts in the wake of Constantine's conversion that led to what he perceived as a "watering down" of the faith. Nevertheless, in an attempt to correct the present circumstance, Cassian insisted that the application of *condescensio* was a temporary measure. Over time, the recipient was expected to outgrow its use.

Internalizing the Spiritual Battle

Cassian's internalization of the spiritual contest marks a pastoral departure from his predecessors. Although Evagrius had been instrumental in the internalization of sin (he emphasized the existence of sin in thoughts rather than acts), it was Cassian who forged the link between Evagrius's λογισμοί and the medieval concept of the seven (eight) deadly sins.[91]

As noted, John identifies eight principal vices (gluttony, lust, greed, anger, despair, laziness, vainglory, and pride) that exist to some degree in every monk.[92] Cassian's arrangement of the vices (like that of Evagrius) begins with the basest (gluttony) and progresses toward the most dangerous (pride). He distinguishes between vices of a physical and of a spiritual origin, as well as those that manifest themselves internally and externally. For example, he describes gluttony and lust as physical but vainglory and pride as spiritual. External causes provoke greed and anger, while despair and sloth originate internally.[93] In the fifth conference, Cassian also discusses the interrelationship of the vices (e.g., how one often leads to another) and provides brief expositions for overcoming them.[94] For example, he writes: "[T]o conquer despair, sadness must be overcome; to drive out sadness, anger must be expelled; to extinguish anger, greed must be trampled under foot; to end greed, lust must first be suppressed; to overcome lust, the vice of gluttony must first be disciplined."[95] He even delves into the many different forms of each passion (e.g., the three types of gluttony or the two kinds of sadness) and offers remedies for their relief.[96]

According to Evagrius, the passions were inextricably linked to individual demons.[97] These demons attacked their prey by enticing the mind with thoughts of temptation (he called these λογισμοί). To safeguard against the λογισμοί, Evagrius provided keys for the monk to recognize demonic presence and strategies to ward off the temptations. For example, he submitted that almsgiving diminished anger and vigils tempered lust.[98]

Though he draws from Evagrius, John's understanding of the passions and his recommendations for their subjugation are distinct. For Cassian, vice exists in every Christian and often operates independently from demons. Instead, the vices use the body or external objects as the instigation of temptation.[99] This is particularly true of the carnal vices: "Gluttony and lust, although they are in us naturally, sometimes arise without the assistance of the mind, but entirely from the provocation of the flesh."[100] In fact, in book 5 of the *Conferences,* which describes the eight passions, John makes few references to demonic instigation. Instead, he emphasizes the natural component of temptation.

Though we can excise the origin of [certain] vices, which have been joined to our nature, we will never be able to free ourselves from gluttony. For we cannot cease to be what we were born by nature, regardless of how much we progress. That this is the case is shown . . . by those who have achieved a more perfect state. For although they are no longer tempted by other passions and go into the desert with a resolute soul and an impoverished body, they are never freed from their concern for food.[101]

Cassian never overtly denies a link between the vices and evil spirits (he does, in fact, allude to it), but his emphasis is not Evagrian.[102] Cassian, more completely than Evagrius, locates the impetus of sin within the individual.[103] In doing so, he furthers the internalizing process because, in his eyes, the source of sin is internal, not external. Ultimately, the intensification of self-inspection fuels the need for spiritual renewal and, in turn, spiritual supervision.

To the extent that Cassian is able to convince his readers that they might unknowingly be the incubators of vice, he simultaneously reinforces the importance of the spiritual father. Only the discerning elder sees the unique manner in which vice corrupts the individual. Through consultation and assisted by grace, the spiritual father identifies those vices that are most active, develops a strategy to counter their threat, and sets the disciple on the path to spiritual recovery.

Book 7 of Cassian's *Institutes* demonstrates the pastoral ramifications of Cassian's enumeration of the vices. Discussing avarice, Cassian argues that the disposition toward greed is more dangerous than the actual possession of material things.[104] In fact, he argues, it is possible for a monk who possesses nothing to suffer from this vice. "For just as the Gospel states that those who are not defiled in body can be adulterers in their heart [cf. Matt. 5.28], so it is possible that those who are in no way burdened by the weight of money may be condemned with a covetous disposition and intent. For they lacked the opportunity to own things, not the desire to do so, and it is this desire rather than need that God is unwilling to crown."[105] Though Evagrius had presented a similar view, he did not identify the spiritual counselor as the safeguard against failure. For Cassian, however, a discerning elder sees through an outward display of poverty and recognizes avarice in his disciple. He then places the monk on the path to recovery. Through his examination of the vices, Cassian not only expands the scale of the spiritual contest but also heightens the importance of the spiritual director.

A second example of interiorization is the concern with the spiritual realm. Recurring references to demonic activity characterize ascetic literature from the fourth century onward. Antony's physical battles with invisible demons and Evagrius's identification of the eight λογοσμοί with demonic assault are prime examples of the spiritual anxiety underlying ascetic literature. David Brakke has recently shown that there was considerable diversity within the ascetic community with respect to the understanding and presentation of the demonic.[106] Whereas Antony's demons were associated with the Fall itself (and therefore not identified with a particular place), Ammonas (his successor) located the ascetic struggle (i.e., with demons) in the desert and Paul of Tamma placed it within the monastic cell.[107]

Cassian's *Institutes* and the *Conferences* contain numerous accounts of demons who deceive even the most accomplished ascetics and, if left unchecked, lead all novices to ruin. Cassian warns in the fourth book of the *Institutes* that "the subtle serpent is constantly watching our heel—in other words, he is waiting for the end of our life. Therefore, it will not be of any use to have made a good beginning and to have eagerly taken the first step toward renouncing the world if it is not accompanied by a similar conclusion."[108] Similar cautions exist throughout his corpus, and in the seventh and eighth conferences Cassian details the demonic powers and their hierarchies. There he carefully notes God's omnipotence and reminds his reader that God never challenges a monk beyond his ability.[109]

Cassian equips his reader with information on the demonic world—in a sense, ammunition for spiritual warfare. For example, he declares that weaker demons prey upon young and inexperienced monks because they are able to offer little resistance, while powerful demons concentrate their efforts on those who have made progress through renunciation.[110] He also tells his readers that a discerning elder not only sees and hears demons but is privy to their sense of accomplishment and failure.[111]

Pastorally speaking, the identification of demonic activity and the articulation of demonic hierarchies and strategies reinforced the need for ascetic action. By linking hunger to the demon of gluttony or sluggishness to the demon of sloth, Cassian, like the ascetics in the East, fostered a self-perpetuating world of spiritual conflict full of suspense and danger. Just like the danger associated with the inner vices, the threat of demonic assault demanded constant introspection and ascetic purgation. It also bolstered the need for spiritual leadership. Whether a deliberate attempt by ascetic leaders to assert their authority (cf. Brakke's assessment of Ammonas) or simply the consequence of a monastic anxiety, the discussion of the demonic invigorated the spiritual father/spiritual model because it promised protection against invisible enemies.[112] The idealized *abba*s of the *Conferences* must have impressed upon Cassian's readers the importance of spiritual leaders who, armed with *discretio,* could protect their flock from demonic assault.

By expanding the scope of the religious battle to include the thoughts, motivations, and temptations of the inner self, Cassian dramatically increased the need for pastoral leadership. The elder did more than instill order and regulate abstinence. He was the only one capable of protecting the average monk from inner temptations as well as external spiritual foes. The interiorization of sin maximized the authority of the spiritual elder. He stood as the principal defender against the devil and, as a result, earned the obedience of his community.

The Balance between Action and Contemplation

A fourth component of John Cassian's pastoral theology was the balance he struck between action and *contemplatio* (contemplation).[113] For Stoic philosophers as well as some early Christian authorities (e.g., Clement, Origen, and Evagrius), action preceded and enabled contemplation, which was the desired state.[114] The monk who was initially πρακτικός, Evagrius taught, eventually became γνωστικός.[115] And while Cassian too recognized that action preceded contemplation, he included among the disciplines of the practical life (*actualis disciplina*) the instruction of disciples. And he even went so far as to require the temporary setting aside of *contemplatio* for the purpose of this tutoring.[116] For Cassian, it was the cenobitic community that fostered the environment most favorable to a balance of action and contemplation.[117]

The privileging of communal life was not always present in Cassian's writing. In his earliest texts, he preferred the eremitic model of monasticism over the cenobitic. In the second book of the *Institutes,* Cassian distinguished between instructions that suited the outer man (the cenobite) and those that suited the inner man (the anchorite).[118] In the preface to his first set of conferences, Cassian made clear his belief that the eremitic life was superior to the communal.[119] We might also observe that Cassian's use of hermits to teach a communal audience further suggests a preference for the anchoritic life.

Commenting on the importance of *contemplatio* in the *Conferences,* Cassian notes that any distraction from contemplation is sinful, even if that distraction is for the purpose of good acts.[120] Nevertheless, certain circumstances demand the temporary cessation of *theoria* for the benefit of the community. Cassian points to the example of St. Paul, who willingly sacrificed his own meditation for the sake of his disciples: "[H]e withdrew his mind, holy and lofty as it was, from heavenly *theoria* for attention to his earthly work."[121] Cassian adds: "[E]ven though in many ways he preferred this greatest of goods [*contemplatio*] to all the fruits of preaching, he still offered himself with love . . . for the benefit of those to whom, like a mother, he was nursing with the milk of the Gospel, and he relinquished his closeness to Christ, which was certainly harmful to him but a necessity for others."[122] Confirming this ideal, Cassian, through the voice of Abba Joseph, maintains that true charity requires the easing of one's own rigorous practice for the benefit of others.[123]

As constructed, the *abba*s of the *Conferences* set aside their own meditations to answer the naive questions of two pilgrims. We can conclude that Cassian expected all experienced ascetics to do the same. But Cassian extends the requirement of communal service to disciples as well. Just as the elder sacrifices his *contemplatio* for the benefit of novices, so too the inexperienced monk is taught that his advancement depends as much upon community service as it does upon private meditation. Note, for example, the importance Cassian places on performing the daily tasks of the monastery.[124]

By the final installment of the *Conferences,* Cassian locates the balance between action and contemplation in the cenobitic monastic experience. In his twenty-fourth conference, he asserts that cenobitic monasticism provides the best avenue to spiritual advancement for the greatest number of persons: "Although the anchoritic life is good, we believe that it is not appropriate for everyone; for many, it not only is unfruitful but is even thought to be dangerous."[125] Monks in isolation are not able to see their own vices as easily as those who live in communities. Likewise, they do not enjoy the advantage of nearby teachers or the opportunity to offer hospitality to a neighbor.[126] While Cassian does not condemn the eremitic life, he does argue that all successful hermits began in a *cenobium.*[127]

As noted, Cassian was one of the first authors in a purely ascetic environment to detail the importance of community service, even when it came at the expense of contemplation. By balancing *actio* and *contemplatio,* he reinforces the importance of pastoral care in the ascetic community. Cassian instructs his readers that experienced renunciants are to sacrifice *theoria* in order to instruct the less experienced—a precedent initially established by St. Paul. By identifying the monastic community as the incubator for spiritual advancement, Cassian envisions an environment where novices not only learn from their elders but also value the community over self and service over personal need. As we will see in the final chapter, Pope Gregory I's desire to balance service and contemplation was so strong that he encouraged monks to leave the monastery and serve the parish.

Exempla

Admonition through saintly example is the hallmark of Cassian's writing. In both the *Institutes* and the *Conferences,* Cassian communicates moral and ascetic lessons through the words and actions of legendary figures. Throughout the *Institutes,* he repeatedly employs Egyptian exemplars. For example, during his lengthy discussion of gluttony in book 5, Cassian includes no fewer than eighteen anecdotes attributed to different hermits.[128] Some are no more than moralizing adages without attribution; others are lengthy stories of an elder's instruction to his disciples.

At the very core of the *Conferences,* Cassian conveys his ascetic agenda through the authoritative voice of distant heroes. The fifteen *abba*s of the conferences (some of them are responsible for more than one conference) were probably well-known figures in their day, and it was for that reason that Cassian and Germanus went to them.[129] At the start of every conference Cassian praises the (ascetic) virtues of his interlocutor as a means of establishing his experience and authority. What is more, the *abba*s themselves often rely on other, more authoritative voices of the past to justify or explain their teaching.[130]

The effectiveness of this approach lies in its association with a recognized authority—the ascetic hero. By taking the persona of a reporter, Cassian transmitted his own words as tradition. Practically speaking, the authenticity of the stories was irrelevant.[131] What mattered was Cassian's ability to ascribe his own ideals to the irrefutable voice of Egyptian hermits. But Cassian's use of the saintly exemplar served as more than an effective literary device; it promoted the pastoral ideals of the ascetic community.

As noted in the introduction, the circulation of "sayings" and *vitae* in late antiquity testifies to the use of the saintly exemplar as a pastoral device. In short, it provided a paradigm of instruction, easily communicated to a multitude of audiences. After a monk confessed his sins or doubts to his mentor, the elder was able to offer encouragement and/or instruction through the exemplar. We find many examples of this principle in the *Conferences*. For example, during a conversation with Abba Joseph, Germanus asks a question about lying to conceal the extent to which one fasts. Abba Joseph responds to the question with an event from the life of Abba Piamun.[132] Joseph does this, he tells us, to "stimulate the young men in their faith."[133]

One additional benefit of the exempla was their lasting functionality. Like the *Apophthegmata Patrum* and the various collections of *Vitae Patrum,* Cassian's texts provided subsequent generations of ascetics with a multitude of stories that they could easily employ for pastoral or theological purposes. If a novice sought counseling for his lust, an elder familiar with the *Conferences* could share the advice of any number of Egyptian saints whose teachings were believed to fill the pages of Cassian's text. These stories provided practical spiritual advice that not only addressed the problem at hand but also reinforced the ascetic imperative. In part, the wide circulation of Cassian's corpus was due to the pastoral appeal of the saintly exemplar. As we will see, Pope Gregory I appreciated the pastoral effectiveness of the exemplar and adopted the genre to his own needs through his preaching and especially in his *Dialogues (Dialogorum libri IV)*.

THE SCOPE OF CASSIAN'S PASTORAL MODEL

Of the five authors in this study, John Cassian is the only one who was not elevated to the episcopate; nor does it seem that he actively served a pastoral function outside his ascetic community (at least not after his arrival in Gaul). As a result, he was not challenged by the pastoral tension that other late ancient ascetics faced upon entering the episcopate. His understanding of spiritual direction was, nevertheless, quite important for the development of Christianity and especially for the spread of asceticism (both among monks and Christians more generally) in Gaul and throughout the West.

We might ask, however, to what extent Cassian sought to extend his pastoral theology beyond the ascetic community. Scholars disagree. Some do not believe that Cassian had any interest in reforming the world at large.[134] They maintain that he wrote solely for his small monastic network. More recently, some historians have argued to the contrary. Philip Rousseau, for example, contends that "by paying less attention to hermits, and by focusing on possibly more compromised, certainly more communal, types of asceticism, Cassian opened the way to a closer link between the monastery and the world."[135] For his part, Columba Stewart reminds us that Cassian wrote for an audience that was increasingly called to serve the Church beyond the walls of the *cenobium*—recall that portions of the *Institutes* and *Conferences* were dedicated to monk-bishops.[136]

Cassian may have anticipated the authority conferred on several graduates of the Lerinian community.[137] Its founder (Honoratus), for example, became bishop of Arles in 4 2 7, and others from Lérins went on to important episcopal positions in the Church.[138] By dedicating his works to these men and their associates, Cassian provided the pastoral nexus between *abba* and *episcopus*.[139] On this point, Conrad Leyser has convincingly linked Cassian's ascetic teaching to the pastoral strategies of several of the Lerinian alumni.[140] He also maintains, I believe rightly, that allegiance to Cassian came at the expense of fidelity to the Augustinian tradition.[141] But how far can we push the connection between Cassian's pastoral initiatives and the lay world around him?

On the one hand, Cassian believed that men and women entered a monastery seeking spiritual progress that was unattainable in the world. The *Institutes* and *Conferences* are filled with examples of saintly action that defy the behavior of those tied to the world. What is more, John frequently chastened monks who desired the priesthood.[142] On the other hand, in the *Conferences,* Cassian displayed an increasing concerned for the monk's responsibility to his neighbor, and he emphasized that many of the Egyptian elders were themselves clerics.[143]

John Cassian's texts reflect a vision of the ascetic community that was increasingly common in the early fifth century. His numerous injunctions to obedience, renunciation, and prayer encompass that tradition. What is new in Cassian is the emphasis on spiritual formation displayed most prominently in the obligation to assist one's neighbor. No longer was ascetic perfection found in the monk who lived alone in the desert. Cassian admonished his readers to take responsibility for others, and he elaborated the pastoral mechanisms through which that could be achieved (e.g., discernment, interiorization, and the saintly exemplar). In short, Cassian provided the archetype from which subsequent leaders inclined to the monastic life could extend the ascetic pastoral model to the lay world. Pope Gregory I was one such bishop.

Pope Gregory I and the Asceticizing of Spiritual Direction

Born in 540, Gregory entered life during a period of great upheaval. During the first half of the sixth century, Justinian's armies waged a continuous war against the Goths in Italy. Imperial forces gained the upper hand, but in the process Rome was besieged a number of times.[1] In 568 the Lombards crossed the Alps, posing a new threat to Italian security that lasted for most of Gregory's life. Plague and famine combined with warfare to devastate the population.[2] Pope Pelagius II, Gregory's predecessor, is thought to have died of plague.[3] As Carole Straw notes, "Gregory's times were the stuff of apocalyptic dreams and visions."[4] It would be unrealistic to think that these conditions had no effect on a man as contemplative as Gregory.

Gregory's was an aristocratic Roman family whose wealth derived from extensive landholdings in Rome and Sicily.[5] Beginning in the fifth century, the family took an active role in the Church. Gregory's great-great-grandfather had been Pope Felix III (483–92), and another pope, Agapetus (533–36), was a distant uncle. Gregory's father, Gordianus, was an official of the Roman Church, most likely a *defensor*.[6]

We can assume that Gregory received an education befitting his aristocratic station—one that would have prepared him for an administrative career.[7] Gregory of Tours maintained that Pope Gregory was the most accomplished man in Rome with respect to grammar, dialectic, and rhetoric.[8] The specifics of his education, however, are difficult to ascertain—the pontiff never discussed his schooling, and modern assessments of the education system in Rome at that period are inconclusive.[9] It has been suggested that Roman students no longer studied Greek authors by the middle of the sixth century, but there is some evidence to the contrary.[10] Either way, the core of

Gregory's boyhood studies probably included Cicero, Seneca, and Virgil. Traces of each of these writers exist in Gregory's corpus, but unlike many of his Christian predecessors, he rarely cited classical texts. In fact, Pierre Riché identifies Gregory's reliance upon Scripture (rather than pagan authors) as evidence of the transformation from a late antique to a medieval literary culture.[11]

We can only assume that it was Gregory's education and family connections that enabled him to begin his public career so auspiciously—as prefect of Rome *(praefectus urbi)* in 573. In earlier times, the Roman prefect had judicial authority over the entire city and surrounding area, but by the time Gregory assumed the office, its importance had diminished.[12] And as it turned out, Gregory's secular employment did not last. Recalling his lay career years later, he noted, "[M]y cares began to threaten me so much that I was in danger of being overcome, not only in outward activity, but what is more serious, in my soul."[13] Therefore, in 574, Gregory resigned from his position and embraced the monastic life. He sold his patrimony, endowed six monasteries in Sicily, and transformed his Roman estate into a seventh, St. Andrews, which he entered as a common monk under the instruction of Valentio, the abbot.[14] For the next several years, he subjected himself to an unusually rigorous asceticism and, as a result, suffered ill health the remainder of his life.[15] In 579, Pope Pelagius II ordained Gregory to the deaconate and then appointed him *apocrisiarius,* papal representative to the emperor in Constantinople.[16]

Though Rome was ostensibly the preeminent see in Christendom, Italy was little more than a western province to the Byzantine emperors of the later sixth century, whose military, economic, and political concerns remained in the East.[17] The civil and military authority in Italy rested in a single Byzantine official, the exarch, who governed Italy from Ravenna. Because political and ecclesiastical dignitaries shared civic obligations, the exarch and the bishop of Rome were expected to cooperate. In practice, however, the two often competed for the support of the people as well as the attention of the emperor in Constantinople.[18] As *apocrisiarius,* Gregory's responsibility was twofold: he spoke for the religious concerns of the papacy, and he championed the military, political, and economic interests of the citizens of Rome.

Gregory spent nearly seven years in the Eastern capital in this capacity, living in a Latin district of the city with other Italian monks.[19] At this time, the imperial court still operated in Latin, and it is debated how well Gregory knew Greek, if at all.[20] Constant war with Persia diminished the emperor's interests in Italy, freeing Gregory to pursue other things. He devoted much of his time to personal study and pastoral supervision (he served as the abbot of his community).[21] In this environment, Gregory delivered what became the voluminous *Morals on the Book of Job (Moralia in Job,* hereafter *Moralia).*

In 585, Gregory returned to Rome and St. Andrews, where he quickly assumed the office of abbot. He may have hoped to remain in that position indefinitely, but when Pope Pelagius II died in February of 590, Gregory emerged as his successor.[22] Gregory of Tours's *History of the Franks (Historia Francorum)* (the lone contemporary account) provides only a few lines concerning the appointment.[23] Emphasizing his subject's reluctance, he chronicles Gregory's many attempts to avoid elevation.[24] Once elected, however, Gregory served as pope until his death in 604. His was one of the most dynamic and influential careers in papal history. Some of Gregory's achievements include the daily feeding of Rome's indigent, the refurbishing of the city's dilapidated churches and defenses, the initiation of monastics to the papal curia, and the reintroduction of Roman Christianity to Britain.[25] Added to those pragmatic accomplishments were the pontiff's hagiographic and exegetical works, which shaped the theological landscape of the medieval world.

But perhaps Gregory's most significant contribution, one that had both administrative and theological consequences, was his asceticizing of spiritual direction. By completing the merger between ascetic and clerical strands of the pastoral tradition, Gregory did nothing less than redefine Christian leadership.

Before we delve into Gregory's model of spiritual direction, however, we must pause for a moment to recall that the Mediterranean world had changed in the hundred years between the death of John Cassian and the birth of Pope Gregory I. Politically, Western Europe was transformed by the "barbarian" migrations. The vestiges of Roman rule remained, but the imperial government was located in the East and, as a result, Rome was often left to fend for itself. More importantly, Christianity also evolved during the fifth and sixth centuries.[26] According to Robert Markus, the change in religious perspective was so dramatic that it marked the end of ancient Christianity.[27] With the process of Christianization further along and monasticism becoming more entrenched, Christian authorities of Gregory's era may well have had a different view of the world than those living in the fourth or fifth centuries.[28]

But this new outlook would not have altered Gregory's understanding of his responsibility as a Christian authority to provide effective spiritual direction—a concern that was shared by each of the authors we have examined. What was different was Gregory's solution to the tension between personal contemplation and the service of ministry—he completed the merger between the ascetic and clerical traditions. This was not simply the consequence of living at the close of the sixth century.[29] Gregory imposed an ascetic policy that drew stiff opposition in Rome.[30] In spite of that, his policy provided a new vision for spiritual direction that carried forward and thus informed pastoral care in the Middle Ages.

LIBER REGULAE PASTORALIS

Gregory presented the *Liber regulae pastoralis,* or *Book of Pastoral Rule,* to John, archbishop of Ravenna, in 590 at the beginning of his pontificate.[31] A few years later, he sent a copy to a friend from Constantinople, Leander, then bishop of Seville.[32] The text is the most thorough pastoral treatise of the patristic era. Like previous authors, Gregory distinguishes between who should and who should not "shepherd" the flock, he identifies many of the priest's daily responsibilities, and he anticipates many pastoral challenges. What makes this work unique is the third section, in which Gregory identifies seventy-two personal traits set in opposition (e.g., old and young, rich and poor, male and female) and provides a pastoral regimen for each. Of particular significance is that these recommendations reflect an ascetic approach to spiritual direction. Indeed, Gregory's *Pastoral Rule* conveys the ascetic perspective in at least three ways: it establishes ascetic criteria for the selection of clerics; it seeks to transform the average priest into a spiritual father who uses the pastoral techniques of an abbot; and it communicates its vision of spiritual direction through decidedly ascetic language.

Gregory's terminology in the text is significant. He employs a variety of terms to refer to the pastoral leader, such as *sacerdos, rector, praedicator,* and *pastor.*[33] *Episcopus* is not one of them. Yet many modern commentators believe that he was writing solely about the episcopate.[34] Given Gregory's less than consistent use of these terms in his corpus, it is more likely that he hoped to inspire anyone vested with pastoral authority. The fact that Gregory advanced the same directives to audiences consisting entirely of monks demonstrates that he extended the message of the *Pastoral Rule* to a wider audience.[35]

Selection of Clerics

In his prologue, Gregory notes: "No art is presumed to be taught without first being learned by intent meditation. How foolhardy it is therefore for the unskilled to covet pastoral leadership *[pastorale magisterium]* when the governance of souls *[regimen animarum]* is the art of arts."[36] For Gregory, the ideal shepherd (he uses the Latin word *pastor*) is the experienced ascetic.[37] As pope, he faced a twofold challenge: how to weed out inferior candidates and how to convince those qualified (i.e., the monks) to accept the burden of responsibility. Throughout the text, Gregory characterizes those things that either qualify or disqualify a candidate from office. One of his longer inventories notes: "Therefore, he should be an example of good living, someone who is already dead to the passions and therefore living a spiritual life, who disregards worldly prosperity, who does not fear adversity, who seeks the interior life only; someone who has a healthy balance between a body that is not always weak nor a spirit opposed by discord; someone who does not covet the possessions of others but gives freely of his own; someone who through compassion is quickly moved to pardon, yet never pardons excessively."[38] Many of these attributes convey ascetic ideals. Note the use of renunciatory terms of contrast such as *passions (passiones)* versus *spiritual living (spiritaliter vivit)* or *body (corpus)* versus *spirit (spiritus)* in his description of the consummate priest.

Gregory equally acknowledges the obstacles that prevent one from being ordained. This apophatic approach provides still greater control over the selection process. For example, he extols the importance of intercession by excluding from office those who lack the capacity to engage in it. "How can anyone seize the post of intercession with God for the people, who does not know himself to be in his grace through the merit of his own life? And how can he ask for pardon for others while not knowing whether he is himself reconciled to God?"[39] Additional obstacles to ordination follow, including pride, vainglory, greed, lust, and the pursuit of prestige.[40] In short, any discernible vice is disqualifying.

Illuminating is Gregory's reading of Leviticus 21.17–18 (a list of physical impediments to the Jewish priesthood). Utilizing a hermeneutic of ascetic purity, Gregory restricts the Christian priesthood to professional ascetics. For example, he compares a blind man to "one who is ignorant of the light of celestial contemplation."[41] In other words, a blind man is unfit for pastoral office because he is "oppressed by the darkness of the present life . . . and does not see where to go himself."[42] A second example, a small nose, symbolizes a person who lacks spiritual discernment, *discretio*. Gregory writes, "[J]ust as the nose discerns the difference between a sweet smell and a stench, [a successful pastor] applies discernment [*discretio*] to distinguish between sin and virtue."[43]

Gregory insists that *contemplatio* and *discretio* are the two most important attributes for successful leadership. By the sixth century, *contemplatio* had long been synonymous with the ascetic retreat—a life of quiet meditation.[44] *Discretio,* likewise, had long been used within ascetic literature to describe the key supernatural gift bestowed by God upon a worthy spiritual advisor. John Cassian had dedicated an entire conference to the subject, and Benedict had identified *discretio* as the most critical quality of a potential abbot.[45]

As important as *discretio* and *contemplatio* were, they were not the only requirements. Claiming that priests lead by example, Gregory warns: "[T]here are some who investigate spiritual precepts with great care but trample upon what they analyze by the way in which they live. Hastily, they showcase what they have learned, not by practice, but through reading. And the very words that they preach they impugn by their habits, just as when a shepherd walks on steep hills, the flock follows him to the precipice."[46] Here Gregory seems to disregard Augustine's claim that a sinful preacher injures only himself.[47]

Spiritual direction is so treacherous, Gregory argues, that it easily confuses the mind, not only stalling the development of subordinates but damaging the rector's spiritual condition.[48] To illustrate his point, Gregory recalls the life of King David. As a shepherd, David had been virtuous and forgiving; once he became king, however, he killed his soldiers to satisfy his lust.[49] In short, David lost the purity of the contemplative life once he assumed a position of authority. Though only one of many asides in the *Pastoral Rule,* the story well characterizes Gregory's concerns about the corrupting influence of power. As pope, Gregory was required to fill a number of clerical vacancies. Hoping that his clergy would avoid the corrosive effect of authority, Gregory sought only those candidates whom he believed would maintain their *contemplatio.* It was for this reason that Gregory turned to the monastic ranks.

With the *Pastoral Rule,* Gregory broke several precedents in pastoral literature. One concerned the recruitment of new clerics. The treatises of the
fourth century (those of John Chrysostom, Gregory Nazianzen, and Ambrose of Milan) had, in effect, discouraged ordination by emphasizing the
transcendence of the office of the priesthood. We could summarize their
message as "When in doubt, refuse." Gregory's *Pastoral Rule,* however, encouraged ordination. In part, this is because Gregory sought to justify his
own election.[50] But more importantly, he believed that the Church's survival
depended upon quality leadership. So he turned to the monasteries to fill the
pastoral void.

In part 1 of the *Pastoral Rule,* Gregory rebukes worthy candidates who resist ordination. Acknowledging their qualifications, he begins: "[F]or there
are several who possess incredible virtues and who are exalted by great talents
for training others; men who are spotless in the pursuit of chastity, stout
in the vigor of fasting, satiated in the feasts of doctrine, humble in the long-
suffering of patience, erect in the fortitude of authority, tender in the grace of
kindness, and strict in the severity of judgment."[51] These men possess everything Gregory prizes in a *rector,* yet just a few lines later it becomes clear that
the pontiff is struggling to persuade these men to accept the responsibility
of leadership. "If they refuse to accept a position of spiritual leadership when
they are called, they forfeit the majority of their gifts—gifts that they received not for themselves only but also for others. When these men contem-
plate their own spiritual advantages and do not consider anyone else, they lose
these goods because they desire to keep them for themselves."[52] He characterizes the same men as "preferring the mystery of stillness [and] tak[ing]
refuge in the solitude of [spiritual] investigations."[53]

There is little doubt that Gregory refers here to professed ascetics. Though
he respects their humility, he believes that their resistance is, in effect, selfish-
ness.[54] The pontiff turns to the Gospels to illustrate his point (especially Matt.
5.15: "A city on a hill cannot be hidden" and John 15.16–17: "If you love me,
feed my sheep"). Distinguishing humility from self-interest, Gregory pro-
claims: "For indeed, no one is truly humble if he understands by the judgment
of the Supreme Will that he ought to govern but then refuses."[55]

Gregory understood, all too well, the reluctance of ascetics who relished
the security of the contemplative life. He often bemoaned the secular responsibilities of office.[56] So he uses the *Pastoral Rule* to equip the pastor with the

tools necessary for a successful ministry. Book 2 of the text itemizes the daily spiritual and practical responsibilities of office, and book 3 supplies the reader with a profile of personality types that he will encounter during his ministry. With these sections, Gregory hopes not only to assist inexperienced leaders but also to encourage the easily intimidated. Given Gregory's familiarity with the Benedictine tradition, I believe that he provides this regimen because it is efficient, and moreover because it mirrors Benedict's own systemization, enabling the pope to lure otherwise reluctant Italian monks to accept the pastoral office.[57]

With respect to the recruitment of new clergy, Gregory's *Pastoral Rule* is asceticizing in two ways. First, his evaluation of the ideal candidate is measured in ascetic terms. The privileging of the nobility that we saw in Nazianzen and the concern for rhetorical expertise that characterized Augustine are present in this text, but they are greatly superseded by an overriding concern for ascetic purity. Second, Gregory's bold endeavor to recruit priests from the ascetic community was new in pastoral literature, and it attests to the pope's trust in the ascetic vocation as a precondition to successful ministry.[58] Not only did Gregory finesse ascetics into accepting ordination, he constructed an intricate system to support their needs.[59]

Transforming the Priest into a Spiritual Father

Prior to Gregory, the most influential Latin pastoral treatise was probably Ambrose's *On the Office (De officiis),* which, drawing from Cicero's work of the same title, treated the office of the priesthood like that of a public administrator.[60] Ambrose (like Augustine after him) understood the priest's primary responsibilities to involve three things: instruction in elementary doctrinal beliefs, distribution of the sacraments, and supervision of charity. Neither Ambrose nor Augustine encouraged ascetic struggle, apart from celibacy, in their priests. Neither author emphasized a pastoral relationship in which the priest monitored the gradual spiritual growth of individuals, nor did either actively encourage his clerical subordinates to promote ascetic disciplines in persons under their care. Given those precedents, Gregory's *Pastoral Rule* is exceptional; it transforms the parish priest or bishop into a formidable spiritual father resembling the ascetic elder or *abba.*

Like Nazianzen, Pope Gregory believed that successful pastoral leadership required both renunciation and service. Consequently, his ideal spiritual father balanced the *contemplatio* of the isolated ascetic and the *actio* of the well-trained administrator. As Carole Straw has shown, for Gregory a fusion of two opposites was superior to either on its own.[61] Thus his "active contemplative" was not only a more effective leader but a better Christian than either the recluse or the administrator.[62] The very fact that Gregory valued action and contemplation equally marks a break from previous Latin pastoral treatises.[63]

In book 2 of the *Pastoral Rule,* Gregory describes the tension between action and contemplation (reminiscent of the divide between the clerical and ascetic pastoral traditions) as a healthy pastoral balance. The pontiff disqualifies those who are unable to balance the two. Essentially, the priest must commit himself to the administrative obligations of office without sacrificing *contemplatio:* "[T]he *rector* should not reduce his attention to the internal life because of external occupations, nor should he relinquish his care for external matters because of his anxiety for the internal life. Otherwise, either he will ruin his meditation because he is occupied by external concerns or he will not give to his neighbors what he owes to them because he has devoted himself to the internal life only."[64] Gregory suggests a number of methods to maintain the proper equilibrium, including the reading of Scripture.[65]

As noted, most organized ascetic communities in late antiquity imposed a spiritual father/spiritual disciple hierarchy. The spiritual father or *abba* identified the unique spiritual condition of each subordinate and then laid out a path of correction accordingly. Gregory anchors his *Pastoral Rule* in this approach. The text not only serves as a sourcebook of spiritual profiles (see book 3) but develops many of the techniques employed by the *abba.*

For example, Gregory's shepherd applies *discretio* to assess the spiritual condition of his subordinates: "[Certain vices], however, lie hidden and require keen investigation so that their symptoms may be brought to light. The *rector* must know these great vices by their small signs, and he must investigate the hidden thoughts of his subordinates and then intervene with the proper rebuke before it is too late."[66] For Gregory, *discretio* allows the shepherd to separate true virtue from vice disguised as virtue: "[T]he *rector* ought to know that there are many vices that appear as virtues. For example, greed disguises itself as frugality, and wastefulness is ascribed to generosity. Often, laziness is accounted loving kindness and wrath appears to be spiritual zeal."[67] *Discretio* also facilitates the appropriate remedy. In other words, *discretio* tells the shepherd when to apply *condescensio* and when to enforce the weight of the law.

As previously discussed, *condescensio* refers to a spiritual father's temporary relaxation of a prescribed reprimand. Drawing from Cassian (and others), Gregory encourages his *rectores* to apply *condescensio* as needed. Describing its application, the pope envisions a scenario in which a penitent suffers from two connected but unequal vices. The priest should treat the more egregious sin first, even if the short-term result is an increase in the second. "When the preacher [*praedicator*] does this, he does not aggravate the overall illness but rescues the life of the one infected, thus enabling him to find a more fitting time to administer the [spiritual] medicine for the lesser fault as well."[68]

Though *condescensio* does not license a priest to abandon ecclesiastical discipline, it does give him the authority to determine the appropriate measure of justice. For example, according to Gregory, sins of ignorance deserve light punishments.[69] Pastoral flexibility was an essential part of spiritual direction in the ascetic community. Both Cassian and Benedict, two authors very familiar to Gregory, encouraged its use. The pontiff concurred and imported their terminology and practices into his *Pastoral Rule*.

Once the condition of a subordinate is discerned, the advisor authorizes a long-term path to spiritual recovery based on the unique circumstance of the individual. To assist in this process, Gregory profiles a variety of personality types and supplements those profiles with specific admonitions and warnings. He devotes book 3 of his text (certainly the longest of the four) entirely to this purpose and identifies personality traits in pairs of opposites. For example, he distinguishes traits of men and women, rich and poor, young and old, indicating the spiritual advantages and disadvantages of each.

Gregory's reading of Nazianzen's "Apology for His Flight" may well have inspired the pontiff's conceptualization of personalities in pairs of opposites, but Pope Gregory's discussion displays a much richer analysis.[70] For example, he notes that the distinction between partner traits is not always obvious. A successful shepherd needs to distinguish between persons who possess lifelong chastity and those who do not, or between those who fail to begin good works and those who cannot complete them. Even honorable characteristics are not without potential pitfalls: for example, a priest should investigate whether a patient man is truly patient or whether he harbors resentment toward others.[71]

As we have seen, Gregory was not the first to suggest different pastoral models for individual personalities. In ascetic circles, John Cassian and Benedict noted that fasting guidelines should be tailored to a person's gender, age, health, and spiritual development.[72] And Augustine routinely instructed his preachers to speak to the level of their audience.[73] But no late antique author matched the scope or detail of Gregory's psychological profiles.

I am not suggesting that Christian leaders before Gregory failed to apply pastoral remedies based on individual circumstances—they certainly did.[74] But only Gregory wrote a treatise on the subject. Gregory's ideal priest monitored and corrected the spiritual condition of those under his care with the sort of precision and intrusion heretofore found only in organized asceticism. Gregory took his model of pastoral direction from John Cassian and Gregory Nazianzen. By modeling the lay priest on the image of the spiritual father, Gregory prepared the transformation the parish into a semiascetic community.

Asceticizing Language

While many not distinctively ascetic Christian texts listed characteristics that were either admirable or shameful, Christian ascetics from the fourth century onward developed more specific renunciatory applications for the virtues and vices. Several expressions in the *Pastoral Rule* either derive from ascetic literature or are most easily understood in an ascetic context. We have already discussed Evagrius's λογισμοί and Cassian's *passiones*. As these and other ascetic authors discovered the sources of sin, they routinely provided ascetic rubrics for its subjugation.[75] Gregory's *Pastoral Rule* is steeped in these linguistic and theoretical conventions.

On more than forty occasions, the *Pastoral Rule* references one of nine vices. The most frequent is pride, *superbia,* garnering citations in fifteen different chapters. In his *Moralia,* Gregory had argued that pride was the "source" or "mother" of all other vices, so he did not include it in his catalog of seven vices, which became the normative list for medieval churchmen.[76] Gregory also omitted sloth, *pigritia,* from this register, but he devotes considerable attention to it in his *Pastoral Rule.*[77] Though the virtues receive less attention, each of the standard seven is present, including the most important, humility, *humilitas.*[78]

There are several reasons that Gregory's language of vice should be read as ascetic. First, the terminology is so entrenched in the ascetic literature of the age that Gregory's readers undoubtedly made the association. Second, the language of virtue/vice conveys ideals that are distinctively ascetic. It evinces the internalization of sin characteristic of renunciation.[79] No other medium provides such an in-depth assessment of one's spiritual condition. Virtues such as chastity, charity, and obedience hearken back to, among other things, the vows of Benedictine monasticism; vices such as gluttony, sloth, and pride cut straight to the concerns of Cassian's ascetic athlete.

Third, like Evagrius, Cassian, and others, Gregory details the elaborate interrelationships of various vices—for example, the link between gluttony and lust or between gluttony and sloth.[80] By doing so, he pushes his ascetic agenda—gluttony is menacing not only because it exposes the weakness of the spirit over the body but also because it opens the door to lust and greed. Similarly, Gregory's *Pastoral Rule* establishes a hierarchy of the vices. Through this index, he, like others before him, identifies the most dangerous (and difficult to correct) of the vices. Thus Gregory enables his priests to detect and solve perplexing spiritual problems.

As noted, another characteristic of late antique ascetic literature is its preoccupation with demonic activity. Gregory's frequent use of phrases like "the enemy who lies in wait" or "the ancient foe" suggests that he embraced supernatural phenomena in a way that Augustine never did.[81] For Augustine, all misfortune was linked to Adam's fall, demonic assault included; for Gregory, demons play the role of tempter, generally in association with the vices.[82] By linking hunger to the demon of gluttony or sluggishness to the demon of sloth, Gregory, like the ascetics around him, fostered a self-perpetuating world of spiritual conflict full of suspense and danger. The threat of demons demanded ascetic-like introspection and purgation.[83]

There are still other examples of ascetic language in the *Pastoral Rule*. *Discretio, condescensio,* and *contemplatio* did exist outside the ascetic's milieu, but for Gregory they provided a distinctively ascetic medium. It is not the similarity of expression that is important but the fact that Gregory adopts the techniques of pastoral leadership from the ascetic world (e.g., *discretio, condescensio*) and communicates those techniques through precise ascetic terms.

By appropriating ascetic language, Gregory not only communicated a model of spiritual direction that was distinctively ascetic but also imparted to the priest all of the pastoral authority of the solitary holy man. It was the holy man in late antiquity who possessed the ability to exorcise demons, foresee the future, and intercede for a community.[84] Gregory hoped to empower his priests with the same authority and influence.[85]

Preaching the Ideal

While still a deacon, Gregory offered an oral commentary on Job. Within the first anniversary of his pontificate, he edited and published that commentary.[86] That same year, the pope began a series of homilies (forty survive) on various Gospel passages corresponding to the Roman Lectionary. He addressed both the homilies and the commentary on Job to monks under his supervision, many of whom went on to positions of authority within his ecclesial administration. Both the commentary and the homilies promote a model of spiritual direction consistent with the *Pastoral Rule.*

Moralia

Known as the *Morals on the Book of Job,* Gregory's exegesis is an examination of the Old Testament text through a three-part method of exegesis: historical, allegorical, and moral.[87] Although he was not the first Christian author to identify Job as a model for ascetic imitation, his was certainly the most comprehensive treatment.[88] But Job afforded Gregory more than an ascetic exemplar; he also provided a model of spiritual leadership.

Using Job's life as a paradigm, Gregory advances a vision of spiritual direction that is consistent with his *Pastoral Rule.* For example, Gregory is able to extrapolate from Job the desire to balance action and contemplation.[89] Commenting on Job 33:15, Gregory states: "[T]hough their office requires them to serve external ministries, holy men always return to the secrets of their hearts and from there ascend to the summit of intimate contemplation."[90] Gregory insists that the best Christian leaders are those who imitate Job and therefore embrace pastoral responsibility without losing *contemplatio.*

Notwithstanding his desire to attract qualified candidates, Gregory warns of the challenges of spiritual leadership. Job, Gregory reminds his reader, endured many difficulties.[91] From this Gregory infers the need for *pastores* to expunge the sin of their subordinates, whatever the consequences.[92] More important, they must avoid pride.[93] He notes that priests are "not kings of men, but shepherds of flocks."[94] Failure in any respect leads to damnation—not only for the priest but for the entire community.[95] To overcome these challenges, a potential leader must purify himself.[96] For Gregory, that purgation takes the form of ascetic training.[97]

The tools of the ascetic pastoral tradition advocated in the *Pastoral Rule* figure prominently in the *Moralia*. According to Gregory, a clear sign of a candidate's aptitude is the gift of *discretio*—a charism present in Job and all of the saints.[98] A leader who correctly discerns the needs of his subordinates knows whether to apply *condescensio* or rigor.[99] Using Job's treatment of inferiors as his model, Gregory highlights the importance of pastoral discretion. Without *discretio,* Gregory warns, an advisor is unable to apply *condescensio*. Consequently, he is unlikely to apply moderation in his correction, diminishing the prospects of spiritual progress.[100] Elsewhere Gregory notes that *discretio* allows a "learned preacher" to refrain from giving his disciples the "food of sublime instruction" if he "discerns" that they have not yet adequately bewailed their past sins.[101]

Gregory, like his ascetic predecessors, believed that every person had unique spiritual gifts and weaknesses.[102] Those peculiarities often required an equally singular spiritual regimen.[103] Commenting on Job 38:36 ("Or who has given the cock understanding?"), Gregory introduces his seventy-two diametrically opposed personal traits.[104] The list presented in the *Moralia* is identical to that of the *Pastoral Rule*. Although Gregory issues brief prescriptions for each scenario, he anticipates an additional treatise on the subject.[105] The very fact that he offers this exhortation to a community of monks not only demonstrates that the spiritual direction of monks is equivalent to that of the laity but also suggests that Gregory expected some of these monks to assume roles in the broader Church.

The most repeated pastoral admonition in the *Moralia* concerns preaching.[106] Gregory extols condescension in preaching—not only because a lofty sermon is of no use to the general populace but because such a sermon is a demonstration of the speaker's pride.[107] Our author extols Job's "preaching" to his wife, friends, and the poor.[108]

Why, we might ask, does the *Moralia* so ardently advance public preaching? After all, Gregory delivered it to a small group of Latin monks who were essentially secluded from the outside world (not only cloistered in their monastery but even isolated by language in the Byzantine capital). Clearly, the future pontiff was preparing his audience for positions of authority in the Church.[109]

Through Job, Gregory advances a distinctively ascetic vision of spiritual direction. Commenting on Job 1:5, he likens Job's blessing of his sons and offering of incense on their behalf to Christ's washing of the feet of the disciples.[110] In both cases, the shepherd discerned vices influencing those in his care and reacted accordingly: Job blessed his sons because they had lost the sight of God through gluttony; Christ washed the feet of his disciples because their preaching had led them to pride.[111] Gregory's pastoral attentiveness and ascetic consciousness are evident in both examples. His final emphasis on the phrase "and so Job did this continually" confirms Job as the quintessential spiritual father.

Gregory's interpretation of Job's reaction to his wife provides another example.[112] Following the loss of their property, Job's wife encourages him to abandon God. Gregory reads Satan's influence into the woman's words. He moves on to distinguish between Job's spiritual wealth and his wife's temporal ambitions. Because Job seeks the Lord only, his loss of property is of no consequence. Not only does he maintain a proper respect for God, but his spiritual strength enables him to offer sensitive yet persuasive instruction to his wife.[113] The ascetic in Gregory welcomes Job's loss of family and wealth; the pastor in Gregory appreciates Job's measured remarks to wife and friends.

The *Moralia* combines Gregory's pastoral model and ascetic vision in other ways. While distinguishing between "things that are good and things that are better," Gregory presents the example of marriage and celibacy. Marriage is an acceptable way of life, but celibacy is superior—a popular position among Christian leaders of the era.[114] On the one hand, Gregory offers a pastoral opinion that gently admonishes his audience in a certain direction. On the other hand, that direction is unabashedly ascetic.

As the text progresses, a subtle transition occurs in Gregory's terminology. Early on, Gregory refers to Job's actions with the phrase "The holy man *[sanctus vir]* did . . ." Further in the narrative, he is less specific: "We see that holy men *[sancti viri]* will . . ."[115] By employing the plural form, Gregory implies that all who wish to be holy must follow Job's example. It is one thing to encourage an audience by saintly example; it is quite another to suggest that "all" persons favored by God must behave similarly.

This initial rhetorical shift links Job to ascetic action. But later the evolution continues from "holy men" to "holy preachers" *(sancti praedicatores)* and occasionally "holy teachers."[116] The use of *rector* and *rectores* also increases in the second half of the text.[117] The substitution of terms is, of course, deliberate. Gregory hopes to make priests of his monastic audience. By linking Job's actions to the toil of preachers, Gregory suggests that not only Job but all those who preach the Gospel are holy. Moreover, he implies that anyone who seeks the favor of God must consent to preaching. In Job, Gregory finds both a pastor and an ascetic—or better still, an ascetic who provides pastoral direction to the laity.

The Homilies

A few months after he ascended the papal throne, Gregory began preaching to a community of monks possibly already incorporated into the papal administration.[118] Of the forty homilies that survive, the majority correspond to specific feasts of the Roman calendar. The pontiff employed historical, allegorical, and moral interpretations of the Gospels and on most occasions trusted a secretary to deliver the message (owing to the pope's frequently poor health).[119] Though the format of the homilies differs considerably from the *Moralia,* the message is consistent.[120]

The brevity of the homilies presented Gregory with certain constraints that he did not face in his examination of Job. In the *Moralia,* Gregory had been free to pursue a theological question or moralizing principle before finally returning to the figure of Job and a more literal interpretation of the text.[121] This was not possible in the homilies. There are few in-depth theological diversions—only brief digressions designed to support a moralizing lesson. Nevertheless, these sermons provide some of Gregory's clearest statements on spiritual direction and (the benefit of) ascetic renunciation.

Commenting on the parable of the talents, Gregory warns his audience, "[W]e who have something more than others in this world will be judged more severely by the Creator of the world. When his gifts to us increase, our accountability for them also grows."[122] Not surprisingly, he then interprets "hiding a talent in the earth" as "wasting one's abilities in worldly affairs."[123] Gregory was looking for priests—not just administrators or dispensers of charity but true spiritual fathers. As he had intimated in his *Moralia* and *Pas-*

toral Rule, Gregory sought men who could combine *contemplatio* with love of neighbor.[124]

One means for this combination was preaching. Commenting on Matthew 12:46–50 ("Who is my mother?"), Gregory notes that a person "becomes Christ's brother or sister through faith but becomes his mother through preaching."[125] A preacher, quite like a mother, brings forth life, though unlike the mother a preacher brings forth spiritual life.[126] On another occasion Gregory compared a preacher's gradual correction of the laity to the description of John the Baptist as one who would make "the crooked straight and the rough ways smooth" (Luke 3:9).[127]

Gregory also uses these homilies as an opportunity to articulate the requirements for clerical service. In Homily 5, he extols the willful poverty of the apostles.[128] Responding to a question concerning the necessary extent of poverty, Gregory answers: "[W]e must consider the natural feeling rather than the amount. . . . For Zachaeus it was half his worth; . . . for Peter and Andrew it was worth the nets and boat they left behind; for the widow, it was worth two small coins [see Mark 12:42]; to another person it was worth a cup of cold water [see Matt. 10:42]. The kingdom of God, as I said, is worth everything you have."[129] Similarly, in Homily 14 he rebukes those who enter office for self-promotion.[130] It is for that reason, he maintains, that the Church lacks quality clerics: "The world is full of priests, but seldom do we find a laborer in God's harvest."[131] As he had in the *Pastoral Rule,* Gregory also uses the homilies to catalog the attributes of a successful minister.[132] He underscores the importance of *discretio, condescensio,* and the need for gradual correction.[133] But more important, he notes that shepherding requires the purgation of vice and the presence of virtue.[134]

Though underdeveloped in the *Moralia* and *Pastoral Rule,* the apocalypticism of the homilies further evinces Gregory's ascetic outlook.[135] Apocalypticism had always been a part of the Christian perspective, but with the triumphant conversion of Constantine it gradually receded from the Church at large and became increasingly the conceptual property of the ascetic during the fourth and fifth centuries. As we will see more completely in his correspondence, Gregory often associated the deterioration of the Roman state in the sixth century with the coming of the end. He not only linked the fall of Rome to the inability of Christians to live piously but also identified social discord as a sign of the coming apocalypse.[136] This twin interpretation further demonstrates Gregory's ability to deliver an asceticizing pastoral message for any situation—on the one hand, Christians needed to adopt renunciatory behavior to forestall the collapse of Rome; on the other hand, they needed to repent because the end of the world was at hand.

As much as any element of his written corpus, the homilies employ the internalizing language of virtue and vice. These discussions not only communicate the hopes and fears of an ascetic's spiritual battle but also promote Gregory's sense of pastoral correction. Take, for example, his discussion of Adam's fall in Homily 16. Gregory describes the event in terms of Adam's gluttony, avarice, and pride. Linking Adam's sin to a lack of abstinence was not new (Tertullian had done so as early the second century), but Gregory transforms a theologically sophisticated event into a simple pastoral message.[137] He not only communicates the story of the Fall in ascetic terms but enables members of the audience to learn how to prevent their own "fall." Another example is Homily 14, where the devil attacks the "sheep" through vice and temptation. Naturally the metaphor of the shepherd caring for a flock represents an ideal of spiritual direction, while "the devil" and "vice" signify the dangers of an ascetic's milieu.

Most important, however, is Gregory's approach to the homilies. With each address the pope seeks either to assist those in his audience directly or to provide a model for others to develop. The terminology, methods, and patterns of direction stem from Gregory's own ascetic experience. Consequently, the homilies, like the *Moralia,* demonstrate Gregory's asceticizing of pastoral direction.

Enforcing the Ideal

Gregory the Great possessed one of the most exhaustive correspondences of the late ancient world. Over eight hundred letters survive, ranging from friendly greetings to theological confrontations, from enjoinders to the contemplative life to requisitions for grain and lumber. These communications were not only frequent but far-reaching, Gregory wrote to aristocratic women in Constantinople and England and discussed theology with John Climacus (the abbot on Mt. Sinai) and Leander of Seville. These letters reflect the pastoral ideas and ideals of his *Pastoral Rule.*

Through his correspondence, Pope Gregory asceticized pastoral care in at least four respects: (1) he encouraged clerics to embrace the ascetic life; (2) he promoted ascetics to important positions; (3) he privileged ascetics over lay persons and bishops; and (4) he consistently employed the pastoral techniques of the ascetic community.

Interestingly, the correspondence reveals a tension between Gregory's encouragement of asceticism, particularly his advocacy of the monastic life, and his desire to bring accomplished ascetics out of the monasteries and place them in positions of pastoral authority. Gregory tried to resolve this tension by reviving Nazianzen's idea of the "active contemplative." Like Nazianzen, he found it difficult to strike the perfect balance.

Encouraging Asceticism

In 590, Gregory told a female correspondent that monasticism was the only adequate preparation for the loss of a loved one.[138] In 591, he cautioned a former ascetic from Syracuse that his abandonment of the cloister and return to secular life jeopardized his soul.[139] And in 594, Gregory commended a patrician from Constantinople for his recent pilgrimage to the famous monastery at Mt. Sinai.[140] These are but a few examples of Gregory's attempts to encourage his lay correspondents to adopt ascetic behavior. More frequent, however, were Gregory's letters to the clergy—letters that often rebuked the less-than-ascetic practices of their recipients.[141]

The pontiff's handling of clerical celibacy is particularly instructive—it combined ascetic encouragement with pastoral skill. Canonically, priests were permitted to marry so long as they did so prior to ordination.[142] In the West, however, many influential churchmen, Gregory included, insisted that a cleric must, upon his ordination, cease physical relations with his spouse.[143] In 591, Gregory advised Peter, his agent in Sicily, to inform local bishops that they should not ordain married men to the subdeaconate unless those men agreed to live in continence.[144] According to Gregory, the Sicilian Church had agreed, three years prior, to conform to the Roman regulation concerning clerical celibacy.[145] But, he acknowledged, it was exceedingly harsh to impose such a rule on men who had not promised celibacy at their ordination. Therefore, those who were unable to adhere to the provision were permitted to retain their rank and their wives, but they were not eligible for further ordinations.

To prevent future problems, Gregory forbade the ordination of anyone who still lived with his wife.[146]

Gregory's own reluctance to serve further testifies to an ascetic perspective. On a number of occasions, he confided to friends and colleagues that the secular burdens of office overwhelmed him.[147] In his inaugural confession of faith he bemoaned the loss of *contemplatio*.[148] For Conrad Leyser, these protestations (what he calls a rhetoric of reluctance) were a critical part of Gregory's initiative to sustain his authority.[149] On one occasion, his lamentation waxed poetic:

> I am so shaken in this position by worldly cares that I am unable to steer into port this old and decaying ship that I have received by the hidden dispensation of God. Now the waves rush in from the front, now heaps of foamy sea swell up from the sides, now the tempest continues from behind. And disoriented by all of this, I am compelled to turn into the very face of the opposing waters, sometimes turning the ship aside to avoid a head-on collision with the waves. I lament because through my neglect the sea of vices increases and the storm attacks the vessel as the already decaying planks sound of a shipwreck. With tears I recall that I have lost my calm shore of stillness *[quietis]*, and with sighs I see the land at a distance that I am unable to grasp because of winds blowing against me.[150]

Addressed to a good friend, Leander of Seville, this epistle conveys two sources of anxiety often repeated in the early years of Gregory's pontificate: the enormous responsibility of leadership and the loss of monastic *otium*. For Gregory, the absence of *contemplatio* made the pastoral life unbearable. For this reason, he insisted that clerics maintain a healthy contemplative life.

Promoting Ascetics to Positions of Authority

As pope, Gregory had the authority and resources to transform the institutional organization for much of Western Christendom. He shuffled the administrative wing of the papal regime, for the first time bringing monks into the Curia.[151] He also overhauled the management of the papal patrimony.[152] Overseeing each of the patrimonies was a *rector*, hand-chosen by the pope. A typical *rector* in the sixth or seventh century had the ecclesiastical rank of sub-deacon but occasionally the lesser rank of *defensor*.[153] Gregory ensured that every *rector,* whether in Italy or abroad, was a member of the Roman clergy.[154] Personally selecting these men enabled Gregory to guarantee that they met his standards of discipline and skill; it also gave him the opportunity to cast further the net of ascetic influence.

At the outset of his pontificate, Gregory focused his attention on Sicily.[155] He charged Peter, the *rector* of the papal patrimony in Sicily, to assess the condition of parish churches in the cities.[156] In those places where the presbyters were not competent, Gregory instructed Peter to replace them with the lower clergy or men from local monasteries.

> If any of the cities of the province of Sicily is known to be without spiritual direction *[pastorali regimine]* through the lapse of their priests on account of sin, you ought to inquire, by first assessing the gravity of their character, whether there are any who are worthy of the rank of the priesthood either from the monasteries or from the lower ranks of the clergy and then send them to us so that the flock of each place should not become destitute for any long period of time because of the lapse of its shepherd.[157]

In short, Gregory gave a subdeacon the authority to remove established priests and replace them with lay monks.[158] Gregory writes as though Peter will be able to achieve the pope's wishes. As it turned out, Peter's intrusion caused such a stir that Gregory needed to appoint a trusted friend and former monk to govern the Church in Sicily.[159]

Ravenna, like Sicily, attracted Gregory's interest. In this period, Ravenna served as the Byzantine outpost in the West. The magnificent architecture and dazzling mosaics scattered throughout the city attest to the Byzantine presence and influence in Italy during the sixth and seventh centuries.[160] On a number of occasions, Gregory found himself at odds with the exarch, whose primary responsibility was protecting Italy from the Lombards.[161] The potential for political and economic difficulties posed by the Greeks made Gregory's need for a trusted ecclesiastical ally in Ravenna all the stronger.[162] Thus, when John, the archbishop of Ravenna, died in 595 at the height of tension with the Lombards, Gregory ensured the election of a trusted monk to the vacant see.

He selected Marinianus for two reasons: he was a loyal ascetic, and he was not Donatus (the man promoted by the Byzantine exarch).[163] Gregory explained the circumstances of Marinianus's election:

> Those persons having been removed [from consideration], we urged the parties to choose someone from among themselves, but they lamented that they did not have anyone qualified for this office; . . . [eventually] they solicited with a unanimous voice our venerable brother, the priest Marinianus, whom they knew to have been with me for a long time in a monastery. Though at first he refused, he was at last persuaded to accept their petition. . . . And I have great confidence that Almighty God, who has chosen to place this man over his flock, will both enable him to maintain the internal [life] and, at the same time, grant him the grace of kindness to administer external responsibilities.[164]

While Gregory's tidy description of events is somewhat suspicious, the letter is revealing of Marinianus's appeal. According to John the Deacon, Marinianus entered the clergy from Gregory's own monastery at St. Andrews in Rome.[165] There could be no surer way for Gregory to know a man's credentials or anticipate his methods of leadership. As if scripted by Gregory, Marinianus went on to promote the pope's ascetic, theological, and political ideals.[166]

By campaigning for an ascetic candidate for the vacant See of Milan, Gregory reached beyond the traditional limits of his Roman jurisdiction. Initially, Gregory wrote to the clergy of Milan assuring them that he had no interest in interfering in their procedures.[167] Having received word from two Milanese clerics that they supported a deacon, Constantius, the pope extended his approval.[168] With great joy, Gregory reported that Constantius was an excellent candidate (they had known each other in Constantinople).[169] Gregory then promised to send a witness, not a participant, to the election. In a subsequent letter to one of his deacons, Gregory presented his involvement rather differently. He wrote:

> Because the Apostolic See, by God's arrangement, is preeminent among the churches, it has many concerns, and our attention is solicited for many things, especially when an episcopal election is delayed while wait-

ing for our opinion. Following the death of Laurentius . . . the clergy reported that they had unanimously consented in the election of our son Constantius. But because their report was not subscribed, it is necessary that we omit nothing in the way of caution and send you immediately to Genoa, supported by the authority of this order.[170]

We might assume one of two scenarios. Either the clergy in Milan were truly planning to elect Constantius and Gregory simply wanted to hasten the process; or a faction in Milan supported Constantius against some other candidate and Gregory did what he could to ensure the election of the man he favored. The pope finessed the initial letter in such a way as to assert his will, all the while claiming not to interfere. Whichever scenario more closely resembles the truth, it is clear that Gregory had a hand in the election of a monk who had been his disciple in Constantinople.[171]

Though the evidence demonstrates that Gregory consistently promoted ascetics to the clergy, two associated issues require attention. The first concerns the relationship between newly ordained priests and their former monasteries. On two separate occasions, Gregory issued strong warnings against priests returning to their communities to requisition supplies.[172] At issue were the autonomy and security of the monasteries. Gregory, though he strongly encouraged ascetics to assume the responsibility of pastoral leadership, was not willing to gain those new priests at the expense of the monasteries themselves. If for no other reason, he did not want to alienate his talent pool of future clerics.

A second issue is simony. Anyone familiar with Gregory's correspondence knows of his endless critiques (he mentions it in over fifty letters). One explanation focuses on the prevalence of simony in Gregory's era. I would stress, however, that simony was particularly despised by Gregory because it ran counter to his ideals. As far as he was concerned, the most qualified candidates were those who had to be brought against their will from the monasteries, not the politicians who craved the advantages of office. Making his case to Antoninus, the *rector* of the patrimony in Dalmatia, Gregory insisted: "[A]nd above all, you must ensure that this election contains neither bribery nor the patronage of any persons; for if one is elected through the patronage of others, he is obliged out of deference to them to comply with their wishes after his ordination."[173]

Perhaps the most significant advancement of ascetics was the mission to the Angli. In September of 595, Gregory instructed Candidus, the newly appointed *rector* of the papal patrimony in Gaul, to use a portion of his revenue to purchase clothing for English slave boys so that they might be educated in monasteries.[174] According to the letter, these boys were to be sent to Rome under the care of a priest and brought up in the monastic profession. Shortly thereafter, Gregory sent lay monks, not priests or bishops, to the far reaches of Europe in the name of spreading the Gospel. Less than a year after this initial letter, Gregory dispatched Augustine, a monk from his monastery in Rome, along with a group of companions to convert the "heathen" English. Gregory not only appointed Augustine *abba* of the mission but also named him papal ambassador to the bishops and aristocrats encountered en route.[175] In time, Gregory conferred control of the entire Church in England to Augustine.[176] According to Markus, the pontiff's plans for the English were an integral component of a much larger initiative to rejuvenate the Church as a whole.[177] The fact that Gregory conferred this responsibility upon a small band of monks demonstrates his commitment to their distinctive brand of leadership.

Privileging Ascetics over Their Rivals

Gregory issued numerous rulings on legal and theological conflicts. On many occasions, these emerged among monastic communities and the secular clergy or laity. In almost every case (more than fifty), Gregory found in favor of the ascetic party. There may be no clearer sign of his loyalty. The following are a few examples arranged in three categories: monks and bishops, financial disputes, and imperial legislation.

There is a tension in Gregory's correspondence between a monastery's sovereignty and a bishop's responsibility to provide for its needs. On the one hand, Gregory establishes the rights of monasteries and rebukes bishops who ignore those rights. On the other hand, he just as frequently criticizes bishops for failing to provide assistance to monasteries. In both circumstances, the pontiff sides with the ascetic community.

Gregory outlines the privileges of monasteries in many epistles. These include the freedom to choose the abbot/abbess; the security of property from clerical encroachment; and the right to refuse an episcopal chair in the monastery church.[178] In a letter dating to 598, Gregory extended three additional privileges.[179] First, all abbots could appeal to the bishop of Rome.[180] Second, the expense of an episcopal visit was to be paid by the bishop. And third, it was necessary for a bishop to consult the abbot before he removed a monk from one monastery to fill a vacancy in another monastery or in a lay parish. This final provision had a dual purpose: it maintained the sovereignty of the monastery and ensured that the monk's spiritual advisor approved of his ordination.

Not surprisingly, Gregory's episcopal correspondents rarely accepted these regulations. In 595, the pontiff reproached Castorius, bishop of Rimini, for seizing monastic property. Gregory demanded three things of the bishop: that he desist from his illegal activities; that he not interfere in the selection of new abbots; and that he never again preside over the liturgy at the monastery.[181] Gregory added this third injunction because the bishop's entourage included too many women—an apparent distraction for the monks.[182]

Ironically, Gregory also criticized bishops who paid too little attention to the monasteries in their dioceses. In 593, he rebuked Secundinus, bishop of Tauremenium (Sicily), for failing to assist a local monastery with the remodeling of its church.[183] On another occasion, Gregory upbraided several bishops when he learned that a woman who had begun an ascetic life had been carried away and forcibly married against her will. Not only did the bishops fail to stop the wedding, but they had not done anything to rectify the situation.[184] The same year, he criticized Domicus, the bishop of Carthage, for neglecting an abbot. According to Gregory, whenever the abbot initiated new regulations, many of his monks would leave the monastery and wander the countryside. Gregory thought it the bishop's responsibility to step in and censure the malcontents. This last case is illuminating because Gregory presumes a cooperative relationship between abbot and bishop. Almost everything in the correspondence suggests a less propitious scenario. More often than not, bishops ignored or manipulated the monasteries in their dioceses. Gregory probably hoped that an asceticized episcopacy would improve the situation.

One way to guarantee the success of monasteries was to ensure that they were financially viable. It is not surprising, therefore, that Gregory consistently ruled in favor of monastic communities in cases involving money or property. Often these disputes involved inheritance laws. For example, a letter from 598 reports that a woman's will had assigned her husband to use a portion of his inheritance to build a monastery. According to Gregory, the husband was dragging his feet. Gregory instructed Romanus, his agent in Sicily, to pressure the husband.[185] In another letter, Gregory wrote to Januarius complaining of a certain priest who had stolen property that had been bequeathed to a monastery.[186] Apparently, the priest had "directed the actions" (i.e., been a spiritual advisor) of the deceased woman while she was alive and had chosen to keep her inheritance for himself.

Occasionally, these financial disputes involved persons intent on joining a monastery. For example, there was a wealthy woman, previously engaged, who desired the monastic life.[187] The jilted groom seized a portion of what would have become his dowry. Gregory instructed the local bishop that this property should be returned to the woman and thus to the monastery. Even more scandalous was an incident involving a wealthy woman who became a nun, relinquishing her property to the monastery. The woman then had an affair with a bishop, producing a child, and the three of them absconded with the funds formerly donated to the monastery. Gregory ordered the two adults to ecclesiastical trial and the money returned.[188]

Gregory's relationship with the imperial government was, for the most part, friendly and cooperative.[189] There were, however, certain laws with which Gregory took exception. In particular, he resisted imperial legislation that prevented slaves and soldiers from entering the monastic life.[190] While the logic of the imperial position is obvious to the modern reader, Gregory believed that it would lead to the loss of souls. He wrote: "[T]his legislation, I confess to your excellency, has terrified me greatly. Through it, the way to heaven has been closed to many and what until now has been lawful has become illegal. Indeed, there are many who are able to maintain the religious life while living in the world. But there are many more who cannot be saved with God unless they give up all [worldly] things."[191] Not surprisingly, the pope also rejected, out of hand, the government's position that many were adopting the monastic life with dubious motives. Eventually, the two sides reached a compromise.[192]

Gregory's deliberate rulings in favor of ascetics went past traditionally accepted limits. He established the rights of monasteries at the expense of episcopal authority; he guaranteed the financial viability of ascetic communities by checking the abuse of would-be swindlers; and he paved the way for men otherwise restricted by imperial decree to pursue the contemplative life.

Gregory's soteriology demanded that all participate in their salvation through ascetic endeavor.[193] By liberating ascetic communities from episcopal, financial, and legal burdens, the pontiff made the "angelic" life a viable option for a greater number of people. In recognizing Gregory's loyalty to these communities and their way of life, we further understand why he advanced a model of asceticized pastoral direction.

Implementing the Pastoral Ideal

The most significant and innovative way in which Gregory asceticized pastoral direction was the transformation of spiritual leadership in the lay environment. The pontiff's correspondence demonstrates that he personally applied the pastoral techniques of the *Pastoral Rule* and admonished others to do the same. Throughout, we see him applying the pastoral tools of the ascetic community.

According to Gregory, the spiritual advancement of an individual subordinate required a specific, long-term plan. When, for example, a correspondent returned to secular life after a brief stint as a monk, Gregory cautiously criticized him, insisting only that he continue to consult the pope in the future.[194] And despite the many successes of Augustine of Canterbury (including his numerous miracles), Gregory continued to monitor and correct the spiritual state of his most famous disciple.[195]

In addition to his own pastoral practice, Gregory encouraged his correspondents to adopt similar methods of individualized correction. Advising the newly appointed abbot of Lérins, Conon, Gregory extolled moderation during the instruction of individual monks: "[T]herefore, let the good know your sweetness, the bad your correction. Yet even in correction, observe this command that you love individuals and address their faults. If you act otherwise, correction will turn into cruelty and you will destroy those you wish to amend. For you should cut away the tumor without damaging what is healthy."[196] Individuals required a unique regimen, but every regimen was to be gradual.

Gregory also issued more general, though no less important, messages about the gradual correction of entire congregations. In a well-known letter to Serenus, bishop of Marseilles, Gregory accused the bishop of stifling the spiritual growth of his flock.[197] At issue was Serenus's destruction of the images of the saints—icons. The pope submitted that icons provided a useful tool for the gradual teaching of the (illiterate) laity.[198] Just as an abbot taught his subordinates through texts, bishops were to employ icons for the instruction of the laity.

A long-term plan for spiritual advancement was particularly necessary when one was attempting to convert Jews or pagans. While he encouraged his addressees to pursue conversions, Gregory opposed the use of force, especially with Jews.[199] In 591, the pope excoriated a bishop who had twice obstructed Jewish worship.[200] Not only should the bishop permit Jewish ceremonies, he ought to realize that "those who dissent from the Christian religion must be brought to the unity of the faith by gentle, kind, and persuasive admonitions . . . not by threats or intimidation."[201] Gregory's Jewish policy was, however, not without its own coercive tactics. In 594, he advised Cyprian, the steward of the patrimony in Sicily, to reduce by a third the rent of any Jewish tenant living on papal lands who converted to Christianity.[202] Though some would convert for the financial advantage only, in the long run, Gregory argued, this tactic would be spiritually beneficial. Ultimately, "the souls of their children would be rescued" because they would be raised as Christians. Perhaps this was gradual conversion taken to an extreme.[203]

The example par excellence of Gregory's policy of gradual conversion comes from England. Having sent Augustine and a band of monks to the island in the summer of 596, Gregory faced a dilemma with respect to the pagan temples. Scholars continue to squabble about his solution. The controversy stems from two letters sent within weeks of one another, one to King Ethelbert (Epistle 11.37) and one to a monk, Mellitus (Epistle 11.56).

In the first letter, Gregory encourages the newly baptized king to embrace the responsibilities of Christian kingship.[204] He writes: "[M]ake haste to extend the Christian faith to the people under your care, multiply the zeal of your rectitude in their conversion, censure the cult of idols, destroy their temples, build up the practices of your subjects in great purity of life by exhorting, by terrifying, by enticing, by reforming, and by demonstrating examples of good works."[205] Some historians have constructed a Gregorian policy of conversion from this letter.[206] In other words, they believe that Gregory's standard missionary maneuver was to employ the "coercive power" of a potentate.[207] This interpretation, however, does not adequately account for the subsequent letter to Mellitus or Gregory's pastoral touch.

When Mellitus received Gregory's letter, he was already en route to England with additional monks and supplies for Augustine.[208] Gregory tells Mellitus to convey the following to Augustine:

> Tell him that I have been thinking long and hard about the case of the Angli; it is now clear to me that by no means should the temples of idols in that nation be destroyed, but that the actual idols that are in them should be. Let holy water be prepared and sprinkled in these temples, and altars constructed, and relics deposited, because, as long as these temples are well built, it is necessary that they should be transformed from the cult of demons to the service of the true God. For when the people themselves see that these temples were not destroyed, they will lay aside the error of their heart, and knowing and adoring the true God, they will flock with more familiarity to the places to which they are accustomed.[209]

With his decision to convert pagan temples into Christian churches, Gregory put to work many of his pastoral techniques. For example, he allowed the uniqueness of the situation to dictate a singular prescription for the gradual conversion of an entire nation.[210] Nazianzen, Augustine, and Cassian had urged spiritual advisors to link pastoral decisions to circumstance. Here Gregory applied that idea on a much larger scale.

As for the different instructions presented to Ethelbert and Mellitus (one to destroy the temples, another to use them), they are more consistent with one another than generally recognized. Both letters record Gregory's commitment to gradual correction, and the letter to Ethelbert is an example of Gregory's individualized approach. In other words, Epistle 11.56 stresses the king's position as a leader of a Christian populace. Gregory's instructions reflect the king's role as a Christian leader and his responsibility to the religious development of his subjects.[211] The letter to Mellitus gives different instructions but shares the same long-term goal—the eventual conversion of the Angli. Typical of Gregory's good common sense, his advice to his monks is to play the hand they have been dealt. It is the second letter, not the first, that most represents Gregory's conversion policy.[212]

The letter to Mellitus is also a fine example of Gregory's use of *discretio* and *condescensio*. Discerning the difficulty of Augustine's efforts, Gregory made

what he believed to be a necessary concession in the hope that it would hasten the true conversion of pagans. This was not his only use of *condescensio*
concerning the English.

According to the Church historian Bede, Augustine of Canterbury requested Gregory's assistance with twelve pastoral questions.[213] The pope issued specific answers to Augustine's queries (known as the *Responsa*), which
are laden with pastoral concessions. For example, Gregory permitted the marriage of second cousins and reduced the impediments to communion.[214] But
in doing so, Pope Gregory explained the pastoral necessity of *condescensio:* "[A]t
this time, indeed, the holy Church corrects some things through fervor, tolerates some things through clemency, suppresses some things with consideration and at the same time endures the same things, such that it often happens
that she might subdue what is withstood by enduring and suppressing."[215]
Though some scholars have disputed the authenticity of the *Responsa,* the defense offered by Deansley and Grosjean is more than sufficient, and this is further confirmed by the fact that the *Responsa* are so consistent with Gregory's
pastoral approach.[216]

Naturally, Gregory encouraged *discretio* and *condescensio* outside England. In
one example, he wrote to the sister of the emperor, Theoctista, after learning that she had come under heretical influence.[217] In a manner typical of his
sensitivity, the pontiff congratulated her for her piety, then identified the errors of "other persons" residing in the capital—never accusing her openly.
Gregory employed similar methods when he tried to convince Brunchild,
queen of the Franks, to condemn the Three Chapters.[218] In both cases, he
perceived the situation and tailored his advice accordingly.

Through the medium of ascetic language, Gregory further advanced his
model of pastoral authority. He congratulated the emperor's physician for
his great charity, a new abbot for his abstinence, and a patrician woman for
her chastity.[219] Reciprocally, he decried the avarice, lack of humility, and uncontrolled feasting of bishops who did not meet his ascetic standards. Just
as he had admonished future clerics in the *Pastoral Rule,* Gregory's own approach to subordinates was to reward what was commendable and critique
what was lacking.[220] Typically, he promoted a particular virtue in the context of correcting an existing vice. For example, he admonished Paul, the
bishop of Naples, to the spiritual advantages of long-suffering as a means
to counter his despair.[221]

As he had in the *Pastoral Rule, Moralia,* and homilies, the pontiff also offered long lists of virtues and vices in the correspondence.[222] The significance lies in the fact that Gregory typically employed this language in the context of spiritual direction. Whenever he directed subordinates or advised other clerics in the art of pastoral care, Gregory used terms and concepts that were distinctively ascetic.

His language was also full of demonic imagery. Writing to Rusticiana, a wealthy woman, Gregory warned that any hesitation in pious action opened the door to "the cunning plotter who strives to ensnare the soul."[223] Elsewhere he attributed vice and the disruption of good to the work of the devil and his demons: "The spite of the ancient enemy has a way of its own; in the case of those whom he cannot delude, because God has resisted him, he maims their reputation for a time by false reports."[224] And just as he had in his homilies and *Dialogues,* Gregory triumphantly reported in his letters the power monks held over the demons.[225] Through such descriptions of demonic activity, Gregory warned his correspondents of the pressing danger in their lives and reminded them of their need for authoritative assistance.

Gregory's apocalypticism was perhaps most pronounced in the correspondence. The constant threat of invasion combined with a crumbling city and frequently poor health to fuel his apocalyptic vision.[226] On a number of occasions, Gregory warned friends and acquaintances of the coming end.[227] The year 600 seems to have been particularly bleak. On two occasions he wrote to bishops (one in Africa and one in the Balkans), noting the collapse of the previous world.[228] According to Gregory, it would still be some time before the actual end, and things were going to get worse, but God had graciously provided Christians the opportunity to repent before the apocalypse.[229]

As noted previously, apocalyptic imagery provided Gregory with a method for communicating the urgency for complete (i.e., monastic-like) repentance. St. Paul had cautioned in 1 Corinthians that it was advisable to live as though tomorrow might not come. Gregory adopted that message, not only because it was part of his apocalyptic hermeneutic, but also because it promoted ascetic behavior.

Thus it is not surprising that Gregory, like St. Paul, encouraged celibacy. In nearly a dozen letters, Gregory openly promoted the ascetic life over marriage. He encouraged wealthy orphans to consider monasticism instead of wedlock.[230] And he rebuked a bishop who failed to assist a female ascetic carried off by a spurned fiancée.[231] But perhaps one of the most revealing examples concerns a woman who complained that her husband had left her to become a monk.[232] Writing to Adrian, notary of Panormus, Gregory assumed one of the following three scenarios: (1) the wife had committed fornication, which constituted grounds for the husband to leave her; (2) the wife had promised to become a nun herself but had then changed her mind, also justifying her husband's actions; or (3) the man simply left without her blessing. Only the final possibility required that the husband return to his wife.[233] We might recall Augustine's different response to a similar situation.[234]

With each use of the ascetic's vocabulary (e.g., virtues/vices, demonology, and apocalypticism), the bishop of Rome linked his monastic past to an idealized vision of the future. Gregory's correspondence not only demonstrates his use of the pastoral methods outlined in the *Pastoral Rule* but conveys its message through an ascetic idiom. And while it is true that other authors of this period were increasingly employing a language and hermeneutic initially born in the ascetic community, Gregory, more than any author of his generation, conveyed that tradition to the Middle Ages.

BENEDICT AS MODEL FOR THE PRIESTHOOD

There has been a heated discussion in recent years concerning the authenticity of Gregory's *Dialogues (Dialogorum libri IV)* (a collection of Italian saints' lives). Some have tried to rescue Gregory from himself by arguing that Gregory was too sophisticated to circulate "legendary" accounts like those of the *Dialogues*.[235] I am not the first to believe that such a position is not borne out by the sources.[236] I raise the subject of the *Dialogues,* particularly the life of St. Benedict, because it confirms Gregory's interests in pastoral direction. In the same way that Athanasius's *Life of Antony* may tell us more about the author than about the subject, so too Gregory's *Dialogues* reveal much about Gregory's own pastoral concerns.[237] And unlike other presentations of late antique ascetic holy men, Gregory's *Life of Benedict (Vita Benedicti)* subordinates its hero's renunciatory prowess and emphasizes his pastoral skills.

If we survey those lives of the saints to which Gregory had access (such as those of Symeon the Stylite, Antony, Hilarion, and Martin of Tours), we see that they follow a common story line.[238] In each account, a young man, eager for the ascetic life, begins as member of community or under the tutelage of one or more elders (e.g., Symeon spends ten years in a monastery, Antony visits a number of hermits, and Martin studies under Hilary of Poitiers).[239] After his training, the ascetic is able to perform heroic *askesis*. Challenges often include demons, the elements, and various temptations.[240] After the hero overcomes these threats, he reigns triumphant, able to share his power with others through miracles and instruction. In nearly every case the saint heals the sick, exorcises demons, and teaches a community of disciples. But these stories never wander far from their subjects' ascetic achievements.

Though similarities exist, Gregory's *Life of Benedict* does not follow this pattern. For example, Benedict begins as a fully accomplished ascetic. Gregory informs us that the saint did not need a mentor or spend time in a community, yet possessed perfect renunciation and enacted miracles from his youth.[241] Throughout the text, Benedict displays many ascetic gifts, but we never learn how he cultivated those skills.

Benedict's struggles are also unique. In the biographies of most ascetic saints, conflict resides in the renunciatory struggle.[242] In the *Life of Benedict,* however, both the conflict and the resolution hinge upon the saint's pastoral responsibilities. As a solitary, Benedict is unfulfilled. Gregory exonerates him only after he successfully combines *contemplatio* with service.

Both subordinates and demons challenge Benedict's authority. In chapter 12, we are told that the monks of Monte Cassino are not permitted food outside the monastery. But a pair of monks traveling for the needs of the monastery forego this regulation. Upon their return, Benedict, discerning the truth, asks them where they have eaten. When the monks respond with a lie, Benedict exposes their deception and solicits a confession. Through this account, Gregory emphasizes Benedict's *discretio* as well as his *condescensio* (he does not treat them harshly; rather he pardons them, confident that they have learned an important lesson).[243]

The *vita* also contains dozens of anecdotes that display Benedict's judicial leadership. It equally features Benedict's perseverance in the face of hostility. For example, we are told that while he lived in the area of Subiaco Benedict organized twelve separate monasteries. According to Gregory, Benedict's success and ensuing fame stirred envy in the heart of a local priest. The priest tried, over and again, to destroy Benedict (once he offered the saint poisoned

bread, later he sent prostitutes to defile the monastery).[244] Each time, however, Benedict avoided the trap and protected his flock.

What makes this story significant is the pastoral way in which Benedict
responds to these challenges. Not wanting to be the source of another's sin,
Benedict appoints abbots for each of the monasteries and then departs. Within
minutes of the saint's exit, God strikes down the jealous priest. A novice from
one of the monasteries rushes to Benedict, rejoicing that his master can now
return. Benedict's response, however, is not what the young man expected.
Gregory writes: "Benedict was overcome with sorrow and regret on hearing
this news, for not only had his enemy been killed, but one of his own disciples
had rejoiced over his death. And for showing pleasure in such news, he gave
[the monk] a penance."[245] Benedict's withdrawal is justified by God's ultimate
intervention and the death of the saint's enemy. In the process, Gregory casts
Benedict as a man who anticipates divine action and never loses his ability to
offer pastoral directives whenever they become necessary.

Elsewhere in the account, Benedict overcomes the obstinacy of subordinates. Early in his career, the saint is asked to govern a monastery whose
abbot has recently died. Benedict is concerned that the monks will not be
able to endure the austerities that he plans to impose. Nevertheless, he accepts the position and sets in motion a series of reforms. The monks are so
resistant to these new regulations that they poison Benedict's wine. Gregory
narrates Benedict's reaction: "[S]till calm and undisturbed, he rose at once
and, after gathering the community together, addressed them. 'May God
have mercy on you,' he said. 'Why did you conspire to do this? Did I not tell
you that my way of life would never harmonize with yours?' . . . Then he
went back to the wilderness he loved, to live alone with himself in the presence of his heavenly Father."[246] Peter, Gregory's interlocutor in the *Dialogues,*
protests that Benedict forsook his responsibility by abandoning the monastery. Gregory responds with a protracted defense of the saint's action. Ultimately, an advisor's success depends upon the willingness of his subordinates.[247] But more important, a spiritual father must weigh his own needs
against those of the community. In other words, he must strike a balance
between action and contemplation. Benedict, the pontiff reasons, would no
doubt have forfeited his own salvation had he remained in that environment.
That is why he returned to the wilderness "to live with himself in the presence of the heavenly Father."

Like the heroes of other late antique Christian biographies, Benedict encounters the devil and his demons. But unlike the dark forces that threatened Antony and Martin, Benedict's spiritual foes pose pastoral rather than ascetic challenges. Upon the suggestion of his bishop, a tormented cleric goes to Benedict for healing. After exorcising the demon, Benedict instructs the man to abstain from meat and to accept no further ordinations. For the next several years, he remains free of demonic assaults. But as time advances and he sees younger men passing him in priestly rank, the cleric presents himself for ordination. "Instantly," Gregory writes, "the man was seized by the devil and tormented mercilessly until he died."[248] Gregory's emphasis in this account lies not with Benedict's exorcism of the demon but with the saint's ability to provide the appropriate pastoral prescription. Had the cleric fulfilled Benedict's instructions, he would have survived. This story simultaneously confirms Benedict's pastoral skill and warns of the danger of disobedience.

In another example, we find the saint alone in the wilderness when the devil appears to him in the form of a blackbird. Benedict crosses himself and the bird flies away, but our hero instantly suffers a violent temptation: "The evil spirit reminded him of a woman he had once seen and, before he realized it, his emotions carried him away."[249] Throwing his garment aside, Benedict dives into a nearby thistle and rolls around until he "drains the poison of temptation" from his body.

Naturally, an ascetic reading of this passage is viable. I believe, however, that this story equally speaks to spiritual direction. The episode is situated early in the text, at the beginning of chapter 2. In the closing lines of the previous chapter, we learn that Benedict had, for the first time, taken on pastoral responsibility. Adalbert de Vogüé argues convincingly that this temptation scene is directly related to Benedict's new role as a spiritual guide.[250] Just as the demons attacked Antony at the first signs of his *askesis*, here Benedict's pastoral success similarly draws the assaults of the evil one.[251] Interestingly, Benedict never again suffers from this or any other temptation. The implication is that ascetic renunciation is a precondition for pastoral leadership. It is on the heels of this spiritual victory that Benedict becomes an abbot. What is more, in the dialogue between Peter and Gregory that follows this scene, Gregory insists that all clerics must maintain chastity.

Discipleship provides another distinction between the *Vita Benedicti* and other popular ascetic *vitae*. Antony, Hilarion, and Symeon all have followers who imitate their way of life; Martin, of course, becomes the bishop of Tours. The authors of those texts, however, rarely develop models of spiritual leadership or a pastoral theology through their encounters with these disciples. In fact, the novices do little more than confirm the heroes' ascetic greatness. In the *Life of Antony,* for example, the monks that congregate around the hermit witness the saint's physical battles with demons and serve as a sounding board for their master's ascetic theology. Athanasius points to Antony's role as spiritual father, but he does not elaborate on Antony's methods.

In the *Life of Benedict,* however, the community of subordinates plays a more defined role. Time and again, Benedict assists (often miraculously) the novices under his instruction.[252] This interaction between saint and disciple allows Gregory to promote Benedict's gifts of spiritual direction. In chapter 16, Gregory explains the source of his hero's power. Anyone, Gregory informs Peter, who observes the commandments of God understands his secrets because that person is united with the Lord.[253] Benedict achieves this union by "meditating continually on the words of holy Scripture."[254] But it is because the saint willingly accepts the responsibility of pastoral leadership that he is, in the eyes of Gregory, the holy man par excellence.

While the span of nearly two hundred and fifty years helps to explain many of the differences between the *Dialogues* and the *Life of Antony,* there is little denying the shift in emphasis. Gregory's *Life of Benedict* redefines both the purpose of ascetic purgation and the summit of perfection in terms of spiritual supervision. In short, Benedict is a model of sanctity because he accepts his true calling—as a spiritual father. We have seen in his *Pastoral Rule* and correspondence how Gregory actively recruited monks to fill the pastoral void. By establishing Benedict as the greatest of all spiritual fathers, Gregory simultaneously provides his priests with a model of pastoral leadership and reminds his monastic audience that service, not contemplation, paves the road to sanctity. According to Gregory, that is most easily performed by joining the clergy. Perhaps the clearest indication of Gregory's interest in Benedict derives from a passage near the end of the *vita:* "There is one thing that I cannot allow to remain hidden. Despite the fame that the holy man received for his many miracles, his words of instruction were equally important. He wrote a rule for monks that is honored for its *discretio* and clarity of message. Anyone who wants to know more about his character and life is able to discover in this rule what he was like as a teacher; for the life of a holy man does not differ from his teaching."[255]

This chapter has documented the ascetic dimensions of Pope Gregory I's vision of spiritual direction. Throughout his career, the pontiff advocated techniques of pastoral care that originated in the ascetic community. In his *Pastoral Rule,* written at the outset of his pontificate, Gregory fixed the criteria for ordination to ascetic achievement. He encouraged the use of many pastoral techniques in vogue in the ascetic community. And he presented his vision of leadership through ascetic language. In short, Gregory's *Pastoral Rule* transformed the lay priest into an engaging spiritual father similar to the monastic *abba.* By doing so, Gregory became the first bishop in the Christian West to articulate a distinctively ascetic approach for the spiritual direction of the laity.

This chapter has also explored the pastoral and ascetic dimensions of Gregory's other writings. The pope's pastoral strategies are on display in his biblical commentaries and homilies (he delivered both to the men who served his administration). Through the correspondence, Gregory further advanced his asceticizing agenda in Rome and abroad. As he had in his *Pastoral Rule,* Gregory required asceticism from all *rectores.* Whenever possible, he promoted ascetics to positions of authority and privileged ascetics over their rivals. Most important, through his correspondence Gregory advanced the asceticized techniques of spiritual guidance that he first advocated in his *Pastoral Rule.* Even the *Life of Benedict* demonstrates Gregory's ability to unite ascetic renunciation and pastoral leadership. Benedict, as much as anything else, symbolizes for Gregory the willingness of great men to condescend to the pastoral necessities of the community. If there was anything Gregory claimed to know, it was the sacrifice of pastoral service.

Gregory's asceticizing of spiritual direction had important implications. First, by identifying ascetic experience as the principal qualification of ordination, Gregory was able to promote those candidates that shared his ideals (ascetic and otherwise). He hand-selected men like Maximianus (bishop of Syracuse) and Marinianus (archbishop of Ravenna) from his monastery in Rome. Operating from a position of strength, Gregory controlled the episcopal elections of several sees and named an untold number of clerics to lesser orders. In return, Gregory's appointees supported his asceticizing program as well as his theological and secular initiatives.

Second, through his pastoral initiatives, Gregory expanded the influence of the ascetic community in the Church at Rome and abroad. While some historians have suggested that the ascetic takeover of the Western Church had occurred prior to Gregory's pontificate, I believe that he was largely responsible for the transformation of the Church in Rome. By restaffing the Curia, Gregory placed ascetics in positions previously held by civil servants. With these men, Gregory had the mechanisms in place to implement his many plans. Consequently, Gregory altered the balance of power in the Roman Church. Ascetics, not career bureaucrats, now controlled the purse strings and set the spiritual and political agendas of the papal machinery.

Outside Rome, Gregory's asceticizing program is also apparent. In scores of parishes, Gregory installed experienced ascetics and encouraged them to employ the pastoral techniques of the *cenobium*. When successful, these priests would have blurred the line between monastery and lay Church. Gregory believed that all Christians, married and celibate alike, should avoid temporal pleasure and redirect their worldly desire into activities that engendered spiritual growth.

Third, Gregory's interest in spiritual direction overrode all other concerns. If we take him at his word, the laity were unable to succeed on their own. It was the priest, as disseminator of the sacraments and interpreter of God's word, who served, taught, counseled, and assisted those in need. More specifically, it was the discerning spiritual father who understood the needs of his disciples and set them on the path to salvation. If we are to appreciate any aspect of Gregory's thought or career, we must first recognize the extent to which pastoral care occupied his attention.

Conclusion

Pope Gregory I died on March 12, 604. During Gregory's tenure, the underprivileged in Rome had grown accustomed to the pope's beneficence, enjoying a daily distribution of grain and bread. This generosity, however, had come with a price—Gregory had, in effect, depleted the papal treasury. According to later biographers, Gregory died just before a famine struck central Italy. Gregory's successor, Sabinianus, had not been won over by Gregory's asceticizing initiatives or his handling of the Curia. Moreover, he was either unwilling or unable to continue Gregory's policy with respect to the poor and began to sell (rather than freely distribute) the grain from the papal estates.[1] Long after Sabinianus's death, legends circulated that Gregory had appeared to Sabinianus in his dreams and scolded him for his avarice. According to one account, however, Sabinianus was not the only malcontent. Certain agitators (probably enlisted by Sabinianus and the pre-Gregorian clerical establishment) were able to convince a Roman mob that Gregory's excessive liberality was the source of their misfortune. Unable to get direct justice from a dead pope, the group turned toward Gregory's former assistants and attempted to burn his books.[2] According to this account, Peter (who was Gregory's trusted deacon) was able to dissuade the mob only by convincing them that he had witnessed the Holy Spirit speaking to Gregory.[3]

It is often difficult to accept hagiography as historical fact, especially in those cases where the authors postdate their subjects by more than one hundred and fifty years. But both John the Deacon's and Paul the Deacon's biographies record a type of resistance to Gregory's legacy in the period after his death that we might otherwise have expected them to suppress. If there is any truth to their stories, the resentment that they convey may signify a resurgent opposition to Gregory's asceticizing agenda. Gregory had made wholesale changes to the Roman Church, dismissing a number of career bureaucrats and replacing them with men from his monasteries—acts that must have provoked a great deal of hostility among the previously entrenched clergy.[4] In turn, Sabinianus reversed Gregory's policies by restricting the distribution of free grain and releasing Gregory's monks from the Curia.[5] It seems as though Gregory's asceticizing of spiritual direction was too much for the Roman clergy of the early seventh century.

Despite the attempt to restore the Roman Church to its pre-Gregorian condition, Gregory's ascetic program continued to influence spiritual direction long after his tenure as pope. In the East, Gregory's *Pastoral Rule* was translated into Greek and disseminated among the Eastern bishops by imperial order—a rare honor for a Latin author.[6] In the centuries that followed, the Western Church came to refer to Gregory as "the Great" because of the effect that he had on the development of the priesthood. There is no denying the popularity of the *Pastoral Rule* in the Middle Ages. Over six hundred manuscripts (an astonishing number) survive in libraries from Moscow to Madrid. Furthermore, Gregory's blueprint for leadership influenced more than the clergy in the Middle Ages. It also was cited as a model for civil government in the ninth century by Alfred the Great, who was responsible for the translation and circulation of the text in England.

But how does one explain the shift in spiritual direction from Athanasius's ambivalence to Gregory's systematic integration of the ascetic and clerical traditions? The evolution of spiritual direction that occurred between the middle of the fourth and the end of the sixth century was an uneven one. I have, quite consciously, not tried to sketch the entire story; instead, I have centered my study on five influential authors who characterize just some of the variability in pastoral care in the late ancient period. By selecting these five authors, I hope to have conveyed three things. First, the legalization of Christianity produced something of a pastoral crisis. Within a few generations of Constantine's conversion, the pastoral realities of monastic and lay life were moving in opposite directions. Quite naturally, each community promoted its authorities and cultivated a type of leadership that best addressed its individual situation. But when monks began to enter the clergy at the end of the fourth century, many of them faced a real pastoral dilemma in that they had to find a way to balance their ascetic ideals with the reality of leadership in the broader Church. Second, Athanasius, Nazianzen, Augustine, Cassian, and Gregory I each resolved that tension in a different way. Although similarities exist, each author responded to his pastoral challenges in ways that not only addressed the issues of his era but also addressed them in accordance with his own vision of spiritual direction. The differences between these authors demonstrate both the complexity of the tension and the extent to which serious consideration of spiritual direction was something new to the post-Constantinian Church and therefore not yet codified. Third, with time, the spiritual direction of the lay Church became more ascetic. Many of the tenets of the clerical model persisted (e.g., the authority of the clergy, the emphasis on preaching, and a concern for administrative competence), but even those considerations evolved to reflect ascetic ideals. For example, Pope Gregory I understood authority to belong to the clergy but identified ascetic experience as the most important criterion for ordination.

An exhaustive comparison of these authors is problematic because each of the five reflected on spiritual direction to varying degrees (e.g., only Nazianzen and Gregory I authored pastoral treatises) and each writer operated in a distinct historical setting. Nevertheless, a few points of contact require some reflection. For example, Athanasius and Augustine offered little (if any) endorsement of the spiritual father/spiritual disciple model of supervision. Athanasius described Antony as a spiritual father, but he never developed the model for himself; Augustine seems to have ignored it altogether. Perhaps this is because both Athanasius and Augustine spent much of their episcopates in the throes of theological conflict. In Athanasius's case, we know that some of his opponents had promoted a type of study group where non-ordained teachers instructed lay persons. For Athanasius, that system was a threat to the authority of the clergy. His reluctance to embrace the spiritual father model for himself might be explained by an unwillingness to mirror the didactic model of his theological competitors. There is less direct evidence for Augustine's resistance. It is possible that the spiritual father/spiritual disciple model of leadership reminded him of his experience with the Manicheans or that it conformed too closely to what he knew of Pelagian asceticism. It is also possible that he never benefited from such a relationship during his early years as a Christian, so the idea never made much of an impression on him. Any conclusion in this regard, however, remains speculative.

Another interesting point of connection/contention for our authors was their attitude toward education as a requirement for leadership. Both Gregory Nazianzen and Augustine understood the need for a well-educated and articulate clergy. In part, we can explain their interest in education as an extension of their own training and rhetorical talents. But both authors developed a thoughtful defense for elevating the educational standards of the clergy. During the late fourth and early fifth centuries the Christian Church struggled for a consensus with respect to the doctrines of the Trinity and Jesus Christ. In the midst of those controversies, Nazianzen and Augustine understood the priest's most important role to be the dissemination of orthodox teaching to the faithful. A priest who was pious and orthodox but unable to explain specific points of doctrine was of little use against the wolves who devoured the faithful through the spread of heresy.

John Cassian, a contemporary of Augustine, provides an interesting contrast. Although Cassian wrote for an aristocratic and educated audience, he provided a vision of spiritual authority in which ascetic experience and *discretio* surpassed all other qualities as the markers of effective leadership. By the time Gregory I assumed the papal throne, many of the doctrinal questions about Christ and the Trinity seemed to have been settled. To be sure, there were theological questions at the end of the sixth century, but Gregory was not a strong proponent of any contentious position—he relied on the authorities of the past. As a consequence, orthodox teaching was just one of many responsibilities of Gregory's priest. For Gregory, unlike Augustine, preaching served more than doctrinal formation—it was also a vehicle to shape the ascetic behavior of the laity. As a result, it was less important for Gregory than it had been for Nazianzen or Augustine that the priest be well educated. Like Cassian, Gregory's spiritual leader was to be a man of ascetic experience who could exercise pastoral discernment.

In general, each of our authors recognized the need for the spiritual director to tailor his message to the specific needs of an audience. This is not surprising; the idea can be found in Scripture, and it was a familiar theme in late ancient oratory. Where our authors differed was in relation to how the *pastor* was to distinguish between subordinates. For Augustine, the most important distinction was between those who were educated and those who were not. Such a partition made sense, especially to a cleric who was responsible for catechesis. Nevertheless, we can contrast this position with that of John Cassian, who believed that novice monks should be instructed according to their spiritual status. It is with the two Gregorys that we find the most elaborate scheme for distinguishing between disciples. Indeed, both Nazianzen and Pope Gregory show a real concern for understanding the specific circumstances of the members of their flock before offering any pastoral advice.

The only direct borrowing of pastoral ideas between the five authors seems to have been Gregory I's reading of Gregory Nazianzen's "Apology for His Flight."[7] The pope cites Nazianzen in the opening lines of his prologue, quoting the Cappodocian's famous line that pastoral care is "the art of arts and science of sciences." More importantly, Gregory I also took from Nazianzen the pairing of opposite conditions as a means to describe the multiplicity of spiritual conditions and the need to develop a unique solution for each situation. Pope Gregory expanded this list and provided greater detail for both the symptoms and the remedies. It is perhaps ironic that Nazianzen's innovation in this regard had, through Pope Gregory's elaboration, a greater circulation in the medieval West than it did in the Byzantine East, where John Chrystostom's *On the Priesthood* became the most popular treatise on pastoral care.

Spiritual direction took many forms in early Christianity. The criteria by which Christian authorities selected their successors and the pastoral techniques that they passed on to these men varied widely, especially in the period after Constantine's conversion. As episcopal vacancies became increasingly filled by ascetics, so too did ascetic notions of spiritual direction gain ascendancy in the lay Church. This evolution, however, was not smooth, and many influential men offered competing ideas about the extent to which ascetic ideas about spiritual direction should be absorbed by the entire Church. With time, Christians in both the East and West came to embrace a synthesis of the clerical and ascetic models in which authority resided with the clergy but ascetic experience became one of the principal criteria for the selection of new bishops. Moreover, many of the pastoral techniques that had originated in the ascetic community became entrenched in medieval religiosity.

Abbreviations

Series

CCSL: Corpus Christianorum, Series Latina
CSEL: Corpus Scriptorum Ecclesiasticorum Latinorum
GCS: Griechischen Christlichen Schriftsteller
PG: Patrologia Graeca
PL: Patrologia Latina
PLS: Patrologiae Latinae Supplementum
SC: Sources chrétiennes

Ancient Sources

Ammonas
Ep.   *Letters [Epistulae]*. Derwas J. Chitty and Sebastian T. Brock, trans., *The Letters of Ammonas, Successor of Saint Antony* (Oxford: SLG Press, 1979).

Antony
Ep.   *Letters [Epistulae]*. Samuel Rubenson, ed. and trans., *The Letters of St. Antony: Monasticism and the Making of a Saint* (Minneapolis: Fortress Press, 1995).

Ath.   Athanasius of Alexandria
Apol. Const.   *Apology to Constantine [Apologia ad Constantium]*. Jan M. Szymusiak, crit. ed. (SC 56).
Ep. Ammoun   *Letter to Ammoun [Ad Amunem]*. J.-P. Migne, ed. (PG 26).
Ep. Drac.   *Letter to Dracontius [Ad Dracontium]*. J.-P. Migne, ed. (PG 25b).
Ep. Fest.   *Festal Letters [Epistolae festales]*. For those preserved in Greek, J-P. Migne, ed. (PG 26); for those preserved in

	Coptic (Letters 24, 29, 39, 40), trans. in David Brakke, *Athanasius and Politics of Asceticism* (Oxford: Clarendon Press, 1995), 320–34.
Ep. Hor. 2	*Second Letter to Horsisius [Epistola II ad Orsisium].* J.-P. Migne, ed. (PG 26).
Ep. Marc.	*Letter to Marcellinus [Ad Marcellinum].* J.-P. Migne, ed. (PG 27).
Ep. Mon. 1	*First Letter to Monks [Ad monachos I].* J.-P. Migne, ed. (PG 25b).
Ep. Mon. 2	*Second Letter to Monks [Ad monachos II].* J.-P. Migne, ed. (PG 26).
Ep. Rufianus	*Letter to Rufianus [Ad Rufianum].* J.-P. Migne, ed. (PG 26).
Ep. Ser.	*Letter to Serapion [Ad Serapionem].* J.-P. Migne, ed. (PG 25b).
Ep. Vir. 1	*First Letter to Virgins [Epistula virginibus II].* Trans. in David Brakke, *Athanasius and Politics of Asceticism* (Oxford: Clarendon Press, 1995), 274–91.
Ep. Vir. 2	*Second Letter to Virgins [Epistula virginibus II].* Trans. in David Brakke, *Athanasius and Politics of Asceticism* (Oxford: Clarendon Press, 1995), 292–302.
V. Ant.	*Life of Antony [Vita Antonii].* G. Bartelink, crit. ed. (SC 400).

Aug.   Augustine of Hippo

Conf.	*Confessions [Confessiones].* L. Verheijen, crit. ed. (CCSL 27).
De civ.	*On the City of God [De civitate Dei].* B. Dombart, crit. ed. (CCSL 47–48).
De doc.	*On Christian Teaching [De doctrina christiana].* I. Martin, crit. ed. (CCSL 32).
De pecc. mer.	*On the Guilt and Remission of Sins [De peccatorum meritis et remissione]* C. F. Urba, crit. ed. (CSEL 60).
De rud.	*On Catechizing the Ignorant [De catechizandis rudibus].* I. Bauer, crit. ed. (CCSL 46).
Ep.	*Letters [Epistulae].* A. Goldbacher et al., crit. ed. (CSEL 34, 44, 57, 58, 88); but for the *Letters Recently Discovered* (nos. 1*–29*), see Johannes Divjak, crit. ed. (CSEL 88).
Serm.	*Sermons [Sermones].* J.-P. Migne, ed. (PL 38–39; PLS, vol. 2).

Basil

Ep.	*Letters [Epistulae].* Yves Courtonne, crit. ed. 3 vols. (Paris: Les Belles Lettres, 1957, 1961, 1966).

Bede

> HE   *Ecclesiastical History of the English People [Historia ecclesiastica gentis Anglorum]*. Bertram Colgrave, crit. ed. (Oxford: Clarendon Press, 1969).

John Cassian

> *Conl.*   *Conferences [Conlationes]*. M. Petschenig, crit. ed. (CSEL 13).
>
> *Inst.*   *Institutes [Institutiones]*. M. Petschenig, crit. ed. (CSEL 17).

Gregory I

> *Dia.*   *Dialogues (Dialogorum libri IV)*. Adalbert de Vogüé, crit. ed. (SC 251, 260, 265).
>
> *Ep.*   *Letters [Registrum epistularum]*. D. Norberg, crit. ed. (CCSL 140, 140A).
>
> *Hom.*   *Homilies on the Gospels [Homiliae in Evangelia]*. R. Étaix, crit. ed. (CCSL 141).
>
> *Mor.*   *Morals on the Book of Job [Moralia in Job]*. M. Adriaen, crit. ed. (CCSL 143, 143A, 143B).
>
> *PR*   *Book of Pastoral Rule [Liber regulae pastoralis]*. F. Rommel, crit. ed. (SC 381–82).

Gregory of Tours

> *HF*   *History of the Franks [Historia Francorum]*. R. Buchner, crit. ed. (Berlin, 1955).

Lib. Pont.   *Book of Pontiffs [Liber pontificalis]*. L. Duchesne, crit. ed. (Paris, 1886–92).

Naz.   Gregory Nazianzen

> *Ep.*   *Letters [Epistulae]*. 2 vols. P. Gallay, crit ed. (Paris: Les Belles Lettres, 1964). Also *Theological Letters* (101, 102, 202) *[Epistulae]*. P. Gallay, crit. ed. (SC 208).
>
> *Or.*   *Orations [Orationes]*
> > Nos. 1–3. J. Bernardi, crit. ed. (SC 247).
> > Nos. 4–5. J. Bernardi, crit. ed. (SC 309).
> > Nos. 6–12. M.-A. Calvet-Sebasti, crit. ed. (SC 405).
> > Nos. 13–19. J.-P. Migne, ed. (PG 35).
> > Nos. 20–23. J. Mossay, crit ed. (SC 270).
> > Nos. 24–26. J. Mossay, crit. ed. (SC 284).
> > Nos. 27–31. P. Gallay, crit. ed. (SC 250).
> > Nos. 32–37. C. Moreschini, crit. ed. (SC 318).
> > Nos. 38–41. C. Moreschini, crit ed. (SC 358).
> > Nos. 42–43. J. Bernardi, crit. ed. (SC 384).

Possidius

    V. Aug.   *Life of Augustine [Vita Augustini]*. J.-P. Migne, ed. (PL 32).

Rufinus

    HE   *Ecclesiastical History [Historia ecclesiastica]*. Theodore Mommsen, crit. ed. In *Die Kirchengeschichte,* vol. 2.2 of *Eusebius Werke,* rev. F. Winkelmann (Berlin: Akademie Verlag, 1999).

Siricius

    Ep.   *Letters [Epistulae]*. J.-P. Migne, ed. (PL 13).

Socrates Scholasticus

    HE   *Ecclesiastical History [Historia ecclesiastica]*. G. C. Hansen and M. Sirinjan, crit. eds. (GCS, NF 1).

Sozomen

    HE   *Ecclesiastical History [Historia ecclesiastica]*. J. Bidez, crit. ed. (Paris: Éditions du Cerf, 1983).

Notes

Introduction

1. Cassian, *Conl.* 18.5.

2. By "lay" Christian, I mean both married and unmarried men and women who understood themselves to be members of the Christian community but who did not wish to adopt the more rigorous life of organized asceticism.

3. A more precise but perhaps overly technical term would be *pyschagogy,* meaning "guidance of the soul." The spiritual director had a prominent place in the philosophical schools of the ancients. Christians borrowed the idea and developed it to suit their needs (sometimes quite differently). Throughout the text, I will use the terms *spiritual direction* and *pastoral care* almost interchangeably. The term *pastoral care* conveys a certain set of modern preconceptions about clerical ministry, but it was also a term employed by late ancient Christians, especially Pope Gregory I, to describe the responsibilities of spiritual leadership. Concerning spiritual direction in classical philosophy, see the collective works of Pierre Hadot, especially his *Philosophy as a Way of Life: Spiritual Exercises from Socrates to Foucault,* trans. Michael Chase (Oxford: Blackwell, 1995).

4. It is, of course, unlikely that priests or monks in the fourth, fifth, or sixth centuries would have understood their formation of disciples to be composed of a series of "pastoral techniques." Nevertheless, it is possible (even necessary) to employ this terminology in order to differentiate between pastoral traditions.

5. Christians did not invent the practice of asceticism—the Greco-Romans had a long tradition of philosophical *askesis* or "training" that was suppose to clear the mind of all distractions, enabling philosophical contemplation. In Christian hands, *askesis* took on physical characteristics that were designed to train both the body and soul to shun those things that distracted a person from God.

6. For the scholarly debate over an acceptable definition of *asceticism,* see Vincent Wimbush's introduction to *Ascetic Behavior in Greco-Roman Antiquity* (Minneapolis: Fortress Press, 1990), 1–11.

7. Here too, *parish* is an awkward and anachronistic term. Nevertheless, it well conveys to a modern reader the environment of a lay Christian community under the leadership of an ordained and orthodox clergy.

8. For a concise presentation of the technical difference but practical similarity between a professed ascetic and a monk, see Susanna Elm, *Virgins of God: The Making of Asceticism in Late Antiquity* (Oxford: Clarendon Press, 1994), 13–14.

9. See Conrad Leyser, *Authority and Asceticism from Augustine to Gregory the Great* (Oxford: Clarendon Press, 2000).

10. See James Goehring, "The Encroaching Desert: Literary Production and Ascetic Space in Early Christian Egypt," *Journal of Early Christian Studies* 1 (1993): 281–96.

11. For example, see Ignatius, *Epistle to the Ephesians* 3–5, in *Letters [Epistulae]* (J. B. Lightfoot, crit. ed., pt. 2, vols. 1–3 of *The Apostolic Fathers* [1885; repr., Peabody, MA: Hendrickson, 1989]).

12. See John Behr, *The Way to Nicaea* (Crestwood, NY: St. Vladimir's Seminary Press, 2001), 81–83.

13. Irenaeus, *Against Heresies [Adversus haereses]* 3.3.4 (A. Rousseau and L. Doutreleau, crit. ed., SC 100, 152–53, 210–11, 263–64, 293–94); Tertullian, *The Prescription against Heretics [De praescriptione haereticorum]* 32 (R. F. Refoulé, crit. ed., SC 46).

14. Chrysostom, *On the Priesthood [De sacerdotio]* 3.4 (A. M. Malingrey, crit. ed., SC 272). Here and elsewhere in this book, all translations from primary sources are my own unless otherwise indicated.

15. Ibid., 3.5.

16. Ibid. John typically uses the vague term ἱερωσύνης (priesthood), which implies both the priest and the bishop. See Anne-Marie Malingrey, ed., *Jean Chrysostome: Sur le sacerdoce* (Paris: Éditions du Cerf, 1980), 72–73.

17. *Didascalia Apostolorum* 2.33. I am relying on R. H. Connolly's translation of the Syriac text; see R. H. Connolly, ed. and trans., *Didascalia Apostolorum: The Syriac Version Translated and Accompanied by the Verona Latin Fragments* (Oxford: Clarendon Press, 1929).

18. 1 Tim. 3:2–4.

19. Ignatius, *Epistle to Polycarp* 3, in *Letters*.

20. *Didascalia Apostolorum* 2.25. See Georg Schöllgen, *Die Anfänge der Professionalisierung des Klerus und das kirchliche Amt in der syrischen Didaskalia* (Münster: Ashendorffe Verlagsbuchhandlung, 1988), 34–100.

21. Claudia Rapp, *Holy Bishops in Late Antiquity: The Nature of Christian Leadership in an Age of Transition* (Berkeley: University of California Press, 2005), 31.

22. *Didascalia Apostolorum* 2.25.

23. Ibid., 2.20.

24. Ibid., 2.1.

25. See Claudia Rapp, "The Elite Status of Bishops in Late Antiquity in Ecclesiastical, Spiritual and Social Contexts," *Arethusa* 33 (2000): 379–99.

26. Aug., *De doc.* 4.2.3 ff.

27. See Rapp, "Elite Status of Bishops," esp. 386–87. See also her *Holy Bishops,* 183–88. See also A. H. M. Jones, *The Later Roman Empire, 284–602,* 2 vols. (1964; repr., Baltimore: Johns Hopkins University Press, 1986), 1:93.

28. On the episcopal court system, see Jill Harries, *Law and Empire in Late Antiquity* (Cambridge: Cambridge University Press, 1999), 199–211, and John Lamoreaux, "Episcopal Courts in Late Antiquity," *Journal of Early Christian Studies* 3 (1995): 143–67.

29. *Didascalia Apostolorum* 2.5.

30. Ibid., 2.18.

31. Origen, *Commentary on the Gospel According to Matthew [Commentaria in Evanglium secundum Matthaeum]* 12.11 (J.-P. Migne, ed., PG 13) .

32. Ibid., 12.14.

33. Rapp, *Holy Bishops,* 35–36. Origen cautions, "[I]f [the bishop] is tightly bound with the cords of his sins, he will be unable to bind and loose." Origen, *Gospel According to Matthew* 12.14.

34. Origen, *Gospel According to Matthew* 12.14.

35. Ammonas, *Ep.* 4, 12. I have relied on Chitty's and Brock's translation from the Syriac.

36. Ammonas, *Ep.* 12.

37. Ammonas, *Ep.* 6.

38. Ammonas, *Ep.* 6.

39. Ammonas, *Ep.* 11. "And if I, who am your spiritual father, had not formerly obeyed my spiritual parents, God would not have revealed His will to me."

40. See, for example, Antony, *Ep.* 6. I have relied on Rubenson's translation of Antony's *Letters*; see Samuel Rubenson, ed. and trans., *The Letters of St. Antony: Monasticism and the Making of a Saint* (Minneapolis: Fortress Press, 1995).

41. Antony, *Ep.* 6.

42. Ammonas, *Ep.* 4.

43. Ammonas, *Ep.* 4. As the consequence of trial, see *Ep.* 10.

44. Ammonas, *Ep.* 4.

45. See Joseph Lienhard, "On 'Discernment of Spirits' in the Early Church," *Theological Studies* 41 (1980): 505–29.

46. The premier study of the role of the spiritual father in ascetic culture is still Irénée Hausherr's *Spiritual Direction in the Early Christian East,* trans. A. Gythiel (Kalamazoo, MI: Cistercian Publications, 1990). Note also John Chryssavgis, *Soul Mending: The Art of Spiritual Direction* (Brookline, MA: Holy Cross Orthodox Press, 2000), esp. 49–58; Philip Rousseau, *Ascetics, Authority and the Church in the Age of Jerome and Cassian* (Oxford: Oxford University Press, 1978), 19–32 and 49–55.

47. See Hausherr, *Spiritual Direction,* 99–122, and Rousseau, *Ascetics, Authority,* 56–67.

48. Cf. Basil, *Longer Rules [Regulae fusius tractatae]* 54, in *Ascetic Works [Ascetica]* (J.-P. Migne, ed., PG 31); see also Philip Rousseau, *Pachomius: The Making of a Community in Fourth-Century Egypt* (Berkeley: University of California Press, 1985), 104–18.

49. Rousseau, *Pachomius*; see also Claudia Rapp, "'For Next to God, You Are My Salvation': Reflections on the Rise of the Holy Man in Late Antiquity," in *The Cult of the Saints in Late Antiquity and the Middle Ages: Essays on the Contribution of Peter Brown,* ed. J. Howard-Johnston and P. Hayward (Oxford: Oxford University Press, 1999), 63–81.

50. The philosopher, according to Hadot, would harness all of his rhetorical resources, not so much to supply an exhaustive explanation of reality as to enable his disciples to orient themselves to their world in a way that would bring assurance and peace to the soul. See, for example, the chapter "Forms of Life and Forms of Discourse in Ancient Philosophy," in his *Philosophy,* 49–77, esp. 63–64. See also the book's introduction by Arnold I. Davidson, 20–22.

51. In its present form the *Apophthegmata* was probably compiled during the sixth century, but it is the product of several editorial redactions and additions. The earliest material stems from the fourth century.

52. Benedicta Ward, trans., *The Sayings of the Desert Fathers* (Kalamazoo, MI: Cistercian Publications, 1975), xxii.

53. Ammonas, *Ep.* 8.

54. Ammonas, *Ep.* 8.

55. Ammonas, *Ep.* 8.

56. Basil, *Longer Rules* 41.

57. Ammonas, *Ep.* 11.

58. Ammonas, *Ep.* 11.

59. John Climacus, *Ladder of Divine Ascent [Scala paradisi]* 4 (J.-P. Migne, ed., PG 88). See Chryssavgis, *Soul Mending,* 59–72.

60. See Antony, *Ep.* 3, 4, 5, and 6.

61. See Ammonas, *Ep.* 4, 5, 8, and 12.

62. Basil, *Longer Rules* 25.

63. Naz., *Or.* 2.16. A phrase borrowed by Gregory I, *PR* prol. 1 (F. Rommel, crit. ed., SC 381–82).

64. Cf. Basil, *Morals [Moralia],* 60, 70.30, in *Ascetic Works [Ascetica]* (ed. J.-P. Migne, PG 31).

65. Ibid., 72.4–5.

66. Hellenistic examples of discernment include Porphyry's *Life of Plotinus* 11 and *Life of Pythagoras [Vita Pythagori]* 13, 54 (Édouard des Places, crit. ed. [Paris: Les Belles Lettres, 1922]). Even Christians employed different models of discernment. The Roman Synod of 378 claimed that a bishop did not need to resort to torture to ascertain the truth from witnesses (as did secular judges) because he could discern, by the charism of his office, when a witness was telling the truth. See Henry Chadwick, *Priscillian of Avila: The Occult and the Charismatic in the Early Church* (Oxford: Clarendon Press, 1976), 128–29. I would like to thank Kevin Uhalde for his many intriguing observations concerning the episcopal exercises of discernment. For episcopal judgment as an act of discernment, see his monograph *Expectations*

of Justice in the Age of Augustine (Philadelphia: University of Pennsylvania Press, forthcoming).

67. Basil, *Longer Rules* 27.

68. See, for example, Basil, *Morals* 70.20–21.

69. To be sure, many authors conceived of this battle in different ways. See David Brakke, "The Making of Monastic Demonology," *Church History* 70 (2001): 19–48.

70. Ath., *V. Ant.*; Evagrius of Pontus, *Praktikos* (A. Guillaumont and C. Guillaumont, crit. ed., SC 170).

71. In a recent article, James Goehring explores how authors who wrote about the desert saints created an idealized, even mythical, characterization of the ascetic life. In turn, this myth of the desert naturalized the expectations of ascetic behavior for both authors and readers, so that monks who had never actually seen the sands of Egypt could legitimately claim to live "in the desert." James Goehring, "The Dark Side of Landscape: Ideology and Power in the Christian Myth of the Desert," in *The Cultural Turn in Late Ancient Studies,* ed. D. Martin and P. Cox Miller (Durham: Duke University Press, 2005), 136–49.

72. Chrysostom, *On the Priesthood* 3.4–5.

73. To say that confession or penance were understood as "sacraments" during the fourth century would be to overstate the case. The earliest systematic analysis of the sacraments was that of Pseudo-Dionysius, *Ecclesiastical Hierarchy [De ecclesiastica hierarchia]* (J.-P., Migne ed., PG 3), which likely dates to the sixth century.

74. *Didascalia Apostolorum* 2.12–18.

75. Ibid., 2.27–33.

76. On the variation in pre-Constantinian Christianity with respect to which clerical orders could confirm a penitent's readmission to the community, see Rapp, *Holy Bishops,* 95–96.

77. As Basil noted in *Morals* 70.10, "[T]he preacher of the Word should not feel successful by virtue of his righteousness but should know that the moral improvement of those trusted to him is the primary responsibility of the office."

78. See Henry Chadwick, *The Role of the Christian Bishop in Ancient Society,* Protocol Series of the Colloquies of the Center 35 (Berkeley: Center for Hermeneutical Studies in Hellenism and Modern Studies, 1979), 1–14.

79. On the transfer of civic responsibilities, see Rapp, *Holy Bishops,* 279–89.

80. Possidius suggests as much in his account of Augustine. Possidius, *V. Aug.* 19.

81. Chrysostom, *On the Priesthood* 3.16.

82. Although Ambrose went directly from a civic position to the episcopate, he became a dedicated ascetic and encouraged ascetic practices among his flock. See Neil McLynn, *Ambrose of Milan: Church and Court in a Christian Capital* (Berkeley: University of California Press, 1994), 53–67.

83. Chrysostom, *On the Priesthood* 3.15.

84. Naz., *Or.* 2.30–32.

85. Similarly, in the late fifth or early sixth century, Julianus Pomerius, a rather obscure author, issued his *On the Contemplative Life,* which held that the bishop should pursue a balance between the active and contemplative life (see esp. 1.13). For more on Pomerius, see Leyser, *Authority and Asceticism,* 65–80.

86. Ambrose, *On the Office [De officiis]* 1.43, 2.20 (M. Testard, crit. ed. [Paris: Les Belles Lettres, 1984–92]).

87. Naz., *Or.* 2; John Chrysostom, *On the Priesthood.*

88. Ambrose, *On the Office* 1.50.

89. Chrysostom, *On the Priesthood* 3.12. For Augustine's position, see ch. 2. For Siricius, see his *Ep.* 1 and 6. Concerning Siricius, see David Hunter, "Rereading the Jovinianist Controversy: Asceticism and Clerical Authority in Late Ancient Christianity," in Martin and Miller, *Cultural Turn,* 119–35, esp. 120–23.

90. See my review of Leyser's monograph in *Theological Studies* 62 (2001): 831–33.

91. Leyser, *Authority and Asceticism,* 133.

92. Robert Markus, *The End of Ancient Christianity* (Cambridge: Cambridge University Press, 1990), 199–211.

93. Leyser, *Authority and Asceticism,* 133.

94. Andrea Sterk, *Renouncing the World yet Leading the Church: The Monk-Bishop in Late Antiquity* (Cambridge, MA: Harvard University Press, 2004).

95. Rapp, *Holy Bishops,* 450.

96. Men like Basil of Caesarea, John Chrysostom, and Benedict of Nursia, who are not discussed, also played an important role in that history.

97. As for John Chrysostom, it is true that his *On the Priesthood* remains to this day the most read treatise of pastoral literature among the Eastern Orthodox, but many of its ideas are derivative of Nazianzen's. Concerning Gregory's influence on John, see Manfred Lochbrunner, *Über das Priestertum: Historische und systematische Untersuchung zum Priesterbild des Johannes Chrysostomus* (Bonn: Borgengässer, 1993), 39–66.

ONE   *Athanasius of Alexandria and Ambivalence Regarding Spiritual Direction*

1. The discrepancy is significant because if the later date is accurate he would not have been of canonical age when he became bishop of Alexandria in 328. The *Festal Index [Chronicon praevium]* 3 (Annik Martin and Marcelline Albert, crit. ed., SC 317) notes that his election was contested on the grounds that he was not of sufficient age. See Timothy Barnes, *Athanasius and Constantius: Theology and Politics in the Constantinian Empire* (Cambridge, MA: Harvard University Press, 1993), 10.

2. For an introduction to the sources for Athanasius's biography, see Martin and Albert's critical edition of the *Festal Index,* 69–106. See also Barnes, *Athanasius and Constantius,* 3–5.

3. The story is repeated in various forms by Rufinus, *HE* 10.15; Socrates Scholasticus, *HE* 1.15; Sozomen, *HE* 2.17.5–31.

4. Ath., *Apology against the Arians [Apologia contra Arianos]* 9.4 (Jan M. Szymuziak, crit. ed., SC 56); Constantius, (surviving in) *Apol. Const.* 30.3–4.

5. Barnes, *Athanasius and Constantius,* 11. See also G. C. Stead, "Rhetorical Method in Athanasius," *Vigiliae Christianae* 30 (1976): 121–37.

6. Scholars have long believed that two letters, in the name of Alexander, bear traces of Athanasius's hand. See G. C. Stead, "Athanasius' Earliest Written Work," *Journal of Theological Studies,* n.s., 39 (1988): 76–91.

7. The Melitian schism began with the persecution of Maximinus in 305. When Peter, the bishop of Alexandria, withdrew from the city, Melitius, the bishop of Lycopolis, stepped in to perform his duties, including the ordination of priests. Peter objected to Melitius's extradiocesan activities, and when Peter returned to Alexandria he convened a council that excommunicated Melitius. After a period in exile, Melitius returned and established a parallel church. According to the compromise worked out at Nicea, Melitius retained his clerical rank (and his see of Lycopolis). However, the council prohibited Melitius from performing any further ordinations and subordinated his clergy in Alexandria to those ordained by Alexander. See Hans Hauben, "The Melitian 'Church of the Martyrs': Christian Dissenters in Early Egypt," in *Ancient History in a Modern University,* ed. T. W. Hillard (Grand Rapids, MI: Eerdmans, 1998), 2:329–49.

8. Epiphanius, *Refutation of All Heresies [Panarion/Adversus haereses]* 68.7.2, 69.11.4 (K. Holl and J. Dummer, crit. ed., GCS 25, 31, 37).

9. Compare, for example, Socrates, *HE* 1.23, with Sozomen, *HE* 2.17–18. The ninth-century patriarch of Constantinople Photius preserved an Arian account of the events (that of Philostorgius). Photius, *Epitome,* preserved in the manuscript *Cod. Barocc. 142 s. XIV.* See Johannes Quasten, *Patrology* (1950; reprint, Westminster, MD: Christian Classics, 1992), 3:531–32. Modern commentators have been no less divided. See, for example, Leslie Barnard, "Two Notes on Athanasius," *Orientalia Christiana Periodica* 41 (1975): 348–49; Barnes, *Athanasius and Constantius,* 17; Charles Kannengiesser, "Athanasius of Alexandria and the Ascetic Movement of His Time," in *Asceticism,* ed. Vincent L. Wimbush and Richard Valantasis (Oxford: Oxford University Press, 1995), 479; and Duane Arnold, *The Early Episcopal Career of Athanasius of Alexandria* (Notre Dame: University of Notre Dame Press, 1991), 28–31.

10. Constantine continued to pressure Athanasius to readmit Arius to communion. As for the Melitians, in 328 they elected their own bishop, who laid claim to Athanasius's see.

11. Athanasius went to Trier in Gaul. *Festal Index* 8; Epiphanius, *Refutation of All Heresies* 68.6. See also Barnes, *Athanasius and Constantius,* 19–20.

12. Athanasius spent most of this time in Italy. *Festal Index* 11–18.

13. Ath., *Apol. Const.* 30.3–4.

14. Though technically exiled from Egypt, Athanasius once again hid among the monks of the Thebaid. *Festal Index* 35.

15. The new emperor in the East, Valens, ordered all those exiled by Constantius who had regained their see under Julian to forfeit their positions. When a pretender to the throne emerged in Constantinople, Valens rescinded the order in fear that his rival would capitalize on his ecclesiastical positions. See Barnes, *Athanasius and Constantius,* 161–63.

16. Some have questioned Athanasius's authorship of the *vita.* A brief summary of the debate is contained in Philip Rousseau, "Antony as Teacher in the Greek *Life,*" in *Greek Biography and Panegyric in Late Antiquity,* ed. Tomas Hägg and Philip Rousseau (Berkeley: University of California Press, 2000), 89–109, esp. 100–106. I follow the consensus that Athanasius is the author, but like Rousseau I maintain that our appraisal of Athanasius needs refinement.

17. David Brakke, *Athanasius and the Politics of Asceticism* (Oxford: Clarendon Press, 1995), 8–11.

18. Ibid., 4–5.

19. Kannengiesser, "Athanasius of Alexandria," 479. See also Brakke, *Athanasius,* 10.

20. Ath., *On the Incarnation [De incarnatione]* 54.3 (Charles Kannengiesser, crit. ed., SC 199).

21. Ibid., 3.1–5.8.

22. Concerning Athanasius and the consequences of the Fall, see Khaled Anatolios, *Athanasius: The Coherence of His Thought* (London: Routledge, 1998), 53–67, esp. 62–63. Concerning its impact on his theology of asceticism, see Brakke, *Athanasius,* 147–61.

23. As Anatolios explains, Athanasius believes that "the added grace bestowed upon humanity comes with the condition that humanity itself maintains its accessibility to this grace. Its 'likeness' to God is simultaneous with the vocation to strive to retain that likeness." Anatolios, *Athanasius,* 59. Cf. Ath., *Against the Gentiles [Contra gentiles]* 2 (P. Camelot, crit. ed., SC 18).

24. Ath., *On the Incarnation* 3.4.

25. Ath., *Against the Gentiles* 2.

26. In his instructions to virgins, for example, Athanasius informs his readers that they have applied their free will appropriately because they have, as St. Paul advised, become brides of Christ. Ath., *Ep. Vir.* 1.23. Similar injunctions fill the festal letters. For example, see *Ep. Fest.* 14.2–3, 6.3–5, and 10.4. I have followed the newer numbering of Athanasius's festal letters according to Alberto Camplani, *Le Lettere festali di Atanasio di Allessandria: Studio storico-critico* (Rome: C.I.M., 1989), 195–96.

27. Ath., *V. Ant.* 2; cf. Matt. 19:21.

28. Ath., *V. Ant.* 2–3. By providing for his sister, he entrusted her to a convent "of good reputation."

29. Ath., *V. Ant.* 4.

30. "He combined the qualities of each and was eager to cultivate for himself the virtues of all." Ath., *V. Ant.* 4.

31. Ath., *V. Ant.* 5–13. Some examples include demons appearing as wild animals (9) and the devil temping him with silver (11) and gold (12).

32. Ath., *V. Ant.* 14.

33. Concerning his control of animals, see *V. Ant.* 15. For his control of demons, see *V. Ant.* 10. And for his pastoral skill, see *V. Ant.* 15–17, 44, and 48.

34. Athanasius, *V. Ant.* 67.

35. Rousseau maintains that other episodes in the *vita* suggest less passivity toward the clergy and that Antony was willing to assert his authority as teacher. Rousseau, "Antony as Teacher," 99–100.

36. See Brakke, *Athanasius,* 201–65, esp. 202. Brakke identifies Athanasius's contest with the Arians and his anxiety about other desert ascetics as two factors that informed the bishop's description of Antony as a loyal supporter of Athanasius.

37. Further evidence of Athanasius's appropriation of Antony's authority could be seen in the fact that the hermit does not want his body to be venerated and bestows his clothing on Athanasius and Serapion, two bishops. Ath., *V. Ant.* 90–91.

38. Brakke, *Athanasius,* 254; see also 57–65.

39. Rousseau, "Antony as Teacher," 89–109.

40. Rousseau aptly notes that during his trip to Alexandria Antony, with the approval of bishops, teaches the laity. Ath., *V. Ant.* 69. Rousseau, "Antony as Teacher," 99.

41. With one notable exception, Athanasius has little to say about selecting leaders within the ascetic community. The exception concerns the leadership of the Pachomian community. See below.

42. See Leslie Barnard, *The Monastic Letters of Saint Athanasius the Great* (Oxford: SLG Press, 1994), xi–xiii. See also Brakke, *Athanasius,* 99–110.

43. Many late ancient ascetics expressed resistance to ordination. In part, they feared that the responsibilities of office would be too great for them to manage — an indication of the monastic attempt to acquire humility. The rejection of ordination may also sometimes have been due to quite the opposite tendency: disdain for work in the world and/or genuine qualms about the heaviness of civic obligations carried by bishops (e.g., letters of recommendation, patronage of all kinds, and the episcopal courts).

44. Ath., *Ep. Drac.* 2.

45. Ath., *Ep. Drac.* 4.

46. Ath., *Ep. Drac.* 7.

47. Ath., *Ep. Drac.* 7.

48. Jacob Muyser, "Contribution à l'étude des listes épiscopales de l'Église copte," *Bulletin de la Société d'Archéologie Copte* 10 (1944): 115–76.

49. Ath., *Ep. Fest.* 24.2.

50. Ath., *Ep. Drac.* 6.

51. Athanasius had good reason to fear. See Barnard, *Monastic Letters,* xi, and Brakke, *Athanasius,* 100–110.

52. Ath., *Apol. Const.* 71.

53. Ath., *Ep. Fest.* 40.

54. Brakke, *Athanasius,* 101.

55. Ibid., 108–9.

56. See, for example, Rousseau, *Ascetics,* and "The Spiritual Authority of the 'Monk-Bishop': Eastern Elements in Some Western Hagiography of the Fourth and Fifth Centuries," *Journal of Theological Studies,* n.s., 23 (1971): 380–419. See also Leyser, *Authority and Asceticism.*

57. See Sterk, *Renouncing the World,* 163–91.

58. Ath., *Ep. Fest.* 19. 6–7.

59. Brakke makes much of Athanasius's attempt to drive out the intellectuals who presented a challenge to his authority in Alexandria. See Brakke, *Athanasius,* 57–79, esp. 58–59.

60. Ath., *Ep. Ruf.* See Kannengieser, "Athanasius of Alexandria," 486–87.

61. Ath., *Ep. Ruf.*

62. Ath., *Ep. Ruf.*

63. Ath., *V. Ant.* 11–15.

64. Elsewhere Athanasius was less specific, but he did admonish leaders to practice what they preached—otherwise, they would scandalize and disrupt their flock. Ath., *Ep. Fest.* 24.2; *Ep. Drac.* 1. The twenty-fourth letter has been mistakenly transmitted as the second.

65. Ath., *V. Ant.* 16–19.

66. For pride, see Ath., *V. Ant.* 17; for wrath, see *V. Ant.* 21.

67. Ath., *V. Ant.* 19.

68. Ath., *V. Ant.* 21–43.

69. Ath., *V. Ant.* 44.

70. And according to Athanasius, Antony's authority derives from his ascetic experience rather than his intellectual gifts and training.

71. Clarence Glad, *Paul and Philodemus: Adaptability in Epicurean and Early Christian Psychagogy* (Leiden: E. J. Brill, 1995).

72. Examples of spiritual counseling include Ath., *V. Ant.* 55 and 57. Some of Antony's miracles are detailed in Ath., *V. Ant.* 58, 59, 60, 61, 62, 63, and 64.

73. Ath., *V. Ant.* 68.

74. See Brakke, *Athanasius,* 201–3.

75. Ibid., 201–65.

76. It is unlikely that he would have presented an Antony altogether alien from the one already known by the initial readers of the *vita.*

77. Ath., *Ep. Fest.* 11.1.

78. Ath., *Ep. Fest.* 11.1. Athanasius similarly interprets Samuel's lament for Saul and Jeremiah's tears for the Jews.

79. Ath., *Ep. Fest.* 11.2.

80. Ath., *Ep. Fest.* 11.2.

81. Concerning the Christian appropriation of classical models of adaptability in the context of psychagogy, see Glad, *Paul and Philodemus,* esp. 36–52 and 185–332.

82. Ath., *Ep. Fest.* 11.3.

83. Recall that Athanasius waits until the end of the *vita* to describe Antony's orthodoxy. As noted in the introduction, praxis was often more important than doctrinal conformity in the late ancient ascetic community. In the festal letter, however, the bishop suggests that theological instruction is the most important of the pastoral responsibilities.

84. Ath., *Ep. Drac.* 2.

85. Ath., *Ep. Ammoun.*

86. Ath., *Ep. Drac.* 2.

87. See below.

88. Ath., *Ep. Ruf.*

89. Ath., *Ep. Ruf.*

90. Brakke, *Athanasius,* 81–82.

91. Ath., *Ep. Ammoun.*

92. A rhetorical if not heartfelt show of respect. See Barnard, *Monastic Letters,* viii.

93. Ath., *Ep. Ammoun.*

94. Ath., *Ep. Mon. 1* and *Ep. Mon 2.*

95. Ath., *Ep. Mon 1.*

96. Many of the Greek fathers, especially the Cappadocians, who came after Athanasius, would employ apophatic theology. See Vladimir Lossky, *The Mystical Theology of the Eastern Church* (Crestwood, NY: St. Vladimir's Seminary Press, 1976), 7–43.

97. Ath., *Ep. Mon. 1* 2–3.

98. Ath., *Ep. Mon. 2.*

99. Ath., *Ep. Mon. 2.*

100. Ath., *V. Ant.* 82. Brakke argues that this move by Athanasius was a critical strategy in the bishop's attempt to sever the monastic camps from Arian influence. See Brakke, *Athanasius,* 134–35.

101. Ath., *Ep. Mon. 2.*

102. For a detailed study of the matter, see Aline Rousselle, *Porneia: On Desire and the Body in Antiquity,* trans. F. Pheasant (Oxford: Basil Blackwell, 1988), esp. 170–73.

103. Ath., *Ep. Ammoun.* See Leslie Barnard, "The Letters of Athanasius to Ammoun and Dracontius," *Studia Patristica* 26 (1993): 354–59. See also Tim Vivian, "'Everything Made by God Is Good,'" *Église et Théologie* 24 (1993): 75–108, and David Brakke, *Athanasius,* 90–96.

104. Ath., *Ep. Ammoun.* See Alvyn Pettersen, *Athanasius and the Human Body* (Bristol: Bristol Press, 1990), esp. 5–34.

105. Apparently, many in the monastic community understood nocturnal emissions to be an indication of a sinful soul. See Brakke, *Athanasius,* 90–96.

106. Ath., *Ep. Ammoun.*

107. John Cassian, *Conl.* 2, 4, 12, and 22.

108. See Vivian, "'Everything Made by God,'" 101–2.

109. Ath., *Ep. Ammoun.* He uses the same analogy in his *Ep. Vir. 1.*

110. Ath., *Ep. Ammoun.*

111. See Barnard, "Letters of Athanasius," 355; and F. Wisse, "Gnosticism and Early Monasticism in Egypt," in *Gnosis: Festschrift für Hans Jonas,* ed. B. Aland (Göttengen: Vandenhoeck und Ruprecht, 1978), 437.

112. Ath., *Ep. Ammoun.*

113. Ath., *Ep. Ammoun.* Likewise, Athanasius maintains that murder is criminal but that conquering one's enemy is valiant.

114. See Ath., *On Sickness and Health* [*De morbo et valetudine*] (Franz Diekamp, crit. ed., in *Analecta Patristica: Texte und abhandlungen zur griechischen patristik* [Rome: Pont. Institutum Orientalium Studorium, 1938]), 5–6. See Brakke, *Athanasius,* 86–90.

115. See Brakke, *Athanasius,* 98–99.

116. See Rousseau, *Pachomius,* 181–87.

117. See Brakke, *Athanasius,* 120.

118. See ibid., 121–25, and Rousseau, *Pachomius,* 174–91, esp. 189–91.

119. He identified their relationship as a συνεργός based on Rom. 16:3. See Brakke, *Athanasius,* 126.

120. As it turned out, he appointed the once-spurned Horsisius. Ath., *Ep. Hor. 2* 2; *Greek Life of St. Pachomius* 150 [*Sancti Pachomii vitae graecae*] (Francis Halkin, crit. ed., *Subsidia Hagiographica* 19 [1932]). See Brakke, *Athanasius,* 127–29.

121. These two explanations are not mutually exclusive.

122. By the fourth century, it was a commonplace for bishops to consider the supervision of widows and virgins as part of their pastoral responsibility. The New Testament itself had alluded to such obligations (Acts 6:1; 1 Tim. 5:3–13). John Chrysostom identified care for virgins and widows as two of the most time-consuming and debilitating requirements of the pastoral office. John Chrysostom, *On the Priesthood* 3.17. For an in-depth look at Athanasius's handling of virgins in his care, see Elm, *Virgins of God,* 331–72.

123. Ath., *Apol. Const.* 33.

124. See Brakke, *Athanasius,* 18–79, esp. 19–21.

125. Ath., *Ep. Vir. 1* 33. For Athanasius's letters to virgins, I have relied on Brakke's translations from the Coptic in Brakke, *Athanasius,* 274–302.

126. Ath., *Ep. Vir. 1* 36–46.

127. Concerning the baths, see Ath., *Ep. Vir. 2* 15–18. They were even cautioned not to compromise their modesty when bathing at home. Concerning conversations with men, see Ath., *Ep. Vir. 2* 19.

128. Ath., *Ep. Vir.* 2 20–29. See Elm, *Virgins of God,* 334.

129. Ath., *Ep. Vir.* 2 11–14.

130. Ath., *Ep. Vir.* 1 15.

131. Cf. Brakke, *Athanasius,* 35.

132. Ath., *Ep. Vir.* 2 8–10.

133. Ath., *Ep. Vir.* 2 20–29. For his part, John Chrysostom encountered considerable resistance when he attempted to end the practice in Constantinople. For his views on the matter, see John Chrysostom, *Against Those Men Who Cohabit with Virgins [Contra eos qui subintroductas habent virgines]* (J.-P. Migne, ed., PG 47).

134. Ath., *Ep. Vir.* 2 4–7. See Elm, *Virgins of God,* 335–36.

135. Ath., *Ep. Vir.* 2 8. All of the references to "elders" in this section are in the feminine form. See Brakke, *Athanasius,* 294.

136. See Brakke, *Athanasius,* 57–79, and Elm, *Virgins of God,* 348–53.

137. Ath., *Ep. Vir.* 1 45.

138. Ath., *Ep. Vir.* 1 39.

139. For more on Hieracas, see Brakke, *Athanasius,* 44–57, and Elm, *Virgins of God,* 339–42.

140. Ath., *Ep. Vir.* 1 2–3.

141. Ath., *Ep. Vir.* 1 2–3. Athanasius identifies the Virgin Mary as the consummate example of this spiritual marriage. *Ep. Vir.* 1 10–11.

142. Ath., *Ep. Vir.* 1 9–17. For more on Athanasius's instruction to virgins concerning Mary, see Elm, *Virgins of God,* 336–38.

143. Ath., *Ep. Vir.* 1 13.

144. Ath., *Ep. Vir.* 1 14.

145. Ath., *Ep. Vir.* 2 8.

146. Ath., *Ep. Vir.* 1 33–35.

147. At issue is the despair of a group of virgins who have returned from the Holy Land and who now feel unable to muster the piety they had during their trip. Athanasius consoles them by noting that one does not need to be present at the Holy Sepulcher to receive the spiritual benefits of its place in history. Ath., *Ep. Vir.* 2 3. For more on the circumstances of this letter, see Susanna Elm, "Perceptions of Jerusalem Pilgrimage as Reflected in Two Early Sources on Female Pilgrimage (3rd and 4th Century AD)," in *Studia Patristica* 20 (1989): 219–23.

148. Of Athanasius's personal letters, only a few convey pastoral instructions (excepting, of course, the letter to Marcellinus). For example, Athanasius's correspondence with the emperors Constantius and Jovinian is bereft of pastoral instruction.

149. Having been forced into exile for his theological views, Athanasius is quick to defend his positions and to set aright the theological allegiances of those he left behind.

150. See, for example, Ath., *Ep. Fest.* 19.3–7.

151. Athanasius's clearest articulation of that doctrine exists in his *On the Incarnation,* possibly written before his elevation in 328. An example of his rendering of free will is recorded in *Ep. Fest.* 19.7.

152. In *Ep. Fest.* 19.7, for example, Athanasius submits that it is impossible to achieve one without the other.

153. Ath., *Ep. Fest.* 24.6. Cf. 1 Cor. 11:2.

154. Ath., *Ep. Fest.* 24.6–7.

155. Ath., *Ep. Fest.* 39. In this letter, Athanasius was the first author to list the twenty-seven books that became New Testament.

156. Ath., *Ep. Fest.* 39. For more on the context of Athanasius's canon of Scripture, see David Brakke, "Canon Formation and Social Conflict in Fourth-Century Egypt: Athanasius of Alexandria's Thirty-ninth Festal Letter," *Harvard Theological Review* 87 (1994): 395–419.

157. For more on this matter, see Anatolios, *Athanasius,* 59–67. See also Brakke, *Athanasius,* 151–52.

158. Ath., *Ep. Fest.* 14.6.

159. According to Athanasius (and the subsequent Eastern Orthodox tradition), Lent occupied the forty days prior to the week before Pascha (i.e., Easter). The fast was suspended for the Saturday and Sunday before Pascha. Monday began a final six days of preparation, which was to be even more rigorous than the preceding forty days. See *Ep. Fest.* 14.6, 24.8, and *Ep. Ser.* See George Demacopoulos, "Liturgical Calendar in the East," in *Dictionary of the Middle Ages,* ed. William Chester Jordan (New York: Charles Scribner's Sons, 2004), 14:327–30.

160. See Ath., *Ep. Fest.* 1.4–7, 3.6, 4.2, 5.1, 5.4, etc.

161. Ath., *Ep. Fest.* 3.5.

162. Ath., *Ep. Fest.* 4.2.

163. Ath., *Ep. Fest.* 6.12. See also *Ep. Fest.* 5.1 and 14.6.

164. Ath., *Ep. Fest.* 1.3, 6.12. He also maintained that sex was for the sole purpose of procreation. However, Athanasius did not believe that sex was sinful or carried guilt. On the contrary, he viewed these restrictions as an opportunity for married Christians to take advantage of ascetic discipline. See Brakke, *Athanasius,* 184–86.

165. Ath., *Ep. Fest.* 14.5 and 1.11.

166. Ath., *Ep. Fest.* 5.6.

167. See Brakke, *Athanasius,* 182–98, esp. 184.

168. Ath., *Ep. Fest.* 10.4.

169. Ath., *Ep. Fest.* 10.4.

170. Ath., *Ep. Fest.* 10.4.

171. Whether the occasion of the text did not lend itself to that discussion or whether Athanasius simply did not employ that type of language is difficult to ascertain.

172. Ath., *Ep. Fest.* 2. This letter was mistakenly transmitted as the twenty-fourth. The text is Coptic and the translation is Brakke's (*Athanasius,* 320–23).

173. Ath., *Ep. Marc.* 1.

174. Ath., *Ep. Marc.* 2 ff. Not only do they contain the Law and Prophets, but they look forward to the incarnation, death, and resurrection of the Word.

175. Ath., *Ep. Marc.* 10.

176. If one has sinned, there are psalms of repentance. If one fears an enemy there are psalms of hope, etc.

177. Ath., *Ep. Marc.* 14.

178. Brakke, *Athanasius,* 144.

179. See ibid., 66–75, 253–58. In the first of his letters to the virgins, Athanasius suggests that they would be better off staying at home and imitating the life of the Virgin Mary than associating with reckless male teachers. *Ep. Vir.* 1 43–45.

TWO   *Gregory Nazianzen's Struggle for Synthesis*

1. It was Gregory's wife, Nonna, who brought him to Christianity. Naz., *Or.* 18.11; *On His Own Affairs [De rebus suis]* vv. 122–27 (J.-P. Migne, ed., PG 37).

2. Indeed, canon law preventing ecclesiastical nepotism was, as yet, undeveloped.

3. There has always been a difficulty in naming Gregory. In the Eastern tradition, Gregory is known as St. Gregory the Theologian, one of only three to bear the prestigious moniker (John the Evangelist and Symeon the New Theologian being the others). Western Christians and scholars of past generations identified him as Gregory of Nazianzus. That title more accurately describes Gregory's father, who was, in fact, consecrated bishop of Nazianzus. I use *Nazianzen,* as do many contemporary scholars, to reflect the fact that Gregory originated from Nazianzus but was never its official bishop.

4. For the volatile relationship of Gregory and Basil, see Raymond Van Dam, *Family and Friends in Late Roman Cappadocia* (Philadelphia: University of Pennsylvania Press, 2003), 155–84.

5. For Gregory's stay in Alexandria and his possible relationships with Didymus the Blind and Athanasius, see John McGuckin, *St. Gregory Nazianzus* (Crestwood, NY: St. Vladimir's Seminary Press, 2001), 44–46.

6. McGuckin, *St. Gregory Nazianzus,* 57.

7. In his autobiographical poems, Gregory attributes his decision for baptism to a nearly fatal sea voyage. Naz., *On His Own Life [De vita sua]* vv. 121–209 (J.-P. Migne, ed., PG 37).

8. Cf. Naz., *Or.* 43.15.

9. Naz., *Or.* 43.21.

10. Naz., *Or.* 43.24.

11. Naz., *On His Own Life* v. 257.

12. Naz., *Ep.* 1.

13. On Gregory's attitude toward the rigors of Annesoi, see *Ep.* 4 and 5.

14. Most believe that the elder Gregory signed the Homoian creed of Rimini as elaborated at the Council of Constantinople in 360. See McGuckin, *St. Gregory Nazianzus,* 106–14.

15. The schism probably lasted two years (362–64). Gregory's Oration 6 presupposes a reconciled community.

16. Naz., *Ep.* 40, 41, 42, and 43.

17. For more on Basil's election, see Philip Rousseau, *Basil of Caesarea* (Berkeley: University of California Press, 1994), 145–51.

18. For Gregory's account, see *On His Own Life* vv. 440–517. For his reaction, see *Ep.* 48.

19. Such is McGuckin's characterization of the events. See McGuckin, *St. Gregory Nazianzus,* 194–205. See also Sterk, *Renouncing the World,* 79–82 and 126–27.

20. For alternate interpretations of Gregory's intentions in the exchange, see McGuckin, *St. Gregory Nazianzus,* 199–203, and Sterk, *Renouncing the World,* 126–27.

21. Naz., *Ep.* 47, 48, 49, and 50.

22. Naz., *On His Own Life* vv. 460–63. While preparing my translations of Gregory's poems, I consulted Denis Meehan's and Peter Gilbert's English translations. Denis Meehan, *St. Gregory Nazianzus: Three Poems* (Washington, DC: Catholic University Press, 1986); Peter Gilbert, *On God and Man: The Theological Poetry of St. Gregory of Nazianzus* (Crestwood, NY: St. Vladimir's Seminary Press, 2001).

23. See McGuckin, *St. Gregory Nazianzus,* 199–203, 232–33. See also Stanislas Giet, *Sasimes: Une méprise de saint Basile* (Paris: Librairie Lecoffre, 1941), esp. 67–82.

24. Some questioned the legitimacy of his election to Constantinople because he had already been appointed to the See of Sasima (which, according to the canons of Nicea, precluded a subsequent appointment). For his response, see Naz., *On His Own Life* vv. 385–550, 1796–1815, and *On Himself and the Bishops [De seipso et de episcopis]* vv. 70–135 (J.-P. Migne, ed., PG 37). See also John McGuckin, "Autobiography as Apologia in St. Gregory Nazianzus," *Studia Patristica* 37 (2001): 164.

25. Scholars offer a number of theories about Gregory's time in Seleukia. For a survey of the possibilities, see McGuckin, *St. Gregory Nazianzus,* 230.

26. According to Gregory, it was Basil, Meletius of Antioch, and Eusebius of Samosata who encouraged Gregory to go to Constantinople. Naz., *On His Own Life* v. 596. There is some debate, however, about the nature of Gregory's "invitation." See Neil McLynn, "A Self-Made Holy Man: The Case of Gregory Nazianzen," *Journal of Early Christian Studies* 6 (1998): 463–84, esp. 474–75.

27. During the Easter vigil of 380, Arians entered the Church of the Anastasia and disrupted the service with a barrage of stones. Naz., *On His Own Life* vv. 655–57, *On Himself and the Bishops* v. 103, *Or.* 22, 33, and *Ep.* 77.3.

28. For Gregory's recollection of the events, see his *On His Own Life* vv. 1574–1679.

29. McGuckin, *St. Gregory Nazianzus,* 352.

30. Naz., *Or.* 42.10, 42.14–15. Concerning the debate about whether he delivered the oration in public or composed it later, see Susanna Elm, "A Programmatic Life: Gregory of Nazianzus' *Orations* 42 and 43 and the Constantinopolitan Elites," *Arethusa* 33 (2000): 411–27.

31. For example, he attacked the monism of the Apollinarians and the "Two Sons" theology of Diodore of Tarsis. See *Ep.* 101, 102, and his poems *On the Incarnation against Apollinarius [De Incarnatione adversus Apolinarium]* (J.-P. Migne, ed., PG 37) and *On His Own Life* vv. 607–51.

32. A different version of this section appeared as an article in *Louvain Studies*: George Demacopoulos, "Leadership in the Post-Constantinian Church According to St. Gregory Nazianzen," *Louvain Studies* 30 (2005): 223–39.

33. Scholars generally point to *Or.* 20 and *Or.* 32 as evidence of his support for episcopal authority. Sections of these orations maintain a sharp divide between leaders and the laity. There are, however, some ambiguities. McLynn argues that *Or.* 32 does not promote clericalism but is instead a critique of most clerics who do not possess Gregory's ascetic qualities. See McLynn, "Self-Made Holy Man," 475–76. Moreover, there are some suggestions in Gregory's later writing that one should not follow bishops who lack the credentials for leadership. In one of his autobiographical poems, Gregory writes that "to avoid such guides is the briefest way and surest precept of salvation." *On His Own Life* vv. 36–37. See also McGuckin, "Autobiography as Apologia," 173.

34. Naz., *Or.* 27.3. The same theme dominates *Or.* 20 and *Or.* 32.

35. Naz., *Or.* 27.3. Elsewhere, Gregory uses the more common Greek synonym for *otium,* ἀπράγμον.

36. For more on Gregory's understanding of *otium,* see Susanna Elm, "The Diagnostic Gaze: Gregory of Nazianzus' Theory of Orthodox Priesthood in His Orations 6 *De Pace* and 2 *Apologia de fuga sua,*" in *Orthodoxy, Christianity, History,* ed. Susanna Elm, É. Rebillard, and A. Romano (Rome: École Française de Rome, 2000), 83–100, esp. 93.

37. Naz., *On Himself and the Bishops* vv. 154–61.

38. Interestingly, Nektarios may well have outranked Gregory. According to Rapp, he was one of the first members of the senatorial class, a former *praetor* of Constantinople, to rise to the rank of bishop—a politician to be sure, but of a higher social rank than Gregory. Rapp, "Elite Status of Bishops," 395.

39. Naz., *On Himself and the Bishops* vv. 212–14.

40. Ibid., vv. 237–38.

41. Naz., *Or.* 2.35.

42. Naz., *Or.* 20.1.

43. McGuckin maintains that Gregory here refers to Nektarios. McGuckin, "Autobiography as Apologia," 169–77.

44. Naz., *Or.* 2. 36–38.

45. Naz., *Or.* 21.6.

46. Naz., *Or.* 21.4.

47. Naz., *Or.* 43.11.

48. Naz., *On Himself and the Bishops* vv. 202–7 and 230–45.

49. For an assessment of the way that some ascetics (e.g., Eustathios) made their Christianity a social manifesto that challenged Roman understandings of class and gender, see Elm, *Virgins of God,* 106–36. See also Charles Frazee, "Anatolian Asceticism in the Fourth Century: Eustathios of Sebastea and Basil of Caesarea," *Catholic Historical Review* 66 (1980): 16–33.

50. Naz., *Or.* 19.10.

51. In the Roman world of late antiquity, the vast majority of persons were slaves and servants. On the local level, the governing class consisted of wealthy landowners, the *curiales,* who were generally born into their position. The army provided the only real avenue for social mobility, and even there opportunities for advancement were limited.

52. In *Ep.* 79, for example, Gregory expresses some concern that a former slave has been raised to the episcopate. See Rapp, *Holy Bishops,* 175.

53. Naz., *Or.* 2.36.

54. Naz., *On Himself and the Bishops* vv. 262–329.

55. Ibid. Perhaps a slight modification of Basil's contention that rhetorical embellishment had no place in the preaching of the Gospel. Cf. Basil, *Morals* 70.25.

56. Rapp, "Elite Status of Bishops" and *Holy Bishops,* 183–95.

57. Over and over again, Gregory asserts his ascetic credentials whenever his authority is challenged. Some examples include *Or.* 6. 3–6, 26.13, 32.12–14, and 36.6. For a general assessment of the way that late ancient churchmen used the rhetoric of asceticism to assert their authority, see Leyser, *Authority and Asceticism,* esp. 160–87 for his treatment of Pope Gregory I.

58. See McGuckin, *St. Gregory Nazianzus,* 95–99.

59. Naz., *Or.* 26.13. Characteristically, Gregory here conflates the philosophic life with that of the Christian contemplative.

60. Naz., *Or.* 2.6.

61. Naz., *Or.* 2.39.

62. Naz., *Or.* 2.39.

63. For more on the difference between Hellenistic and Christian patterns of *askesis,* see the chapter "Ancient Spiritual Exercises," in Hadot, *Philosophy,* 126–44.

64. See, for example, his *Poem of Lament over the Calamities Afflicting His Soul [De animae suae calamitatibus carmen lugubre],* vv. 125–46 (J.-P. Migne, ed., PG 37).

65. Naz., *Or.* 2.3. The reference to the *nous*'s direction of the soul is based upon the Platonic understanding of the tripartite soul, where the *nous* serves as the ra-

tional faculty. The conception became a common one in later Greek theological literature.

66. Naz., *Or.* 2.71.

67. Naz., *Or.* 2.53.

68. Naz., *Or.* 2.55.

69. Naz., *Or.* 2.50–70.

70. In one clever turn, he acknowledges his father's error but delicately chastens the monks for rejecting the authority of their bishop. Naz., *Or.* 6.10–11, 6.13–14.

71. Naz., *Or.* 6.2. See also *Or.* 6.1, 6.3.

72. Gregory rhetorically turns a blind eye to their disobedience by describing it as an error of zealotry. Naz., *Or.* 6.11.

73. Naz., *Or.* 6.11.

74. See Elm, "Diagnostic Gaze," 85–90.

75. The Eunomians were extreme subordinationists (one of the varieties of neo-Arians during the later part of the fourth century) who denied that the Father and Son shared a common essence. For more on the theological context of the five theological orations, see Frederick Norris and Lionel Wickham, *Faith Gives Fullness to Reason* (Leiden: E. J. Brill, 1991), 53–71.

76. "Not to all men, because it is permitted only to those who have been examined and who are already masters in meditation [θεωρία] and who have previously purified [κεκαθαρμένων] their soul and body, or who at the very least are in the process of purifying them." Naz., *Or.* 27.3.

77. Naz., *On Himself and the Bishops* vv. 397–710.

78. Ibid. Some of the charges he levies against them include attendance at stage performances (vv. 397–404) and horse races (vv. 405–15), illegal business practices (vv. 415–31), and debauchery (vv. 620–27).

79. See McGuckin, "Autobiography as Apologia."

80. Elm draws a similar conclusion in "Programmatic Life," 423.

81. Naz., *On Himself and the Bishops* vv. 709–86. McGuckin, "Autobiography as Apologia," 175–76.

82. Naz., *On His Own Life* vv. 40–50.

83. Cf. Elm, "Programmatic Life"; McGuckin, "Autobiography as Apologia."

84. Gregory's funeral orations follow classical topoi for eulogy. The oration for the feast of St. Cyprian is a prime example of the historical inaccuracy of these orations. Gregory clearly confuses Cyprian of Carthage, who was martyred in 258, with Cyprian of Antioch, who was supposedly martyred in 304. Though both were bishops, their lives were very different. For our purposes, Gregory's construction of Cyprian's nobility and education is the most telling. Clearly a trope, it nevertheless well conveys Gregory's understanding of the criteria for authority. Naz., *Or.* 24.6. Near the close of the oration, Gregory also notes that Cyprian cultivated asceticism after his conversion to Christianity. Naz., *Or.* 24.13–14.

85. For Gregory's refashioning of his relationship with Basil through public eulogy, see Neil McLynn, "Gregory Nazianzen's Basil: The Literary Construction of a Christian Friendship," *Studia Patristica* 37 (2001): 178–93.

86. Concerning Gregory the elder's asceticism, see *Or.* 18.21–28; for his pastoral success, see *Or.* 18.16.

87. Naz., *Or.* 18.16.

88. Naz., *Or.* 18.16.

89. Naz., *Or.* 21.2.

90. Naz., *Or.* 21.19.

91. Gregory did not attend Basil's funeral, which was in January of 379. Instead, he delivered the oration after his dismissal from Constantinople, perhaps on the third anniversary of Basil's death. Gregory's oration for Basil has drawn much attention from scholars in recent years. See Frederick Norris, "Your Honor, My Reputation: St. Gregory of Nazianzus's Funeral Oration on St. Basil the Great," in Hägg and Rousseau, *Greek Biography,* 140–59; David Konstan, "How to Praise a Friend," in Hägg and Rousseau, *Greek Biography,* 160–79; and Neil McLynn, "Gregory Nazianzen's Basil."

92. Naz., *Or.* 43.43.

93. Naz., *Or.* 43.43.

94. In a fascinating new article, Susanna Elm maintains that Gregory's endorsement of a "philosophy of action" in his second oration was, in part, motivated by his critique of Emperor Julian's stated policies regarding philosophy. Thus, for Elm, Gregory is simultaneously stating his positions on leadership in the Christian community and engaging in a broader conversation about the nature of philosophy and the life of the philosopher. Susanna Elm, "Hellenism and Historiography: Gregory of Nazianzus and Julian in Dialogue," in Martin and Miller, *Cultural Turn,* 258–77, esp. 266–71.

95. See J. Bernardi's introduction to his critical edition of Gregory Nazianzen's *Orations 1–3,* 20–50.

96. Naz., *Or.* 2.4.

97. Plato, *Republic* 6.489. For Gregory's appropriation of this tradition, see Elm, "Diagnostic Gaze," 92–93.

98. Elm, "Diagnostic Gaze," 93.

99. See Peter Brown, ed., *The Philosopher and Society in Late Antiquity: Protocol of the Colloquy,* Center for Hermeneutical Studies in Hellenistic and Modern Culture, Protocol Series (Berkeley: Center for Hermeneutic Studies, 1980), esp. his introduction, 3–5. Brown is quick to show the differences between the philosopher and the Christian ascetic (see 13–15), but with respect to Gregory that distinction would have been less clear.

100. Elm, "Diagnostic Gaze," 91–93. In the classical tradition (as represented by Symmachus's letters), the candidate accepts his role because of the acclamation

of the people, *vox populi.* In contrast, Gregory's rhetoric of return is a response to the will of God.

101. Naz., *Or.* 2.1, 2.6–9, and *On His Own Life* 337–56.

102. Naz., *Or.* 2.34.

103. Naz., *Or.* 2.34.

104. For Gregory's use of Moses, see *Or.* 2.92–99, 2.114, 20.2, 32.16–17, and 28.2–3. See Sterk, *Renouncing the World,* 124. See also Rapp, *Holy Bishops,* 125–36.

105. Naz., *Or.* 2.50–82.

106. Naz., *Or.* 2.92. Gregory bases this on the fact that Moses alone was permitted to ascend the mountain, enter the cloud, and speak with God.

107. Naz., *Or.* 28.3.

108. Sterk, for example, notes Gregory's praise for Basil and Athanasius, who were able to achieve the balance between action and contemplation (what she calls the "mixed life"), but maintains that Gregory was too Platonic and therefore withdrew from conflict as a philosopher would. Sterk, *Renouncing the World,* 135. See also Elm, "Programmatic Life," 414.

109. A poem from the period just before his father's death, *Poem of Lament over the Calamities Afflicting his Soul,* suggests that Gregory experienced periods of doubt over his loss of the contemplative life.

110. There is some debate as to whether Gregory served as the spiritual advisor for a community of nuns during this time. Either way, he had certainly removed himself from the supervision of the laity. See McGuckin, *St. Gregory Nazianzus,* 229–31.

111. See McGuckin, *St. Gregory Nazianzus,* 357–58.

112. Naz., *On His Own Life* vv. 1424–35.

113. Elm notes, however, that even this picture of Gregory is one of his own self-fashioning and that to absorb it uncritically is to allow Gregory's skill to prevent analytical reading. Elm, "Programmatic Life," 415.

114. Gregory's concept of an active/contemplative balance influenced many subsequent authors, including John Cassian, John Chrysostom, and Pope Gregory I.

115. Indeed, in the first letter to Basil after his ordination, Gregory remarked, "Since [the ordination] has happened, we ought to endure it . . . especially when we consider that we live in an age with so many heretical voices." Naz., *Ep.* 8.

116. Naz., *Or.* 2.35.

117. Naz., *Or.* 2.36.

118. Naz., *Or.* 2.35–37.

119. Naz., *Or.* 2.38.

120. Naz., *Or.* 21.7, 43.43, and 43.63. Ironically, Gregory's eulogy for Basil does not convey the whole story. At times, Gregory censured his friend for shortchanging what he believed to be the fulfillment of the Nicene doctrine. In particular, Gregory criticized Basil's reluctance to extend the term ὁμοούσιος to the Holy Spirit. See Naz., *Ep.* 58 and 59. For an analysis of this, see McGuckin, *St. Gregory Nazianzus,* 215–19.

121. In his *On the Holy Spirit,* Basil made a similar claim against his opponents. Basil, *On the Holy Spirit [De Spiritu Sanctu]* 30.77 (B. Pruche, crit. ed., SC 17).

122. Naz., *On Himself and the Bishops* vv. 310–20.

123. Naz., *Or.* 42.4–6 and 42.8.

124. Naz., *Ep.* 101 and 102, to Cledonius, which, in addition to laying out an orthodox Christology, offer some of the earliest and clearest expressions of the role of the Virgin Mary in Christ's dual natures.

125. Naz., *Ep.* 101 and 102. It was Cledonius who eventually assumed the pastoral responsibilities of the Church in Nazianzus so that Gregory could spend his retirement writing.

126. Naz., *Ep.* 202. Other letters to Nektarios suggest a cool but not hostile relationship between them. See, for example, *Ep.* 91, 151, 185, and 186. McGuckin has sufficiently demonstrated that Gregory's letters to Nektarios are not as warm and cordial as previous generations of scholars have held. See McGuckin, *St. Gregory Nazianzus,* 374–81. For an alternate reading, see Meehan, *St. Gregory Nazianzus,* 21 and 74.

127. Naz., *Or.* 2.30. The same point is reasserted in *Or.* 2.39 and in many subsequent orations, such as *Or.* 14.5 and 19.7. Cf. Cicero's contention that "one single style of oratory is not suited to every case, nor to every audience." Cicero, *On the Making of an Orator [De optimo genere oratorum]* 3 (A. S. Wilkens, crit. ed., in *M. Tulli Ciceronis rhetorica,* vol. 2 [Oxford: Oxford University Press, 1903]).

128. Naz., *Or.* 2.28–29.

129. Naz., *Or.* 2.30–31. Similarly, in his fourteenth oration, Gregory argued that the spiritual journey took many forms (each with its own merit) and that it was Christ who formed the bond between them. Naz., *Or.* 14.5.

130. Cf. Aristotle, *Rhetoric [Ars rhetorica]* 1408a (Rudolph Kassel, crit. ed. [Berlin: De Gruyter, 1971]); Cicero, *Making of an Orator*; Plutarch, *On the Delays of the Divine Vengeance [De sera numinis vindicta]* 549–50 (Robert Klaerr and Yvonne Vernièrre, crit. eds., in *Plutarch's Moral Works,* vol. 7 [Paris: Les Belles Lettres, 1974]). See Glad, *Paul and Philodemus,* 50–52.

131. For example, they distinguished between age, gender, vocation, and social rank. See Glad, *Paul and Philodemus,* 52.

132. Naz., *Or.* 2.32.

133. Naz., *Or.* 2.54.

134. Examples of this in the "Apology for His Flight" are chs. 45 and 48.

135. Naz., *Or.* 18.16.

136. In the oration for Basil, *Or.* 43.40, Gregory maintains that Basil overcomes his enemies with gentleness and good nature rather than by bullying them or tricking them with rhetoric.

137. Note, for example, *Or.* 2.15, 6.9.

138. See Sterk, *Renouncing the World,* 58–59, for a discussion of Basil's application of the spiritual father.

139. Naz., *Or.* 2.78. Elsewhere he offers more dire statements about the danger associated with pastoral supervision. For example, during his nineteenth oration, Gregory turns to the priests in the audience and comments, "[P]riests, wrap your-selves in righteousness. . . . [D]o not scatter and destroy the sheep of our flock. . . . [L]et us fear that judgment will begin with us, as the Scripture warns, let us not re-ceive from the Lord's hand double for all our sins (Is. 40:27) because not only will we be barred, but we will also bar those who are able." Naz., *Or.* 19.9.

140. Naz., *Or.* 17.6.

141. Naz., *Or.* 2. 16. See also Gregory, *PR,* prol.

142. Naz., *Or.* 2.16–18.

143. Naz., *Or.* 2.18.

144. See, for example, *Or.* 2.19–21 and 32.2.

145. Elm, "Diagnostic Gaze," 85. Sterk makes the same observation in *Renounc-ing the World,* 124. See also Rapp for her brief but insightful analysis of Gregory's use of physician imagery. Rapp, *Holy Bishops,* 43–45.

146. In two orations, Gregory speaks directly to imperial officials. In *Or.* 36.11, Gregory addresses the emperor. He directs *Or.* 17 to an imperial governor. On both occasions, he provides specific pastoral advice appropriate to their positions of au-thority. In short, Gregory offers them the opportunity to attain deification through the practice of justice and philanthropy. See Verna Harrison, "Poverty, Social In-volvement, and Life in Christ According to Saint Gregory the Theologian," *Greek Orthodox Theological Review* 39 (1994): 151–64.

147. "My brothers, our faith would be the most unjust thing in the world if it was reserved for only the sophisticated and those who exhibited an extraordinary com-mand of words and logic. For it would lie beyond most people." Naz., *Or.* 32.26.

148. Naz., *Or.* 11.5.

149. Naz., *Or.* 11.6.

150. Naz., *Or.* 14.16.

151. Naz., *Or.* 14.17. The same criticism is extended to the use of cosmetics. In-terestingly, Augustine did not reprove the laity for similar actions. Cf. Aug., *Ep.* 245.

152. Naz., *Or.* 14.18. Concerning Gregory's understanding of the value of mar-ried life versus monastic life, see his two poems *On the Different Walks of Life (De diversis vitae generibus)* and *Blessings of Various Lives [Variorum vitae generum beatitudines]* (both in J.-P. Migne, ed., PG 37), where he suggests that neither has a monopoly on virtue.

153. For a detailed analysis of Gregory's conception of the poor and the contrast to his Hellenistic contemporaries, see Susan Holman, *The Hungry Are Dying: Beggars and Bishops in Roman Cappadocia* (Oxford: Oxford University Press, 2001), 140–67.

154. On the connection between Gregory's encouragement of philanthropy and renunciation, see Harrison, "Poverty, Social Involvement."

155. See Holman, *Hungry Are Dying.* See also Donald Winslow, "Gregory of Nazi-anzus and the Love for the Poor," *Anglican Theological Review* 47 (1965): 348–59.

156. Naz., *Or.* 14.5. In the process, Nazianzen also developed a theology of the poor that, unlike Greco-Roman models of charity, linked the poor (especially lepers) to the body of Christ and identified them as legitimate members of society. See Holman, *Hungry Are Dying,* 142, 148–67.

157. Naz., *Or.* 14.5.

158. Naz., *Or.* 14.37.

159. Naz., *Or.* 6.17.

160. Naz., *Or.* 17.5.

161. A drought coupled with a cattle plague was followed by a devastating hailstorm. His father was so overcome by the disaster that Gregory was forced to address the people of Nazianzus in his father's place. The oration is often known by the title "On His Father's Silence."

162. Naz., *Or.* 16.15.

163. Naz., *Or.* 16.15.

164. Naz., *Or.* 16.13.

165. Naz., *Ep.* 20.

166. Caesarius was a physician and spent time within the emperor's court in Constantinople. For more on his life, see Naz., *Or.* 7.

167. Caesarius agreed to Gregory's request but died unexpectedly within the year.

168. Naz., *Ep.* 11.

169. Gregory delivered the oration in the church at Ikonium, probably in the presence of its bishop, Faustinos. Gorgonia and her husband, Alypios, lived in Ikonium, which was located at the western end of Cappadocia.

170. Naz., *Or.* 8.3, 10, 13.

171. Naz., *Or.* 8.8. For Gregory's negotiation of Gorgonia as both wife and ascetic, see McGuckin, *St. Gregory Nazianzus,* 166–67.

172. Naz., *Or.* 8.8.

173. Naz., *Or.* 8.9.

174. McGuckin, *St. Gregory Nazianzus,* 26–30.

175. Naz., *Or.* 8.10–14. Possibly, Gorgonia took her lead from the female community at Annesoi led by Basil's sister, Macrina the Younger. Concerning her life, see Gregory of Nyssa's biography, *The Life of St. Macrina.*

176. Naz., *Or.* 8.17–18. She had, in fact, gone to the church during an illness, laid her head on the altar, helped herself to the sacrament, and refused to leave until she was healed.

177. See McGuckin, *St. Gregory Nazianzus,* 28–30.

178. Cf. Naz., *Or.* 8.6, 14. For a detailed discussion of Gregory's understanding of female monasticism and its implications for conceptions of gender (as well as Basil's similar perspective), see Elm, *Virgins of God,* 137–83, esp. 154.

179. Given the hagiographical nature of these texts, it is difficult for us to retrieve the "historical" Gorgonia or Macrina. Our knowledge of these women is lim-

ited by the fact that the *vitae* are the literary constructions of male authors (after the death of their subjects). Though the texts reveal much about what the authors what us to believe, they are unreliable as historical witnesses.

180. Gregory, *Prescriptions for Virgins (Praecepta ad virgines)* vv. 96–124 (J.-P. Migne, ed., PG 37).

181. Ibid. See Elm, *Virgins of God,* 154–55.

182. Gregory, *Prescriptions for Virgins* vv. 241–55.

183. See Gregory, *Ep.* 56, 223, and *Ep.* 158, 159 respectively. Again, see Elm, *Virgins of God,* 155–57.

184. Naz., *Or.* 6.10–11.

185. Naz., *On Himself and the Bishops* v. 147; *On His Own Life* vv. 1403–1505.

186. There was, of course, a difference between the Homoians and the more radical Eunomians. Eunomius preached a doctrine of ἀνούσιος, which completely denied the divine nature of the Son (and the Spirit). By way of contrast, the Homoians took the middle-ground position of ὁμοιούσιος, which acknowledged that the Son had an essence "similar" to the Father's. See Norris and Wickham, *Faith Gives Fullness,* 53–71.

187. For the complicated dating of Orations 22 and 23, I follow McGuckin's reasoning that 23 must refer to the issues in Constantinople and not Nazianzus. See McGuckin, *St. Gregory Nazianzus,* 248–49. See also Martha Vinson, *Gregory Nazianzen, Select Orations* (Washington, DC: Catholic University Press, 2003), xvi–xvii, 131 n. 1.

188. Naz., *Or.* 22.16 and *On His Own Life* vv. 1408–20.

189. Naz., *Or.* 23.3. Theodosius seems to have followed Gregory's lead in this matter. When the emperor arrived in Constantinople in 381, only a small minority of the Arian clergy were persecuted (probably the Eunomians, not the Homoians). See McGuckin, *St. Gregory Nazianzus,* 250. Gregory was not alone in this policy, nor was he the only one to be criticized for a lenient policy. See, for example, Basil's *Ep.* 204, 205, and 210 and Sterk's commentary. Sterk, *Renouncing the World,* 46.

190. Naz., *On His Own Life* vv. 1408–17.

191. See also Naz., *Or.* 17.10.

192. Theodore of Tyana, a member of Gregory's clergy at the Church of the Anastasia, sought criminal charges against the agitators of the Arian mob that had disrupted the services with a hail of stones. Gregory, who had been equally threatened in the affair, urged Theodore to forgive the offenders. Naz., *Ep.* 77.

193. Naz., *Or.* 20, 27, and 32.

194. Naz., *Or.* 27.5.

195. "Just as excessively loud sounds injure the ears, or excessive food the body, or excessive burdens injure those who bear them, or excessive rain the earth, so too does the investigation of things beyond our grasp." Naz., *Or.* 27.3.

196. Cf. Naz., *Or.* 14.

197. Cf. Naz., *Or.* 32.10–11.

198. Though Gregory's orations display his familiarity with and endorsement of many of the monastic techniques of spiritual direction, his personal correspondence does not produce sufficient evidence that he routinely put these practices into action. In fact, most of the letters are not pastoral—this will prove to be a sharp contrast to Pope Gregory I, whose correspondence evinces the breadth of his pastoral activities. Even in those letters that do convey pastoral advice, Gregory does not adopt the spiritual father/spiritual disciple model of correction. For example, in his petitions to imperial officials (e.g., *Ep.* 21, 37, 104–6, and 161–65) Gregory operates very much as an aging Greco-Roman statesman rather than a spiritual counselor to public officials.

199. Naz., *Or.* 18.8. The paradigm was quasi-monastic. Referring to his mother, Gregory asks, "[W]ho had a greater love of virginity, while remaining patient of the married life?" Naz., *Or.* 18.9. He also urges his audience to imitate his father's charity, abstemiousness, and common dress. Naz., *Or.* 18.21–25.

200. Naz., *Or.* 21.7, 21.20, and 43.60–63.

201. Naz., *Or.* 21.31 and 43.40.

202. Commemorating Eleazar and the seven brothers "martyred" for their Jewish faith by Antiochus IV Epiphanes, the Seleucid king of Syria (175–64 BC). The story derives from 2 Macc. 6–7. Vinson argues that Gregory was the first to develop a special veneration of the Maccabean martyrs. See Vinson, *Gregory Nazianzen,* 72 n. 2.

203. Naz., *Or.* 15.1.

204. Naz., *Or.* 15.2.

205. Naz., *Or.* 15.12.

206. The twenty-fourth oration, dedicated to the festival of St. Cyprian, functions much like that of the Maccabean martyrs. In many of his other panegyrics (e.g., those for the elder Gregory, Athanasius, and Basil) Gregory has many purposes beyond simple pastoral admonition. In the oration for Basil, for example, Gregory is more concerned with reconciling himself to his old friend (and to the latter's family, who would have been in attendance) than with giving the audience some simple pastoral instructions.

207. Naz., *Or.* 15.3.

THREE   *Augustine of Hippo and Resistance to the Ascetic Model of Spiritual Direction*

1. Cf. Aug., *Conf.* 1.14.23. See also Peter Brown, *Augustine of Hippo* (Berkeley: University of California Press, 1966), 36.

2. As professor of rhetoric, Augustine would deliver the official panegyrics on the emperor. His speeches would receive the attention of the public and the court. See Aug., *Conf.* 5.13.23.

3. There is no shortage of scholarly examinations of Augustine's religious journey. See, for example, Fredrick Russell, "Augustine: Conversion by the Book," in *Varieties of Religious Conversion in the Middle Ages,* ed. J. Muldoon (Gainesville: University Press of Florida, 1997), and Robert Markus, *Conversion and Disenchantment in Augustine's Spiritual Career* (Villanova: Villanova University Press, 1989).

4. Augustine's mother, Monica, had been a Christian, and although she encouraged religious devotion in her son, she did not force baptism upon him. See Aug., *Conf.* 3.12.21.

5. Aug., *Conf.* 3.5.9. In particular, he found the Old Testament whimsical and lacking sophistication.

6. See John Rist, *Augustine: Ancient Thought Baptized* (Cambridge: Cambridge University Press, 1994), 2–3. See also Peter Brown, *Augustine of Hippo,* 40–45.

7. Roughly equivalent to a catechumen. For more on the Manicheans in North Africa, see François Decret, *L'Afrique manichéenne: Étude historique et doctrinale* (Paris: Études Augustiniennes, 1978), and Jason BeDuhn, *The Manichaean Body: In Discipline and Ritual* (Baltimore: Johns Hopkins University Press, 2000).

8. Aug., *On the Usefulness of Believing [De utilitate credendi]* 1.2 (I. Zycka, crit. ed., CSEL 25). For more on Augustine's time as a Manichean, see Samuel Lieu, *Manicheanism in the Later Roman Empire and Medieval China: A Historical Survey* (Manchester: Manchester University Press, 1985), 117–53, and the collection of papers in *Augustine and Manichaeism in the Latin West: Proceedings of the Fribourg-Utrecht Symposium of the International Association of Manichaean Studies,* ed. Johannes Van Oort, Otto Wermelinger, and Gregory Wurst (Leiden: E. J. Brill, 2001).

9. According to his *Confessions,* Augustine grew disenchanted with the Manicheans because of the inability of their leaders to answer some of his most troubling questions about the universe. Especially disheartening was the encounter in 383 with Faustus, a revered intellectual, whom Augustine took to be a charlatan. Aug., *Conf.* 5.6.11–5.7.13. See Peter Brown, *Augustine of Hippo,* 46–60.

10. Cf. Aug., *Conf.* 6.4.5.

11. Aug., *Conf.* 6.11.20.

12. Though his concubine of many years was dismissed because she stood as an obstacle to an arranged marriage (cf. Aug., *Conf.* 6.15.25), he ultimately resisted marriage and turned away a second mistress because of his new religious commitment. It is, of course, possible that Augustine might have entertained the idea of marriage had his initial partner been of an acceptable social class.

13. Aug., *Conf.* 6.12.21–22.

14. Aug., *Conf.* 8.12.29. See Elizabeth Clark, "Asceticism," in *Augustine through the Ages,* ed. Allan Fitzgerald (Grand Rapids, MI: Eerdmans, 1999), 68. See also Lieu, *Manicheanism,* 152–53.

15. Concerning Western Christian appropriations of Roman *otium,* see Jacques Fontaine, "Valeurs antiques et valeurs chrétiennes dans la spiritualité des grands

propriétaires terriens à la fin du IVe siècle occidental," in *Epektasis: Mélanges J. Daniélou,* ed. Jacques Fontaine and Charles Kannengiesser (Paris: Beauchesne, 1972), 571–95.

16. Aug., *Retractions [Retractiones]* 1.1.1 (A. Mutzenbecher, ed., CCSL 57).

17. Cf. Aug., *Against the Academics [Contra academicos]* 1.1.3 (W. M. Green, crit. ed., CCSL 29).

18. Augustine authored four texts while staying at Cassiciacum—*Against the Academics, On the Blessed Life [De beata vita]* (W. M. Green, crit. ed., CCSL 29), *On Order [De ordine]* (W. M. Green, crit. ed., CCSL 29), and *Soliloquies [Soliloquiorum]* (W. Hörmann, crit. ed., CSEL 89)—each exploring religious topics.

19. Possidius, *V. Aug.* 3.

20. Possidius, *V. Aug.* 3.

21. This category includes a large and diverse group. For more on monasticism in North Africa, see Georges Folliet, "Aux origines de l'ascétisme et du cénobitisme africain," *Studia Anselmiana* 46 (1961): 25–44.

22. Especially the ascetics of the Egyptian desert. See Aug., *On the Morals of the Catholic Church [De moribus ecclesiae catholicae]* 31.65–68 (J.-P. Migne, ed., PL 32). See Georges Folliet, "Le monachisme en Afrique de saint Augustin à saint Fulgence," in *Il monachesimo occidentale,* Studia Ephemerides Augustinianum 62 (Rome: Institutum Patristicum Augustinianum, 1998), 291–316, particularly 292–98.

23. By his own account, Augustine had gone to Hippo to interview a man who wished to join his community. Aug., *Serm.* 355. Possidius describes Augustine's reluctance to be ordained, noting that he would go so far as to avoid towns where he knew there to be an episcopal vacancy. Possidius, *V. Aug.* 4.

24. Possidius, *V. Aug.* 5.

25. Folliet offers a concise critique of authenticity. Folliet, "Le monachisme en Afrique," 296–97. The arguments for authenticity are presented by George Lawless, *Augustine of Hippo and His Monastic Rule* (Oxford: Oxford University Press, 1987).

26. Cf. Aug., *Ep.* 210 and 211.

27. For more on Augustine's conversion and ascetic language, see George Lawless, "Augustine's Decentring of Asceticism," in *Augustine and His Critics: Essays in Honor of Gerald Bonner,* ed. Robert Dodaro and George Lawless (London: Routledge, 2000), 142–63.

28. See Aug., *Ep.* 48. See also Leyser, *Authority and Asceticism,* 4 ff.

29. Aug., *Ep.* 21.

30. For example, see Aug., *Lectures on the Gospel of John [In euangelium Ioannis tractatus]* 57.5–6, *Ep.* 22*, 18*, and 84 (R. Willems, crit. ed., CCSL 36). The "*" designates that the letter is one of the twenty-nine newly discovered letters in *Letters Recently Discovered [Epistolae ex duobus codicibus nuper in lucem prolatae]* (Johannes Divjak, crit. ed., CSEL 88).

31. Aug., *De doc.* 4.2.3 ff. Augustine defended the study of rhetoric and was indignant about the rhetorically challenged clergy. In particular, he was critical of the Punic-speaking rustics who staffed the churches of the countryside. See Aug., *Ep.* 22 and 84.

32. Aug., *De doc.* 4.3.4.

33. Possidius, *V. Aug.* 5.

34. For both Ambrose and Siricius, it seems to have been an issue of ritual purity related to the celebration of the Eucharist. For Ambrose, see his *On the Office* 1.50; for Siricius, see *Ep.* 1, 5, 6 and 10. See David Hunter, "Clerical Celibacy and the Veiling of Virgins," in *The Limits of Ancient Christianity: Essays on Late Antique Thought and Culture in Honor of R. A. Markus,* ed. William E. Klingshirn and Mark Vessey (Ann Arbor: University of Michigan Press, 1999), 139–52, and "Rereading the Jovinianist Controversy," 120–23. See also Leyser, *Authority and Asceticism,* 19–32.

35. See, for example, Basil, *Morals* 70.8, and Naz., *Or.* 40.

36. Aug., *Serm.* 355 and 356.

37. Aug., *Ep.* 18*.

38. Aug., *Ep.* 22*.

39. Concerning the decline of the curial class and its relationship to the clergy, see Rapp, *Holy Bishops,* 280–89.

40. Aug., *Ep.* 22*. Ordination did not excuse members of the *curiales* from their tax burden. See Jones, *Later Roman Empire,* 1:732–57 and 2:920–29.

41. Aug., *Ep.* 22*.

42. Nowhere does Augustine insist that the lack of suitable clergy stemmed from a lack of piety, knowledge of Scripture, etc. Moreover, he lists no renunciatory requirements, apart from celibacy and the disposal of personal property.

43. Maureen Tilley, "No Friendly Letters: Augustine's Correspondence with Women," in Martin and Miller, *Cultural Turn,* 40–62, specifically 43–45.

44. It is no wonder that he was awed by Ambrose's calm demeanor in the face of the clamor and confusion of the courtroom. Aug., *Conf.* 6.3.12. For more on Augustine and the courts, see Peter Kaufman, "Augustine, Macedonius, and the Courts," *Augustinian Studies* 34 (2003): 67–82.

45. Possidius, *V. Aug.* 19.

46. See Kauko Raikas, "*Audientia Episcopalis*: Problematik zwischen Staat und Kirche bei Augustin," *Augustinianum* 37 (1997): 476–77.

47. Aug., *Ep.* 60.

48. Aug., *Ep.* 78.

49. Aug., *Ep.* 21*.

50. Aug., *Ep.* 20*.

51. An episcopal consecration required the presence of three bishops.

52. Most of the charges related to Antoninus's exploitation of his diocese for financial gain.

53. For a detailed discussion of this episode, see Jane Merdinger, *Rome and the African Church in the Time of Augustine* (New Haven: Yale University Press, 1997), 154–82. See also Leyser, *Authority and Asceticism,* 19–21.

54. Cf. Aug., *On Baptism, against the Donatists [De baptismo]* (Michael Petschenig, crit. ed., CSEL 51), and *Ep.* 61. For a more complete analysis of Augustine's approach to

Donatist clergy, see Rémi Crespin, *Ministère et sainteté: Pastorale du clergé et solution de la crise donatiste dans la vie et la doctrine de S. Augustin* (Paris: Études Augustiniennes, 1965).

55. Crespin notes that certain Donatist priests were even elevated to the episcopacy after their conversion. Crespin, *Ministère et sainteté,* 171.

56. See Aug., *Ep.* 61.

57. Cf. Aug., *Ep.* 23, 33, 51, etc.

58. See Robert Eno in his commentary for his translation, *St. Augustine: Letters 1*–29** (Washington, DC: Catholic University Press, 1989), 153–54. The Council of Carthage in 411 did not deliver an immediate reconciliation for the African Church, and Donatist reintegration was inconsistent. For more on the incorporation of Donatist clergy, see W. H. C. Frend, *The Donatist Church* (Oxford: Clarendon Press, 1952), 275–99. See also Serge Lancel, *Actes de la Conférence de Carthage en 411,* 4 vols. (Paris: Éditions du Cerf, 1972).

59. For a thorough study of Augustine's text, see William Harmless, *Augustine and the Catechumenate* (Collegeville, MN: Liturgical Press, 1995), esp. 107–55.

60. See ibid., 123–40.

61. Students stood between the two groups. Aug., *De rud.* 8.12–9.13.

62. Augustine was particularly concerned about disingenuous motivations for conversion.

63. As noted in previous chapters, for Christians the tradition goes back to Paul and was a common theme in rhetorical manuals. For a comparison to Nazianzen, see his *Or.* 2.15.

64. Aug., *De rud.* 16.24.

65. Aug., *De rud.* 11.16. Noting his own frustration, Augustine counsels that the speaker's feelings of inadequacy are often more imaginary than real.

66. Aug., *De rud.* 13.18–19.

67. Joseph Christopher has argued that Augustine was the first to appreciate the "question and answer" method in the process of catechism. Christopher, *St. Augustine: The First Catechetical Instruction* (Westminster, MD: Newman Bookshop, 1946), 6.

68. See Harmless, *Augustine and the Catechumenate,* 126–30.

69. Ibid. Also see Joseph Christopher, introduction to *St. Augustine.*

70. Cf. *Didache* 1, 5 (Adolf von Harnack, crit. ed., reprinted in *Die Lehre der zwölf Apostel, nebst Untersuchungen zur ältesten Geschichte der Kirchenverfassung und des Kirchenrechts* [Berlin: Academie Verlag, 1991], vol. 2).

71. Belche offers an alternate interpretation of the text. He prefers to read the text with an eye to Augustine's understanding of conversion. Jean-Pierre Belche, "Die Bekehrund zum Christentum nach Augustins Büchlein *De Catechizandis Rudibus,*" *Augustiniana* 27 (1977): 26–69, esp. 26–35. I believe the text is equally (if not more) informative regarding Augustine's teaching on leadership. The bishop of Hippo designed the text with the stated purpose of assisting the clerical responsibility of catechism. Not only did he provide a sample lecture, he spent considerable time coaching the reader on the art of leadership.

72. Aug., *De doc.* 4.4.6.

73. Aug., *De doc.* 4.4.6.

74. Aug., *De doc.* 4.2.3 ff. Harmless maintains that Augustine, in many ways, circumvented the cumbersome rules of ancient rhetoric to emphasize only those elements that he personally found useful. Either way, Harmless concedes that much of Augustine's advice concerning rhetorical matters was derivative of Cicero. Harmless, *Augustine and the Catechumenate*, 173–80.

75. Aug., *De doc.* 4.10.24.

76. Aug., *De doc.* 4.11.26 ff.

77. Like many late ancient Christian authorities, Augustine turned to classical authors (like Cicero) as authorities for rhetoric and grammar. See Rist, *Ancient Thought Baptized*, 8–9.

78. Concerning the liturgy and praying for one's flock, see Aug., *Ep.* 153 and 228. For the distribution of charity, see Aug., *Ep.* 125.

79. Aug., *Ep.* 245. This is a rare example of Augustine's interfering in the pastoral decisions of others. By way of contrast, Gregory I's close scrutiny of the pastoral practices of his subordinates (and even fellow bishops) yielded over one hundred written injunctions.

80. Cyprian, Ambrose, Jerome, and Chrysostom (and many others) had all condemned these practices, even for the laity. One wonders if Augustine was making a pastoral concession or if he believed those practices were not a hindrance to the salvation of the laity.

81. Markus, *End of Ancient Christianity*, 53.

82. Aug., *Ep.* 191.

83. Aug., *Ep.* 191.

84. Augustine's suggestion that Sixtus exercise restraint might also elicit comparisons to the spiritual fathers' use of *condescensio*. Aug., *Ep.* 191.

85. Even a cursory reading of late ancient ascetic literature from the Egyptian desert will reveal the general lack of concern among ascetic authors with respect to doctrinal matters. See, for example, the *Apophthegmata Patrum* (J.-P. Migne, ed., PG 65).

86. Cf. Aug., *Ep.* 21.

87. Aug., *Ep.* 132.

88. Contrast the lengthy responses that Augustine gives his intellectual peers with those to correspondents of lesser skill. Take, for example, Augustine's terse yes/no answers to Publica's farcical questions. Aug., *Ep.* 47.

89. Aug., *Ep.* 136.

90. Aug., *Ep.* 137.4 ff.

91. Aug., *Ep.* 137.18.

92. Aug., *Ep.* 137.1.

93. For example, see Aug., *Ep.* 54, 55, 186, and 217.

94. Aug., *Ep.* 92.

95. Aug., *Ep.* 92.

96. Tilley, "No Friendly Letters."

97. Ibid., 46.

98. Aug., *Ep.* 130.20.

99. Tilley, "No Friendly Letters," 50–53, 57.

100. I am not suggesting that he actively discouraged ascetic practice but only that the level of encouragement he provided was higher for his female correspondents than it was for men.

101. Ascetic women would, at least in theory, have made a commitment to obedience and were most likely to recognize the authority of their spiritual fathers.

102. Concerning the lack of ascetic prescriptions, see Lawless, "Augustine's Decentring of Asceticism," 145.

103. Johannes Brachtendorf, "Cicero and Augustine on the Passions," *Revue des Études Augustiniennes* 43 (1997): 289–308.

104. Pierre Hadot distinguishes between classical and Christian notions of *askesis*, noting that for the ancients *askesis* designated "inner activities of thought and the will." By extension, it may be that Augustine encouraged *askesis* in the classical sense but not in the manner typical of monastic bishops of his era. See Hadot, the chapter "Ancient Christian Exercises,'" in *Philosophy,* 128.

105. In *Ep.* 36, Augustine responded to a series of statements (made by an unnamed author) concerning the practice and efficacy of fasting. Throughout, he encouraged fasting as prescribed in Scripture, but his advocacy stemmed from questions posted to him concerning controversial practices; he did not issue ad hoc instructions to spiritual disciples.

106. Concerning Augustine's desire to control his appetite, see *Conf.* 10.31.43–47.

107. Aug., *Serm.* 205–11.

108. Aug., *Serm.* 206.1.

109. Aug., *Serm.* 207.2.

110. The only clear sign that it was a Lenten sermon comes from the brief recognition by Augustine that "these are holy days in which we are observing Lent."

111. Never advancing to the status of the "elect," Augustine remained a "hearer," a designation roughly equivalent to a Christian catechumen.

112. For a concise survey of Manichean teaching as it related to Augustine, see J. K. Coyle, "Mani, Manicheanism," in Fitzgerald, *Augustine through the Ages,* 520–25. For a more comprehensive study, see Lieu, *Manichaeism,* and BeDuhn, *Manichean Body.*

113. For Augustine's less than flattering account of their practice, see Aug., *Against Faustus the Manichean [Contra Faustum Manichaeum]* 5.10 (I. Zycka, crit. ed., CSEL 25) and *On the Morals of the Manicheans [De moribus Manichaeorum]* 13.29–16.53 (J.-P. Migne, ed., PL 32).

114. This was not an easy task. As Robert Markus comments, "Augustine's opponents never allowed him to forget the hair's breadth that separated the ascetic ideal from a Manichean denial of the flesh." Markus, *End of Ancient Christianity,* 159.

115. Aug., *On the Morals of the Manicheans* 13.29. This suggested to him that they lacked self-control.

116. Aug., *On the Morals of the Manicheans* 15.36. He had previously identified love of God and control of the passions as the two goals that motivated Catholic piety. Cf. Aug., *On the Morals of the Catholic Church* 31.65 ff.

117. Aug., *On the Morals of the Manicheans* 13.28.

118. Aug., *Against Faustus the Manichean* 30.5.

119. Around the year 393, Jerome issued a treatise against a Roman ascetic, Jovinian, that repudiated the latter's claim that virgins were not superior to married Christians. Jerome's praise of virginity went so far that Augustine read it as an assault on marriage. Jerome, *Against Jovinian [Aduersus Iouinianum]* 1.3–11 (J.-P. Migne, ed., PL 23).

120. Aug., *On the Good of Marriage [De bono coniugali]* 3–4, 7, 15, and *On Holy Virginity [De sancta virginitate]* 12.12 (both in I. Zycha, crit. ed., CSEL 41). Augustine further developed these goods of marriage in later treatises against the Pelagians.

121. Aug., *On the Good of Marriage* 1.

122. For more on Augustine's attempts to appeal to Roman sensibilities, see Peter Brown, *Augustine of Hippo,* 399–400.

123. Aug., *On the Good of Marriage* 5.

124. Aug., *De civ.* 14.10.15–16. Peter Brown offers a fascinating interpretation of this position. At the heart of his argument is the idea that Augustine deliberately embraced the structures of Roman society (i.e., marriage and family life) in order to preserve the unity of the Christian Church. According to Brown, Augustine constructed a sociable vision of paradise by distancing himself from previous exegetes who understood sexuality as a consequence of the Fall. See Peter Brown, The *Body and Society: Men, Women and Sexual Renunciation in Early Christianity* (New York: Columbia University Press, 1988), 399–400.

125. Gregory of Nyssa, John Chrysostom, Ambrose, and Jerome had all posited that sexuality was a consequence of the Fall. See Gary Anderson, "Celibacy or Consummation in the Garden? Reflections on Early Jewish and Christian Interpretations of the Garden of Eden," *Harvard Theological Review* 82 (1989): 121–48. For an expanded discussion, see his *The Genesis of Perfection: Adam and Eve in Jewish and Christian Imagination* (Louisville, KY: Westminster John Knox Press, 2001), esp. 43–74.

126. The schism began with the election of Caecilian to the See of Carthage in 408. The bishops who consecrated Caecilian were accused of *traditio* (i.e., handing over the Scriptures during the persecutions). Equally problematic, Caecilian welcomed back to the Church those who had lapsed during the persecution. The Donatists emerged as a rival, more rigorous faction.

127. Aug., *Against the Letters of Petilian [Contra litteras Petiliani]* 2.32 (M. Petschenig, crit. ed., CSEL 52).

128. Aug., *Ep.* 108.

129. Aug., *Ep.* 35.

130. Peter Kaufman, *Church, Book and Bishop* (Boulder, CO: Westview Press, 1996), 88–89.

131. These phrases are borrowed from Gerald Bonner, "Pelagianism and Augustine," *Augustinian Studies* 23 (1992): 34.

132. Aug., *Against the Letters of Petilian* 2.13.

133. Cf. Aug., *Against Cresconius the Grammarian [Contra Cresconium Grammaticum]* (M. Petschenig, crit. ed., CSEL 52).

134. In other words, Augustine exaggerated the Donatist claims to perfection specifically so that he could poke holes in them. Kaufman, *Church, Book,* 87–88.

135. Cf. Matt. 19:21.

136. John Climacus, for example, described the quest for spiritual perfection as the climbing of a thirty-rung ladder. Each step required the mastery of a specific ascetic quality. As the monk advanced, the attainment of the new steps became more difficult. *Ladder of Divine Ascent [Scala paradisi]* (P.-G. Migne, ed., PG 88). For more on Climacus's ladder, see Irénée Hausherr, "La théologie du monachisme chez saint Jean Climaque," in *Théologie de la vie monastique* (Paris: Aubier, 1961), 385–410.

137. Note, for example, the very first line of Cassian's *Conferences,* which described the reason for his sojourn into Egypt: "[F]or there, in the desert of Skete, dwelled the most experienced *(probatissimi)* fathers of monks and every perfection *(perfectio)*." Cassian, *Conl.* 1.1.

138. Despite Augustine's claims to the contrary, Pelagius did maintain a role for divine grace.

139. Cassian, *Conl.* 13.

140. Cf. Aug., *Conf.* 1.7.11.

141. Augustine's doctrine of original sin came to comprise five tenets: (1) both the actual sin of Adam and its punishment were inherited; (2) human nature became thoroughly corrupted; (3) original sin was transmitted from parent to offspring through the concupiscence associated with procreation; (4) the infant soul was guilty; and (5) salvation required baptism, even for infants.

142. Aug., *On the Grace of Christ and Original Sin [De gratia Christi et de peccato originali]* 10–13 and 23 (C. F. Urba, crit. ed., CSEL 42).

143. Aug., *On Nature and Grace against Pelagius [De natura et gratia contra Pelagium]* 2 (C. F. Urba, crit. ed., CSEL 60).

144. "This grace, however, of Christ, without which neither infants nor adults are saved, is not distributed according to merit but is given freely, on account of which it is also called grace." Aug., *On Nature and Grace* 4.

145. Aug., *On Correction and Grace [De correptione et gratia]* 31 (J.-P. Migne, ed., PL 44), *De civ.* 14.11, *Unfinished Work against Julian [Contra Iuliani opus imperfectum]* 3.118 (M. Zelzer, crit. ed., CSEL 85), and *Ep.* 214. While Augustine maintained that he accepted the freedom of the will, it is clear that he believed that this freedom was confined to the freedom to choose evil.

146. Aug., *On Correction and Grace* 31. Elsewhere, Augustine is quick to show that this control of the will does not destroy the will. See, for example, Aug., *Ep.* 157.

147. Aug., *On Grace and Free Will [De gratia et libero arbitrio]* 6 (J.-P. Migne, ed., PL 44).

148. For more on why Augustine's reading of the Fall did not lead him to an ascetic theology, see Leyser, *Authority and Asceticism,* 14–15.

149. Aug., *On Grace and Free Will* 8.

150. Aug., *On Grace and Free Will* 9.

151. Aug., *Ep.* 214.

152. Ironically, it would be impossible to explain Augustine's doctrine of original sin outside an ascetic context. Its construction required an ascetic worldview in which lust was something to be avoided. Nevertheless, Augustine's system did not reward ascetic behavior.

153. In his thirteenth conference, Cassian maintained that an individual's salvation required both the grace of God and human initiative.

154. See Aug., *Ep.* 214 and 215.

155. Aug., *On Grace and Free Will* 8.

156. Aug., *De pecc. mer.* 3.2 –3.13, *On the Grace of Christ and Original Sin* 42–43, *On Marriage and Concupiscence [De nuptiis et concupiscentia]* 22 ff (C. F. Urba, crit. ed., CSEL 42), and *On Correction and Grace* 28. See Carol Scheppard, "The Transmission of Sin in the Seed: A Debate between Augustine of Hippo and Julian of Eclanum," *Augustinian Studies* 27 (1996): 99 –108. See also Mathijs Lamberigts, "A Critical Evaluation of the Critics of Augustine's View of Sexuality," in Dodaro and Lawless, *Augustine and His Critics,* 176 –97.

157. Aug., *Unfinished Work against Julian* 5.15 and 2.27.2.

158. Ibid., 1.79, 1.91, 2.38, and 3.118.

159. Ibid., 6.22. See Elizabeth Clark, "Vitiated Seeds and Holy Vessels: Augustine's Manichaean Past," in her *Ascetic Piety and Women's Faith* (New York: E. Mellon Press, 1986), 293.

160. Cf. Aug., *Serm.* 355 and 356.

161. Two regional councils in the East, one in Jerusalem, the other in Diospolis, vindicated a repentant Pelagius in 415. More importantly, monastic authorities such as John Cassian vigorously defended a participationist soteriology. It must be noted, however, that the doctrine of predestination is not without its pastoral considerations. See Leyser, *Authority and Asceticism,* 27.

162. Clark, "Vitiated Seeds."

163. Aug., *Retractions* 2.21.

164. Aug., *On the Work of Monks [De opere monachorum]* 2 (I Zycha, crit. ed., CSEL 41). Cf. Matt. 6:25 –34.

165. He went on to provide his own interpretation of several key passages, including Paul's injunction that one must work for his food. Cf. 2 Thess. 3:10.

166. Aug., *On the Work of Monks* 38.

167. Gregory of Tours records that a certain Wulfilach ascended a pillar on Western soil, only to be ordered down. Gregory of Tours, *HF* 8.15. Peter Brown infers from Gregory's writing that, in the late antique West, sanctity was not conferred upon an individual until his death. Brown goes on to contrast this to Eastern notions of holiness represented by the holy ascetic. See his chapter "Eastern and Western Christendom in Late Antiquity: A Parting of the Ways," in *Society and the Holy in Late Antiquity* (Berkeley: University of California Press, 1982), 166–95, esp. 185–86.

168. Aug., *Ep.* 262.

169. See Tilley, "No Friendly Letters," 51–53.

170. Aug., *Ep.* 48.

171. Aug., *Ep.* 48.

172. See Gregory, *Ep.* 7.20, 9.165, 9.205.

173. Leyser, *Authority and Asceticism,* 7–8.

FOUR   *John Cassian and the Spiritual Direction of the Ascetic Community*

1. Cf. Gennadius, *On the Lives of Illustrious Men [De viris illustribus]* 62 (E. Richardson, crit. ed. [Leipzig: J. C. Hinrichs, 1896]). See Henri Marrou, "La patrie de Jean Cassien," *Orientalia Christiana Periodica* 13 (1947): 588–96; see also Theodor Damian, "Some Critical Considerations and New Arguments Reviewing the Problem of St. John Cassian's Birthplace," *Orientalia Christiana Periodica* 57 (1991): 257–80.

2. See Cassian, *Conl.* 14.12.

3. Cassian, *Conl.* 24.1.3.

4. Stewart concludes that Cassian visited the Nile Delta, Scetis, Kellia, and Nitria. He argues that Cassian did not emphasize his time in Kellia or Nitria because of Evagrius's connection to those places. Cassian, no doubt, wanted to distance himself from Evagrius. Columba Stewart, *Cassian the Monk* (Oxford: Oxford University Press, 1998), 8–12.

5. Cf. Palladius, *Dialogue on the Life of John Chrysostom* 3 *[Dialogus de vita Chrysostomi] (*A.-M. Malingrey, crit. ed., SC 341–42).

6. For the many possibilities, see Stewart, *Cassian the Monk,* 13–16.

7. Evidence for Cassian's two monasteries derives from Gennadius, *On the Lives of Illustrious Men* 52. See Stewart, *Cassian the Monk,* 15–24.

8. Prosper of Aquitaine's *Against the Conferencer [Liber contra collatorem]* (J.-P. Migne, ed., PL 51), composed in 432, implies that Cassian is still alive, but this is the last mention of John in contemporary literature.

9. For example, see Philip Rousseau, "Christian Asceticism and the Early Monks," in *Early Christianity: Origins and Evolution to 600. In Honour of W. H. C. Frend,* ed. Ian Hazlett (London: SPCK, 1991), 112–22; Judith Herrin, *The Formation of Christen-*

dom (Princeton: Princeton University Press, 1987), 68–69; Peter Brown, *The Rise of Western Christendom: Triumph and Diversity, 200–1000* (Brighton: Blackwell, 1996), 66.

10. I am indebted to Elizabeth Clark, who has shared with me her (as yet) unpublished paper entitled "John Cassian and the Origenist Controversy," which, among other things, explores the relationship between Cassian and Evagrius. See also Adalbert de Vogüé, "Un morceau célèbre de Cassien parmi des extraits d' Evagre," *Studia Monastica* 27 (1985): 7–12.

11. Cf. Evagrius, *Praktikos* 6–14.

12. Cassian, *Inst.* 1; Evagrius, *Praktikos* prol.

13. Concerning the influence of Evagrius, see Stewart, *Cassian the Monk,* 11–12, 35–36, 43–44, 98, and 114–18.

14. Cf. Cassian, *Conl.* 1. See Elizabeth Clark, "John Cassian," 3–14; *The Origenist Controversy: The Cultural Construction of an Early Christian Debate* (Princeton: Princeton University Press, 1992), 43–84. Concerning Evagrius and *gnosis,* see Susanna Elm, "Evagrius Ponticus' *Sententiae ad Virginem,*" *Dumbarton Oaks Papers* 45 (1991): 97–120.

15. Cassian, *Inst.* prol. 3.

16. Cassian, *Inst.* prol. 8.

17. Stewart aptly notes that the "*Institutes* are inescapably a critique of the native monastic tradition associated with Martin of Tours." Stewart, *Cassian the Monk,* 17. See also Conrad Leyser, " 'This Sainted Isle': Panegyric, Nostalgia, and the Invention of Lerinian Monasticism," in Klingshirn and Vessey, *Limits of Ancient Christianity,* 192–94; Friedrich Prinz, *Frühes Mönchtum im Frankenreich: Kultur und Gesellschaft in Gallien, den Rheinlanden und Bayern am Beispiel der monastischen Entwicklung, 4. bis 8. Jahrhundert,* 2nd ed. (Munich: R. Oldenbourg, 1988), 47–117, 452–80. Rousseau is less convinced. See his *Ascetics, Authority,* 169, 183.

18. The importance of Lérins in the asceticizing of the Gallic Church has been sufficiently documented by others. See Leyser, " 'This Sainted Isle' "; Markus, *End of Ancient Christianity,* 194–96; and Adalbert de Vogüé, "Les débuts de la vie monastique à Lérins," *Revue de l'Histoire des Religions* 88 (1993): 5–53.

19. Cassian, *Conl.* prol. 2.1–2.

20. In recent scholarship, the traditional pitting of Cassian versus Augustine on the issue of grace and human initiative has been correctly tempered. Cassian was just as concerned about Pelagius's errors as he was about Augustine's position — that is why Conference 13 balances the two positions. For more on this issue, see Augustine Casiday, "Cassian against the Pelagians," *Studia Monastica* 46 (2004): 7–23; Leyser, *Authority and Asceticism,* 40; Stewart, *Cassian the Monk,* 18 n. 161; and Markus, *End of Ancient Christianity,* 177–79.

21. Cf. Cassian, *Conl.* 23.12.3–5.

22. He offers the same position in a concise form in *Inst.* 12.10–14.

23. See, for example, Rebecca H. Weaver, *Divine Grace and Human Agency: A Study of the Semi-Pelagian Controversy* (Macon, GA: Mercer University Press, 1996).

24. See, for example, Markus's critique. Robert Markus, "The Legacy of Pelagius: Orthodoxy, Heresy and Conciliation," in *The Making of Orthodoxy: Essays in Honour of Henry Chadwick,* ed. R. Williams (Cambridge: Cambridge University Press, 1989), 215–35; Leyser, "'This Sainted Isle,'" 192.

25. Note, for example, the balance between grace and free will in the *Apophthegmata Patrum* and Ath., *V. Ant.*

26. In 529, the Second Council of Orange condemned the followers of Cassian's participationist soteriology, though Cassian himself was not identified.

27. For example, the *Master* transformed Cassian's ten marks of humility (see *Inst.* 4.39) into twelve degrees of humility. *Rule of the Master [Regula magistri]* 10 (Adalbert de Vogüé, crit. ed., SC 105–7). See Adalbert de Vogüé, "De Cassien au Maître et à Eugippe," *Studia Monastica* 23 (1981): 247–61.

28. Benedict, *Rule of St. Benedict [Regula Benedicti]* 42.3, 42.5, 73.5 (J. Neufville, crit. ed., SC 181–82).

29. In a letter to Respecta, Abbess of St. Cassiani at Massilia (the convent established by Cassian), Gregory discusses the feast of St. Cassian. This is significant because it has generally been assumed that Cassian was not recognized as a saint in the West, except in Marseilles. Gregory's encouragement of Cassian's cult points to the pontiff's acknowledgment of Cassian's sanctity.

30. Leyser, *Authority and Asceticism,* 57.

31. Cassian, *Conl.* 16.3–5.

32. For example, see Cassian, *Inst.* 2.3.

33. Cassian, *Conl.* 1.7.

34. Cassian, *Conl.* 11.8.

35. Cassian, *Inst.* 2.3.

36. Cassian, *Inst.* 2.3. According to Leyser, Cassian's language enabled a rhetorical self-fashioning that extended his authority through a pretext of humility. See Leyser, *Authority and Asceticism,* 47–55.

37. Cassian, *Inst.* 2.3. See Rousseau, *Ascetics, Authority,* 191–92.

38. Cf. Cassian, *Inst.* 12.6, 12.8.

39. Cassian, *Inst.* 12.15.

40. The *Institutes* explore a number of ways that the Egyptian monks attempted to teach obedience to their novices. See, for example, the rigorous tests imposed upon a man who wishes to join a monastery. Cassian, *Inst.* 4.3–10.

41. For Cassian and discernment, see Lawrence S. Cunningham, "Cassian's Hero and Discernment," in *Finding God in All Things,* ed. Michael J. Himes and Stephen J. Pope (New York: Crossroad, 1996), 231–43; John Levko, "The Relationship of Prayer to Discernment and Spiritual Direction for John Cassian," *Saint Vladimir's Theological Quarterly* 40 (1996): 155–71; and Stephan Alexe, "Le discernement selon saint Jean Cassien," *Studia Patristica* 30 (1997): 129–35.

42. Cassian, *Conl.* 2.4.

43. Cassian, *Conl.* 2.1.4.

44. Cassian, *Conl.* 2.2.3.

45. Cassian, *Conl.* 2.2.5.

46. Cassian, *Conl.* 2.2.6.

47. Cassian, *Conl.* 2.1.4.

48. Cassian, *Conl.* 2.10.

49. In his *On First Principles [De principiis]* (Paul Koetschau, crit. ed. [New York: Harper and Row, 1966]), Origen identified the discernment of spirits as a gift of the Holy Spirit that enables the recipient to differentiate between good and evil spirits. John Chrysostom likewise discussed the ability to identify the kind of spirit that speaks through a man (i.e., if the man is a prophet or a deceiver) and to distinguish between spiritual and nonspiritual individuals. Chrysostom, *Homilies on First Corinthians [Argumentum epistolae primae ad Corinthios]* 29 (J.-P. Migne, ed., PG 61). See Lienhard, "On 'Discernment of Spirits,'" 505–29.

50. Ath., *V. Ant.* 14.

51. Though Evagrius did not use the term διάκρισις in his *Praktikos,* he offered sage advice for combating the λογοσμοί.

52. Similar applications of discernment appear in the *Apophthegmata Patrum.* See, for example, Agathon 5 and John the Dwarf 7.

53. Cassian, *Inst.* 4.9.

54. Cassian, *Inst.* 4.9.

55. Cf. Cassian, *Conl.* 2.5.

56. Moses insists that the cultivation of *discretio* begins with obedience to one's elder and respect for the traditions of the ascetic community. Cassian, *Conl.* 2.9.1–2.11.8.

57. Cassian, *Conl.* 2.13.1–3.

58. Book 4 of the *Institutes* describes how the guest master supervises all initiates. Once the novice officially enters the community, he takes a new spiritual father.

59. Cassian, *Inst.* 2.3.

60. Cassian, *Inst.* 2.2.

61. Cassian, *Inst.* 2.3.

62. Cassian, *Inst.* 2.5. In the eighteenth conference he makes a similar claim through the voice of Abba Piamun, though in this case the early Egyptian monks are compared to the community described by St. Luke in the Book of Acts. Cassian, *Conl.* 18.5.

63. On this point, see Leyser, "'This Sainted Isle,'" 203–6, and Markus, *End of Ancient Christianity,* 181–211.

64. For example, the *Rule of the Master* and the *Rule of St. Benedict* incorporated each of these methods.

65. Cf. Cassian, *Inst.* 4.9–10.

66. Cassian, *Inst.* 5.5.

67. Cf. Cassian, *Inst.* 4.9–10.

68. Basil of Caesarea, for example, noted that each monk had gifts and faults that required individualized attention (*Longer Rules* 7). He also insisted that novice monks focus on obedience—only an advanced monk could cultivate theology. Basil, *Longer Rules* 4.

69. Cassian, *Inst.* 4.3.

70. Cassian, *Inst.,* 4.5–7. The elder responsible for guests lived apart from the community near the entrance to the monastery. Cassian argued that it was important to keep the initiates separate from other monks until they had learned the "rudiments of humility and patience."

71. Cassian, *Inst.* 4.7.

72. Cassian, *Inst.* 4.7. Each of these elders supervised up to ten disciples.

73. Cassian, *Inst.* 4.8 ff.

74. Cassian, *Inst.* 4.30. Similar stories occur in many forms by other ascetic authors.

75. Cassian, *Conl.* 5.13. See also *Conl.* 24.8.3 ff.

76. See Cassian, *Conl.* 5.13 ff.

77. Cassian, *Conl.* 1.2.1.

78. Cassian, *Conl.* 1.4.3.

79. Cassian, *Conl.* 1.4.1.

80. Cassian, *Conl.* 1.5.3–4.

81. Cassian, *Conl.* 1.5.4.

82. Cassian, *Conl.* 5.12.1.

83. Cassian, *Inst.* 11.2.

84. The two men had promised to make a short excursion into Egypt and return promptly to their monastery in Palestine. See Cassian, *Conl.* 17.2.1 ff.

85. Cassian, *Conl.* 17.20.2.

86. Cassian, *Conl.* 17.20.8. Cf. 1 Cor. 7:5 and 1 Cor. 3:2.

87. Cassian, *Conl.* 24.5.2.

88. See Boniface Ramsey, "Two Traditions on Lying and Deception in the Ancient Church," *Thomist* 49 (1985): 504–33.

89. Cassian, *Conl.* 18.5.2.

90. Cassian, *Conl.* 18.5.2.

91. Evagrius, *Praktikos* 6–14. See Elizabeth Clark, *Origenist Controversy,* 78–79. It was Gregory I who reduced the number from eight to seven.

92. Books 5–12 of the *Institutes* describe each of the vices in detail. In book 5 of the *Conferences* Cassian offers a concise and more systematic analysis.

93. Cassian, *Conl.* 5.3.

94. Cassian, *Conl.* 5.10–11.

95. Cassian, *Conl.* 5.10.2.

96. Cassian, *Conl.* 5.11.

97. Evagrius, *Praktikos* 5–14, 27–32, and esp. 36.

98. Evagrius, *Praktikos* 20, 22.

99. Cassian, *Conl.* 5.7–10.

100. Cassian, *Conl.* 5.4.1.

101. Cassian, *Conl.* 5.19.4.

102. One such allusion is *Conl.* 5.25–26.

103. In the first of his conferences, Cassian argues that evil thoughts derive from one of two sources, demons or the individual. Cassian, *Conl.* 1.17.

104. Cassian, *Inst.* 7.21.

105. Cassian, *Inst.* 7.22.

106. Brakke, "Making of Monastic Demonology," 19–48.

107. Ibid., 46–47.

108. Cassian, *Inst.* 4.37.

109. Cassian, *Conl.* 7.28.

110. Cassian, *Conl.* 7.20.1–3.

111. Cassian, *Conl.* 7.21.4.

112. Brakke, "Making of Monastic Demonology," 32–41.

113. See Stewart, *Cassian the Monk,* 50–55. See also Markus, *End of Ancient Christianity,* 184–86.

114. Stewart, *Cassian the Monk,* 50.

115. Evagrius, *Praktikos* prol.

116. Cassian, *Conl.* 5.3–7.

117. Cassian, *Conl.* 24.8.3. Markus notes Cassian's gradual shift toward cenobitic monasticism. Markus, *End of Ancient Christianity,* 182–86.

118. Cassian, *Inst.* 2.9.

119. Cassian, *Conl.* prol.

120. Cassian, *Conl.* 23.5.3, 23.4.4.

121. Cassian, *Conl.* 23.4.4. Cf. 2 Thess. 3:8; Phil. 1:22–24.

122. Cassian, *Conl.* 23.5.6.

123. Cassian, *Conl.* 17.19.

124. Cassian, *Inst.* 4.19.

125. Cassian, *Conl.* 24.8.3.

126. Cassian, *Conl.* 24.8.2 ff. Cassian's view is similar to Basil's. See Basil, *Longer Rules* 7.

127. Cf. Cassian, *Conl.* 24.4.2–.6.2.

128. Cassian, *Inst.* 5.24–41.

129. See Boniface Ramsey, introduction to his *John Cassian: The Conferences,* Ancient Christian Writers Series 57 (Mahwah, NJ: Newman Press, 1997), 9.

130. At times, the speakers reference anonymous elders (e.g. Cassian, *Conl.* 9.6.1 ff). Elsewhere, the citations point directly to the teachings of famed ascetics such as Antony. See Cassian, *Conl.* 2.2.1 ff, 2.6.1, 3.4.2, 8.18.1 ff, 9.31, 14.4.1, 18.5.4 ff, and 24.11.1 ff.

131. This does not necessitate that the stories are fictional. Their authenticity lies beyond the historian's purview.

132. Cassian, *Conl.* 18.24.

133. Cassian, *Conl.* 18.24.

134. See Peter Munz, "John Cassian," *Journal of Ecclesiastical History* 11 (1960): 1–22, esp. 2–4. See also Owen Chadwick, *John Cassian: A Study in Primitive Monasticism* (Cambridge: Cambridge University Press, 1950), 105; and J. M. Wallace-Hadrill, *The Long-Haired Kings* (London: Methuen, 1962), 35.

135. Rousseau, *Ascetics, Authority,* 199.

136. Stewart, *Cassian the Monk,* 131–32.

137. Concerning the impact of Lérins on the episcopate in southern Gaul, there is an ever-expanding historiography. See Leyser, *Authority and Asceticism,* 81–100, and "'This Sainted Isle'"; Markus, *End of Ancient Christianity,* 194–96; Vogüé, "Les débuts"; and Prinz, *Frühes Mönchtum im Frankenreich,* 47–87.

138 Hilary (bishop of Arles ca. 430), Lupus (bishop of Troyes in 427), Eucherius (bishop of Lyons ca. 432), Maximus (bishop of Riez ca. 434), Faustus (bishop of Riez ca. 460), and Caesarius (bishop of Arles, beginning in 502). Leyser, "'This Sainted Isle,'" 195, 200. For a complete study of the monastic community at Lérins, see Salvatore Pricoco, *L'isola dei santi: Il cenobio di Lerino e le origini del monachesimo gallico* (Rome: Edizioni dell'Ateneo and Bizzarri, 1978).

139. For the relationship between Cassian and Lérins, see Adilbert de Vogüé, *Les règles des saints Pères* (Paris: Éditions du Cerf, 1982). Also see Markus, who maintains that the Lerinians assumed episcopal responsibility despite Cassian's warnings against it. Markus, *End of Ancient Christianity,* 181.

140. Leyser, "'This Sainted Isle,'" 202–6.

141. Ibid., 204.

142. Cf. Cassian, Inst. 11.14, and Conl. 1.20, 4.11. Cassian contends that priestly ambition demonstrates vanity and pride.

143. The elders who held clerical positions included Archebius, bishop of Panephysis (Conl. 11.2), Piamun (Conl. 18.1), and Paphnutius (Conl. 2.5), who were priests.

FIVE   *Pope Gregory I and the Ascetizing of Spiritual Direction*

1. Procopius Caesariensis, *The Wars [De belli],* 6–8 (J. Haury, crit. ed. [Leipzig: Teubner, 1905–13]). See Robert Markus, *Gregory the Great and His World* (Cambridge: Cambridge University Press, 1998), 3–7. See also Frederick H. Dudden, *Gregory the Great* (New York: Longmans Green, 1907), 25–58.

2. Some estimates put the death toll at one-third of the population. See Pauline Allen, "The Justinianic Plague," *Byzantion* 49 (1979): 5–20.

3. Gregory of Tours, *HF* 10.1.

4. Carole Straw, *Gregory the Great: Perfection in Imperfection* (Berkeley: University of California Press, 1988), 2.

5. Gregory of Tours, *HF* 10.1.

6. *Lib. pont.* 66; John the Deacon, *Life of Gregory [Vita Gregorii Magni]* 1.1, 4.83 (J.-P. Migne, ed., PL 75). In the Roman Church, the office of *defensor* typically involved the administration of property. See Jeffrey Richards, *The Popes and the Papacy in the Early Middle Ages, 476–752* (London: Routledge and Kegan Paul, 1979), 289–306.

7. Pierre Riché, *Écoles et enseignement dans le Haut Moyen Age* (Paris: Aubier Montaigne, 1979), 17.

8. Gregory of Tours, *HF* 10.1. As the two never met, this must, to some extent, be hyperbole.

9. See, Riché, *Écoles et enseignement,* 15–19; and M. L. W. Laistner, *Thought and Letters in Western Europe,* 2nd ed. (Ithaca: Cornell University Press, 1966), 108–12.

10. Joan M. Petersen points to the poet Arator as evidence of Greek learning in Rome. Petersen, "Did Gregory the Great Know Greek?" in *Orthodox Churches and the West,* ed. D. Baker (Oxford: Basil Blackwell, 1976), 121–34. Moreover, we know that Cassiodorus's community at Vivarium translated Greek works into Latin. See Laistner, *Thought and Letters,* 99–101.

11. Riché, *Écoles et enseignement,* 18. According to Riché, it is not the quality of Gregory's Latin but his disdain for the classical past that distinguishes him from earlier writers (Christian and non-Christian alike). For an assessment of Gregory's Latin, see Michel Banniard, *Viva Voce* (Paris: Institut des Études Augustiniennes, 1992), 105–79.

12. The sphere of influence included the guilds and the senate. See Markus, *Gregory the Great,* 9 and 134. See also Jones, *Later Roman Empire,* 1:523–62.

13. Gregory, *Ep.* 5.53. This letter is the prefatory address to Leander, to whom Gregory sent the first copy of the *Moralia.* I have followed the numbering for Gregory's letters in D. Norberg's critical edition (CCSL 140–41).

14. Gregory of Tours, *HF* 10.1. This account is expanded by Paul the Deacon (*Life of Gregory [Vita Gregorii]* 3) (J.-P. Migne, ed., PL 75) and John the Deacon (*Life of Gregory* 1.5–6).

15. Gregory of Tours, *HF* 10.1.

16. Gregory, *Mor.* prol.

17. Concerning the relationship between Rome and Constantinople at the time, see John Meyendorff, *Imperial Unity and Christian Divisions: The Church, 450–680* (Crestwood, NY: St. Vladimir's Seminary Press, 1989), 251–90.

18. During his own pontificate, Gregory was often at odds with the exarch. Much of the conflict centered on peace negotiations with the Lombards. In 593/94, Gregory secured an armistice with the Lombards but was subsequently accused of treason by the exarch. See Gregory, *Ep.* 5.34, 5.36, and 5.40. See Kaufman, *Church, Book,* 121–22.

19. Some of these monks journeyed from Rome with Gregory. Among them was Maximian, whom Gregory later assisted to the See of Syracuse. See Gregory,

Ep. 3.36. Concerning Gregory's time in Constantinople, see Dudden, *Gregory the Great,* 123–57.

20. The traditional position (represented by Dudden, Pierre Batiffol, and Riché) is that Gregory knew no Greek. This was challenged in 1976 by Joan Petersen, who argued that Gregory possessed a reading knowledge of the language. In 1987, Petersen qualified her previous position, admitting that she had overestimated the pontiff's fluency. Peter Brown has more recently suggested that the oft-cited passage in which Gregory claims to be ignorant of Greek (*Ep.* 7.26) is overemployed by scholars, suggesting instead that Gregory had limited ability. Dudden, *Gregory the Great,* 153 and 288. Pierre Batiffol, *Saint Grégoire le Grand* (Paris: J. Gabalda, 1928), 34. Pierre Riché, *Education et culture dans l'occident barbare, VIe–VIIIe siècles,* 2nd ed. (Paris: Éditions du Seuil, 1973), 189. Petersen, "Did Gregory the Great Know Greek?" and "'Homo omnino Latinus'? The Theological and Cultural Background of Pope Gregory the Great," *Speculum* 62/63 (1987): 529–51. Peter Brown, *Rise of Western Christendom,* 138.

21. Gregory, *Mor.* prol.

22. Concerning his satisfaction with monastic life, see Gregory, *Dia.* 1, prol. 3–5.

23. Gregory of Tours, *HF* 10.1.

24. Gregory of Tours, *HF* 10.1. Conrad Leyser argues that Gregory's own discussion of the events employs a "rhetoric of reluctance" that stems from two different rhetorical traditions: the philosopher-king whose worthiness derives from his distaste for power and the moral ruler whose authority stems from his ascetic perfection. Leyser, *Authority and Asceticism,* 161.

25. For his charitable works, see Gregory, *Ep.* 1.1, 1.37, 1.44, etc.; for his refurbishing of Roman churches, see *Lib. pont.* 66; and for the mission to England, see Gregory, *Ep.* 6.52–56 and 11.39–42. For a study of Gregory's urban initiatives and social work, see Georg Jenal, "Gregor der Grosse und die Stadt Rom (590–604)," in *Herrschaft und Kirche: Beiträge zur Enstehung und Wirkungsweise episcopaler und monastischer Organisationsformen,* ed. Friedrich Prinz (Stuttgart: A. Hiersemann, 1988), 123–30.

26. In the realm of spiritual direction, a series of Western authors drew idiosyncratically from the clerical and ascetic traditions. Specifically, Julianus Pomerius, Caesarius of Arles, and Benedict of Nursia developed the ideas of Augustine and Cassian in ways that suited their own communities and interests. A detailed analysis of any of these three authors is beyond the scope of the present study. For more on their development of the language of authority, see Leyser, *Authority and Asceticism,* 65–128.

27. Markus, *End of Ancient Christianity,* xi–xiii.

28. Markus interprets variation between Augustine's and Gregory's policies as the consequence of the overriding shift in Christian perspective and not a direct rejection of Augustine by Gregory. Ibid., 223–28. See also his *Gregory the Great,* 40–41.

29. Both Leyser and Markus suggest that ascetics were already well integrated into Christian society before Gregory's pontificate. As a consequence, Leyser believes

that Gregory's implementation of ascetic authority was a logical transition. Conrad Leyser, "Expertise and Authority in Gregory the Great: The Social Function of *Peritia*," in *Gregory the Great: A Symposium,* ed. John C. Cavadini (Notre Dame: University of Notre Dame Press, 1995), 44; Markus, *End of Ancient Christianity,* 199–214.

30. On the situation in Rome at the time of Gregory's elevation, see Jeffrey Richards, *Consul of God: The Life and Times of Gregory the Great* (London: Routledge and Kegan Paul, 1980), 70–107 and 162–80.

31. Gregory, *PR* prol.

32. Gregory, *Ep.* 5.53.

33. *Sacerdos* is used nineteen times, *rector* forty-three times, *praedicator* twenty-one times, and *pastor* nineteen times.

34. See Wilhelm Gessel, "Reform am Haupt: Die Pastoralregel Gregors des Grossen und die Besetzung von bischofsstühlen," in *Papsttum und Kirchenreform: Historische Beiträge. Festschrift für Georg Schwaiger zum 65,* ed. Manfred Weitlauff and Karl Hausberger (St. Ottilien: EOS Verlag Ezabtei, 1990), 17–36. See also Robert Markus, "Gregory the Great's *Rector* and Its Genesis," in *Grégoire Le Grand,* ed. Jacques Fontaine (Paris: Éditions du Centre National de la Recherche Scientifique, 1986), 137–45.

35. Cf. Gregory's *Moralia.*

36. Gregory, *PR* 1.1. The phrase "art of arts" (*ars artium*) derives from Gregory Naziansus's second oration, "Apology for His Flight." Leyser makes much of Gregory's description of pastoral authority as an *ars.* Leyser, "Expertise and Authority," 50–51.

37. For the role of ascetic experience in the Gregorian ideal, see Leyser, "Expertise and Authority," 38–61.

38. Gregory, *PR* 1.10.

39. Gregory, *PR* 1.10.

40. Gregory, *PR* 1.11.

41. Gregory, *PR* 1.11.

42. Gregory, *PR* 1.11.

43. Gregory, *PR* 1.11.

44. Cf. Cassian, *Conl.* 10; *Inst.* 5.

45. Cassian, *Conl.* 2; Benedict, *Rule* 2.

46. Gregory, *PR* 1.2.

47. Cf. Aug., *De doc.* 4.27.59–60.

48. Gregory, *PR* 1.3–6.

49. Gregory, *PR* 1.3. Cf. 2 Kings 11:3.

50. Gregory, *PR* prol.

51. Gregory, *PR* 1.5.

52. Gregory, *PR* 1.5.

53. Gregory, *PR* 1.5.

54. Concerning the humility related to resistance, see Gregory, *PR* 1.7.

55. Gregory, *PR* 1.6.

56. See, for example, Gregory, *Ep.* 1.3, 5.42, 6.33, and 11.21.

57. Gregory is the author of the *Life of St. Benedict (Vita Benedicti),* contained in the *Dialogues.* In it, he identifies the *Rule* as a masterpiece of discretion. There are numerous links between Gregory's *Pastoral Rule* and Benedict's *Rule.* Note, in particular, the qualifications for leadership and the discussions of conforming admonitions to the individual.

58. Although Gregory Nazianzen (and others) required clerical candidates to be active ascetics, he did not use his pastoral treatise to recruit ascetics to office.

59. Gregory clearly recognized the need for structure. As he knew all too well, the most accomplished ascetic could easily lapse into spiritual laziness once he became a bishop. Such had been the situation of a close friend. Gregory, *Ep.* 4.33.

60. Though Pomerius's *On the Contemplative Life [De vita contemplativa]* (J.-P. Migne, ed., PL 59) was probably read by many in southern Gaul and anticipates many characteristics of Gregory's synthesis, there is less evidence of its circulation.

61. Straw's thesis is that Gregory forged complementarity from contrary conditions. By virtue of his creativity, Straw argues, Gregory derived new meaning through a dialectic of opposites. Whether they were spiritual and carnal, active and contemplative, or good and evil, the merger was harmonious. For example, he believed that both the active and the contemplative life were dangerous in isolation; when combined, however, the two not only counterbalanced but actually enhanced one another. Straw, *Gregory the Great,* 236–60.

62. He often describes this balance in the *Moralia.* See, for example, Gregory, *Mor.* 5.45 and *Mor.* 6.36.56.

63. I refer here to pastoral literature written by episcopal officials, primarily that of Augustine and Ambrose. As noted, Pomerius clearly appreciated the value of contemplation.

64. Gregory, *PR* 2.7.

65. Gregory, *PR* 2.11. For a fuller analysis of this component of Gregory's plan, see Bruno Judic, "La Bible miroir de pasteurs dans la *Règle pastorale* de Grégoire le Grand," in *Le monde latin antique et la Bible,* ed. Jacques Fontaine and Charles Pietri (Paris: Beauchesne, 1985), 455–73.

66. Gregory, *PR* 2.10.

67. Gregory, *PR* 2.9.

68. Gregory, *PR* 3.38.

69. Gregory, *PR* 2.10.

70. As noted in previous chapters, the techniques of adaptability and versatility in the process of instruction were part of rhetorical training in the classical period. Pope Gregory's education would have included these ancient theories—they would have been part of his intellectual arsenal. But his conception of rhetorical styles

would also have been supplemented and reinforced by Nazianzen's appropriation and transformation of these Hellenistic models.

71. Gregory, *PR* 3.9.

72. Cassian, *Inst.,* 4.5; Benedict, *Rule* 34.

73. See, for example, Aug., *De rud.* 9.13–10.15 and 15.23.

74. This, in fact, is the thrust of Hausherr's examination of the role of the spiritual father in the early Christian East. Hausherr, *Spiritual Direction.*

75. See ch. 4.

76. Gregory, *Mor.* 31.45.87. See Kallistos Ware's introduction to John Climacus's *Ladder of Divine Ascent* for a comparative analysis of the lists of Evagrius, Cassian, Gregory, and Climacus. Ware, introduction to *John Climacus, Ladder of Divine Ascent,* trans. C. Luibheid and N. Russell (New York: Paulist Press, 1982). See John Climacus, *Ladder of Divine Ascent* 62–66.

77. In *PR* 3.15 Gregory distinguishes between a slothful and a hasty subordinate. Gregory also examines sloth in *PR* 3.4 and *PR* 3.16.

78. Others include abstinence, chastity, charity, patience, obedience, and long-suffering. Straw argues that Gregory's use of the virtues is distinctively ascetic. Straw, *Gregory the Great,* 181–82.

79. Hausherr, *Spiritual Direction,* 224.

80. Gregory, *PR* 3.19.

81. See Gregory, *PR* 3.14. Robert Markus has shown us how Gregory understood his world to be filled with demons and angels. Markus distinguishes Gregory's casual discussions of the spiritual realm from Augustine's more cerebral tendencies. He then points to this "sacralization" as evidence of the end of ancient Christianity. Markus, *End of Ancient Christianity,* 204 and 228.

82. Aug., *De civ.* 22.22.

83. Though a fear of demons does not dominate Gregory's *Pastoral Rule* as it does his *Moralia* or homilies, its presence further testifies to the author's ascetic outlook. Some examples of Gregory's attention to the "demonic" are *PR* 3.23, 3.28, 3.29, and 3.32.

84. Cf. Peter Brown, "The Rise and Function of the Holy Man in Late Antiquity," *Journal of Roman Studies* 61 (1971): 80–101.

85. Gregory's *Dialogues,* homilies, and correspondence included powerful tales of these ascetic holy men.

86. It is almost impossible to distinguish between the original exegesis and the subsequent revision. For this reason, my examination of the *Moralia* follows the discussion of the *Pastoral Rule.*

87. The historical was a literal interpretation of the text; the allegorical sought to identify some part of Christ's saving ministry or the trials of the Church through prefiguration in Job; and the moral, which was the longest, served as the basis for applying the whole of Scripture to Christian ascetic living. While Gregory applies all

three methods to a few early verses, he typically employs only one for most verses. For Gregory's explanation of his method, see the introductory letter to Leander.

88. Both John Chrysostom and John Cassian had attributed ascetic virtues to Job. See Chrysostom, *On Job [Fragmenta in beatum Job]* (J.-P. Migne, ed., PG 51), and Cassian, *Conl.* 6.8–11.

89. Carole Straw makes great use of the *Moralia* when she argues, in *Gregory the Great,* that perfection for Gregory lay in a combination of extremes.

90. Gregory, *Mor.* 23.20.38. See also *Mor.* 6.37.56 ff, 18.43.70, 28.13.33, 30.2.8, and 31.25.49.

91. Concerning persecution, see Gregory, *Mor.* 31.25.50; cf. *PR* 2.8. Concerning ungrateful subordinates, see *Mor.* 13.2.2 and 13.5.5. Cf. *PR* 2.8 and *On First Kings [In I Librum Primum Regum]* 4.5 (P. Verbraken, crit. ed., CCSL 144).

92. Gregory, *Mor.* 29.12.17. Cf. *PR* 2.8.

93. A clear sign of a priest's pride is the consistent and harsh punishment of subordinates. Gregory, *Mor.* 24.16.41.

94. Gregory, *Mor.* 21.14.22: "non tam reges hominum quam pastores pecorum."

95. Gregory, *Mor.* 19.35.43–44 and 24.25.53–54; cf. *PR* 1.1–2. Nevertheless, subordinates should never rush to judge their leaders but should endure their faults willingly. Gregory, *Mor.* 25.15.36–37.

96. Gregory, *Mor.* 22.4.7; cf. *PR* 2.2.

97. Gregory, *Mor.* 31.24.44. Concerning qualifications, see Gregory, *Mor.* 23.13.21; cf. *On First Kings* 4.3.

98. Gregory, *Mor.* 28.11.26.

99. Gregory explores two situations requiring *condescensio:* (1) when a subordinate accepts a reprimand but is incapable of completing the standard penance and (2) when a subordinate commits multiple sins but lacks the strength to excise all of them at once. Concerning the first, Gregory writes: "[I]t ought to be known that there are some whom Mother Church tolerates, nursing them with the breast of charity, whom she leads gradually *[incrimenta perducat]* to spiritual heights." Gregory, *Mor.* 31.13.24. Concerning the second, he adds: "[W]hen the mind is constrained by both great and minor sins *[peccata],* if no outlet of escape exists without sin, the minor sin is always preferred." Gregory, *Mor.* 32.20.39.

100. Gregory, *Mor.* 2.15.27–2.16.29.

101. Gregory, *Mor.* 30.9.33–34.

102. Gregory, *Mor.* 24.8.19, 28.10.21–24. As this final example demonstrates, Gregory's spiritual anthropology likely derived from his reading of 1 Cor. 12.

103. Gregory, *Mor.* 34.15.29.

104. Gregory, *Mor.* 30.3.11–13. The connection between the cock and the preacher, according to Gregory, is that both know the appropriate time to proclaim their message to the world.

105. Gregory, *Mor.* 30.3.11–13.

106. Nearly the whole of books 27 and 30 and a good part of 31 concern that subject.

107. Gregory, *Mor.* 30.13.48; cf. *PR* 3.39. Concerning pride in preaching, see *Mor.* 20.2.4, 23.12.25. This particular explanation is absent in the *Pastoral Rule*.

108. Gregory, *Mor.* 16.21.25.

109. We know, for example, that Leander of Seville was in attendance. Gregory, *Ep.* 5.53.

110. Gregory, *Mor.* 1.22.30 ff.

111. Gregory, *Mor.* 1.22.31; cf. Luke 18:8.

112. Gregory, *Mor.* 3.9.15 ff.

113. Likewise, Job admonishes his friends to worship God. Gregory, *Mor.* 3.11.19 ff.

114. Gregory, *Mor.* 26.26.44.

115. In books 1–18, Gregory uses *sanctus vir* sixty-eight times in the singular form versus only twenty-six in the plural. In books 19–36, however, the singular drops to twenty-eight occurrences while the plural increases to forty.

116. Gregory employed "holy preachers" only five times in the first half of the text but at least twenty times in the second half.

117. Six examples of the term are used in books 1–18, compared to twenty in books 19–36.

118. Internal evidence informs us of a few exceptions: Gregory delivered *Hom.* 2 to an audience that included women; *Hom.* 17 acknowledged that priests and bishops were present; and he presented *Hom.* 23, 27, and 36 to the laity. I have followed Étaix's numbering of the homilies.

119. Gregory, *Hom.* 21 was a special exception because Gregory delivered it himself—no doubt in honor of the feast of the Resurrection.

120. The *Moralia* was a running commentary, unrelated to the daily worship cycle. In contrast, Gregory offered his homilies during the liturgy, following the Bible readings. There was no continuity from one sermon to the next. Each contained three elements: (1) a reconstruction of the biblical passage; (2) a clarification of the more complicated messages; and, most important, (3) an overtly asceticizing moral lesson. This final component was often achieved through the example of past or present ascetic saints.

121. If we imagine that Gregory confined his daily exposition of the *Moralia* to a few hours, his audience may well have gone entire days without hearing the name of Job.

122. Gregory, *Hom.* 9.

123. Gregory, *Hom.* 9.

124. For example, see Gregory, *Hom.* 38.

125. Gregory, *Hom.* 3.

126. Gregory, *Hom.* 3.

127. Gregory, *Hom.* 20.

128. This particular homily comes on the Feast of St. Andrew the Apostle. Gregory stresses Andrew's willingness to forsake his livelihood at the moment he heard the call of Christ.

129. Gregory, *Hom.* 5. Gregory does not insist upon complete poverty for his clergy. But he consistently emphasizes the renunciation of worldly desire.

130. Gregory, *Hom.* 14.

131. Gregory, *Hom.* 17. Several things contributed to this problem: some priests led sinful lives, others were reluctant to punish their subordinates, still others lacked *discretio,* etc. See Gregory, *PR* 1.11. A similar complaint is leveled against bishops in *Hom.* 26.

132. For example, humility, willingness to suffer, gentle, gradual correction of subordinates, hatred of public acclaim, distaste for wealth.

133. Gregory, *Hom.* 26. Other discussions of the criteria for spiritual authority include *Hom.* 10, 13, 14, 20, 29, and 33.

134. Gregory, *Hom.* 34.

135. For Gregory's apocalypticism, see Leyser, *Authority and Asceticism,* 150–57.

136. Gregory, *Hom.* 35.

137. Tertullian, *On Fasting, against the Psychics [De jeiunio adversus Psychicos]* (Franciscus Oehler, ed., in *Tertulliani quae supersunt omnia* [Liepzig: J. B. Hirschfeld, 1853]).

138. Gregory, *Ep.* 1.11.

139. Gregory, *Ep.* 1.33.

140. Gregory, *Ep.* 4.44. Gregory hinted that had he been the pilgrim he would never have returned.

141. In 592, Gregory censored Natalis, the bishop of Salona, for his frequent feasting, lack of spiritual reading, and general lack of discipline (*Ep.* 2.17); later the same year, Gregory openly rebuked the same man for drunkenness (*Ep.* 2.34). In 596, Gregory wrote to his deacon in Ravenna about Archbishop Marinianus, a once accomplished ascetic who Gregory feared had, since his promotion, abandoned his ascetic way of life for the leisure life of the nobility (*Ep.* 6.33). Gregory also rebuked Desiderius, the bishop of Vienne, for his continued interest in secular learning. It was bad enough, Gregory wrote, for lay persons to read pagan authors, it was entirely unbefitting a person of Desiderius's position to do so (*Ep.* 11.34).

142. Cf. Canon XIV and XV of the Council of Chalcedon.

143. Cf. Ambrose, *On the Office* 1.50.

144. Gregory, *Ep.* 1.42.

145. Pope Pelagius II had ordered the Sicilian Church to adopt the Roman practice in 588. Whether the Sicilian Church actually accepted this decree is a matter of speculation.

146. Gregory, *Ep.* 1.42. See also *Ep.* 4.34 and *Ep.* 9.111.

147. A few of the fifty or so examples are Gregory, *Ep.* 1.5, 1.4, 2.50, and 5.36.

148. Gregory, *Ep.* 1.5. Customarily, a bishop newly elected to one of the five patriarchates (Alexandria, Antioch, Constantinople, Jerusalem, or Rome) sent a statement of faith to each of the others. Gregory in his letter went on to promote an ascetic ideal and introduce his vision of the priesthood. Not surprisingly, several lengthy passages from this letter reappeared in the *Pastoral Rule* a few months later. For example, see Gregory, *PR* 2.1, 2.3. 2.4, 2.5, 2.6, and 2.7.

149. According to Leyser, Gregory struggled to maintain authority in Rome. To ensure his survival, Leyser submits, Gregory restaffed the Papal Curia with like-minded ascetics and maximized his authority by identifying pastoral care as an art and asserting that the most effective shepherd was the one who protested his unworthiness. Leyser, "Expertise and Authority," 54–56; *Authority and Asceticism,* 142. While it may be true that Gregory's survival in Rome was not guaranteed, Leyser's reading may be unnecessarily cynical. Gregory employed this "rhetoric of reluctance" in the *Moralia,* which he drafted before his elevation to the pontificate. Moreover, similar language fills a number of letters addressed to Gregory's own agents—men from whom he stood to gain no political advantage (e.g., Gregory, *Ep.* 1.9 and 2.50). Leyser is right to recognize the rhetorical flourish in the epistles addressed to the Eastern patriarchs and imperial court—those letters were thoughtfully crafted. But the language of reluctance appears too frequently in Gregory's corpus for us to dismiss it as insincere.

150. Gregory, *Ep.* 1.41. The image of the bishop as the pilot of the ship goes back to the apostolic fathers (cf. Ignatius's *Letter to Polycarp*) and was repeated by many of the fathers, including Tertullian, Cyprian, and Pomerius. Note, however, the extent to which Gregory has asceticized the image by identifying the ship as "decaying" and linking it to worldly responsibilities.

151. Gregory, *Ep.* 5.57.

152. By Gregory's tenure, the Roman Church had accumulated fifteen regional patrimonies scattered throughout Italy and abroad. Eleven of the regional landholdings were in Italy proper (including Sicily and Dalmatia), and four extended beyond the political control of the Byzantine exarch of Ravenna. Those included relatively small districts in Gaul, Sardinia, Corsica, and North Africa. Each consisted of multiple estates that were rented to tenants *(conductores)*. See Richards, *Popes and the Papacy,* 307–22.

153. Within the administrative wing of the papal machinery, there were three *scholae:* (1) *notores,* who were responsible for the papal correspondence and records; (2) *defensores,* whose primary responsibility was estate management; and (3) deacons, who served the central administration and oversaw poor relief. See ibid., 289–306.

154. The responsibilities of the *rector* fell into two categories: the administrative (e.g., collecting rents, orchestrating grain shipments, poor relief) and the ecclesiastical (maintaining clerical discipline, overseeing episcopal elections, acting against heresy). During Gregory's tenure, both roles took on increased importance. On the

one hand, the papal lands provided much of the grain needed by the city of Rome. On the other hand, Gregory increasingly employed his *rectores* as papal ambassadors abroad, entrusting them to administer his personal policies.

155. Unlike the patrimonies scattered throughout the Italian mainland, the Sicilian estates were free of the Lombards. As such they were of particular value to Rome, and Gregory was able to effect ecclesiastical as well as agricultural gains.

156. Peter served as *rector* of the papal patrimony and vicar of all Sicily from September of 590 until 592, when he was recalled to Rome. The variety of tasks assigned to Peter by Gregory is evidence of the great faith the pontiff had in his abilities. See Gregory, *Ep.* 2.50.

157. Gregory, *Ep.* 1.18.

158. Though surprising, this was not without precedent. Pope Pelagius I (556–61) had instructed his *rector* in Sicily, John, to remove the pallium from a disagreeable bishop and send the man to Rome for trial. Pelagius, *Ep.* 41.

159. Gregory, *Ep.* 2.5. According to John the Deacon (*Life of Gregory* 2.11–12), Maximianus had, for a time, been abbot of Gregory's monastery of St. Andrew in Rome. He also accompanied Gregory to Constantinople and was the subject of one of the miraculous stories of the *Dialogues* (3.36; cf. *Hom.* 34).

160. Concerning Ravenna's art and architecture, see Otto von Simson, *Sacred Fortress: Byzantine Art and Statecraft in Ravenna* (Chicago: University of Chicago Press, 1948).

161. The most notable dispute arose in 595, when Romanus Patricius, the exarch of Ravenna, withdrew the imperial troops, leaving Rome unprotected, and then broke the truce with the Lombards. As a consequence, the Lombards besieged Rome, enslaving many of the capital's citizens and forcing Gregory to negotiate peace with King Agilulph. In turn, Romanus accused Gregory of treason. See Gregory, *Ep.* 5.34 and 5.36.

162. Markus has rightly argued that Gregory understood himself to be a faithful citizen of the Byzantine Empire. The pontiff's arguments with the exarch did not compromise his loyalty. See Markus, *Gregory the Great,* 144–56.

163. Gregory wrote to a colleague of Donatus's candidacy: "We wished to consent to the will of the most excellent Lord Patricius as to Donatus the archdeacon. But since it is a very dangerous thing for the soul to lay hands on anyone rashly, we chose to investigate thoroughly his life and deeds. And because many things have surfaced, as we wrote to the Lord Patricius, that disqualify him from the episcopate, we did not consent to his ordination." Gregory, *Ep.* 5.51.

164. Gregory, *Ep.* 5.51.

165. John the Deacon, *Life of Gregory* 37.

166. Gregory's trust in Marinianus is evidenced by multiple letters. See Gregory, *Ep.* 7.39, 9.139, 9.140, and 9.156. But Gregory also expressed concern about the bishop's actions in *Ep.* 6.33.

167. Gregory, *Ep.* 3.29.

168. The proceedings took place in Genoa, not Milan, out of fear of the Lombards.

169. Obviously the man was one of Gregory's disciples living in the capital.

170. Gregory, *Ep.* 3.30.

171. Gregory also promoted ascetic candidates in Naples and the Balkans, two regions, like Sicily, that were traditionally understood to be part of the papal jurisdiction. For Naples, see Gregory, *Ep.* 10.19. For the Balkans (Salona), see *Ep.* 3.46.

172. Gregory, *Ep.* 7.40 and *Ep.* 8.17. A third letter reports a similar circumstance in which an abbot in charge of a group of monks running a hospital was elevated to the episcopacy. Gregory decrees that no future abbots of this hospital may rise to the rank of the episcopacy without first relinquishing their role as abbot. At issue was the property of the hospital. Gregory, *Ep.* 13.9.

173. Gregory, *Ep.* 3.22.

174. Gregory, *Ep.* 6.10.

175. Cf. Gregory, *Ep.* 4.52, 6.53–56, and 6.60.

176. Gregory, *Ep.* 11.39. Though Augustine was granted complete control of England, Gregory had different plans for the island upon Augustine's death. There were to be two metropolitans (London and York), who were each to have eleven supporting bishops. Despite these ambitious plans, the administrative system of the English Church grew slowly.

177. Markus, *Gregory the Great,* 186.

178. See Gregory, *Ep.* 7.12 and 13.10.

179. Gregory, *Ep.* 8.17.

180. This was a serious infringement upon the traditional model of authority within a diocese. It can also be understood as an expansion of Petrine authority.

181. Gregory, *Ep.* 5.49. The case is first introduced in *Ep.* 5.47. There are other examples of bishops seizing monastic property. See *Ep.* 6.24, 7.40, and 8.32.

182. In a similar episode, Gregory rebuked Felix, bishop of Pisaurum, for installing an episcopal chair in a local monastery and frequently presiding over public liturgies. Gregory submitted that this infringed upon the rights of the monks; if the monks desired more services, the bishop should appoint a priest to serve them. Gregory, *Ep.* 6.46.

183. Gregory, *Ep.* 3.56.

184. Gregory, *Ep.* 9.225.

185. Gregory, *Ep.* 9.165.

186. Gregory, *Ep.* 9.205.

187. Gregory, *Ep.* 7.20.

188. Gregory, *Ep.* 4.6.

189. See Markus, *Gregory the Great,* 144–56.

190. Gregory, *Ep.* 3.61. The law had been issued by the emperor, Mauricus, the previous year.

191. Gregory, *Ep.* 3.61. Gregory's comments were a sharp contrast to Augustine's attempt to discourage a soldier from monasticism. See Aug., *Ep.* 17*.

192. In a letter addressed to several Western bishops, Gregory informed them that they were not to accept into the clerical or monastic ranks persons who owed civil responsibilities (soldiers, bureaucrats, etc.) unless it could be determined that they did so for the profit of their souls and not to escape their secular responsibilities. Gregory, *Ep.* 8.10.

193. For more on Gregory's soteriology, see George Demacopoulos, "The Soteriology of Pope Gregory I: A Case against the Augustinian Interpretation," *American Benedictine Review* 54 (2003): 312–27.

194. Gregory, *Ep.* 1.33. Gregory counseled the man for many years. See *Ep.* 6.42 and *Ep.* 11.18.

195. Gregory, *Ep.* 11.36. Commenting on Augustine's ability to perform miracles, Gregory remarks: "For I know that Almighty God has displayed great miracles through your love in the nation that he has chosen. Wherefore you should rejoice with fear and trembling for this heavenly gift. Rejoice because the souls of the Angli are drawn by outward miracles to inward grace; but tremble because these signs that are performed through you . . . might give rise to vainglory."

196. Gregory, *Ep.* 11.9.

197. Gregory, *Ep.* 11.10.

198. "For what writing provides to those who read, the icon provides to the unlearned who see. And more specifically, an icon is used in place of reading by foreigners *[gentibus]*. You especially ought to have attended to this since you live among foreigners. . . . If you had seasoned zeal with *discretio,* you would have obtained what you sought and not scattered a collected flock." Gregory, *Ep.* 11.10.

199. That flexibility did not, however, allow Jews to own Christian slaves. See, for example, Gregory, *Ep.* 2.4, 3.37, 4.9, and 4.21.

200. Gregory, *Ep.* 1.34.

201. Gregory, *Ep.* 1.34. See also the circumstances of *Ep.* 1.45, 9.196, and 13.13.

202. Gregory, *Ep.* 5.7.

203. It is appropriate to note a common trope in Gregory's exegesis—that of the blinded Jew, ignorant of God's ultimate will. Robert Markus has recently argued that Gregory is not so much interested in presenting a description of Jewish error as in employing passages in Scripture to develop the important distinction between secular and contemplative life. Thus the Jew serves as a symbol of worldly concern and ambition, which ought to be replaced by divine *contemplatio.* See Robert Markus, "The Jew as a Hermeneutic Device: The Inner Life of a Gregorian Topos," in Cavadini, *Gregory the Great,* 1–15.

204. As per his custom, Gregory admonished this king to follow the example of Constantine the Great. For the date of Ethelbert's conversion, see Robert Markus, "The Chronology of the Gregorian Mission to England: Bede's Narrative and Gregory's Correspondence," *Journal of Ecclesiastical History* 14 (1963): 16–30.

205. Gregory, *Ep.* 11.37.

206. See Robert Markus, "Gregory the Great and a Papal Missionary Strategy," *Studies in Church History* 6 (1970): 29–38.

207. Ibid., 34–35. See also Claire Stancliffe, "Kings and Conversion: Some Comparisons between the Roman Mission to England and Patrick's to Ireland," *Fruhmittelalterliche Studien* 14 (1980): 59–94, esp. 60–61.

208. It is also quite likely that Mellitus was carrying the letter to Ethelbert.

209. Gregory, *Ep.* 11.56.

210. Successful or not, it is Gregory's approach that is at issue.

211. Note additionally the letter sent to Bertha, Ethelbert's wife, with the individualized mandates regarding her role as Christian queen and wife. Gregory, *Ep.* 11.35.

212. Markus argues that the second letter is an anomaly, inconsistent with Gregory's approach to conversion. He believes that the letter to Ethelbert was indicative of an overarching missionary strategy of coercive power for the conversion of all peoples. Markus, "Gregory the Great," 34–35.

213. Bede, *Ecclesiastical History of the English People [Historia ecclesiastica gentis Anglorum]* 27 (Bertram Colgrave, crit. ed. [Oxford: Clarendon Press, 1969]).

214. Gregory, *Responsa [Libellus responsionum]* 6, 8 (in Bede, *HE*).

215. Gregory, *Responsa* 7.

216. Margaret Deanesly and Paul Grosjean, "The Canterbury Edition of the Answers of Pope Gregory I to St. Augustine," *Journal of Ecclesiastical History* 10 (1959): 1–49. Heinrich Brechter raised the original objection in 1941. See his *Die Quellen zur Angelsachsenmission Gregors des Grossen* (Münster: Aschendorff, 1941). See also Paul Meyvaert, "Le libellus responsionum à Augustin de Cantorbéry: Une oeuvre authentique de saint Grégoire le Grand," in Fontaine, *Grégoire le Grand,* 543–50.

217. Gregory, *Ep.* 11.27.

218. Gregory, *Ep.* 8.4.

219. Gregory, *Ep.* 5.46, 7.29, and 9.86 respectively.

220. E.g. Gregory, *Ep.* 9.86; cf. *PR* 2.6.

221. Gregory, *Ep.* 3.2. He offers the same message in *Ep.* 10.12 and 10.15.

222. See, for example, the list of vices in the letter to Abbot Connon. Gregory, *Ep.* 11.9.

223. Gregory, *Ep.* 2.24.

224. Gregory, *Ep.* 2.29.

225. For example, note the story of a group of monks, aided by St. Andrew, who overcame demonic possession. Gregory, *Ep.* 11.26.

226. More than fifty letters attest to the threat posed by the Lombards or the dilapidated state of the city. As for Gregory's illnesses, see Gregory, *Ep.* 2.38, 8.29, and 9.176.

227. For example, note Gregory, *Ep.* 9.157 to the bishops of Greece, *Ep.* 9.232 to a wealthy friend in Italy, and *Ep.* 11.37 to Ethelbert, king of the Angli.

228. Gregory, *Ep.* 10.20 and 10.15 respectively.

229. Gregory, *Ep.* 10.20 and 10.15.

230. Gregory, *Ep.* 11.59.

231. Gregory, *Ep.* 11.225.

232. Gregory, *Ep.* 11.30.

233. In a letter addressed to a new abbot, Gregory, *Ep.* 6.49, Gregory cautioned that the abbot should refuse any man whose wife was not also willing to enter a monastery.

234. Aug., *Ep.* 262.

235. Francis Clark, *The Pseudo-Gregorian Dialogues* (Leiden: E. J. Brill, 1987).

236. Throughout his corpus, Gregory describes the world of spirits and demons, miracles and wonders. Many of the stories presented in the *Dialogues* are retold in the correspondence and homilies. See William McCready's excellent treatment of the miraculous in Gregory's corpus. McCready, *Signs of Sanctity: Miracles in the Thought of Gregory the Great* (Toronto: Pontifical Institute of Medieval Studies, 1989). See also Paul Meyvaert, "The Enigma of Gregory the Great's Dialogues: A Response to Francis Clark," *Journal of Ecclesiastical History* 39 (1988): 335–81.

237. Cf. Brakke, *Athanasius.*

238. For Gregory's "library," see Joan M. Petersen, *The Dialogues of Gregory the Great in the Late Antique Cultural Background* (Toronto: Pontifical Institute of Medieval Studies, 1984), 151–88. Petersen argues that Gregory had access to a number of Greek texts in Latin translation, including the *Apophthegmata Patrum,* the *Lausiac History,* the *History of the Monks,* the *Life of Antony,* and possibly the *History of Monks of Syria* of Theodoret of Cyrus (which includes the life of St. Symeon Stylites).

239. Theodoret of Cyrus, *Life of St. Symeon,* in his *History of the Monks of Syria [Historia Religiosa]* 26.6 (P. Canivet and A. Leroy-Molinghen, crit. eds., SC 234, 257); Ath., *V. Ant.* 3–4; and Sulpicius Severus, *Life of St. Martin of Tours [Vita Martini]* 5 (J. Fontaine, crit. ed., SC 133–35). With respect to Symeon, I refer to the *vita* by Theodoret. This was not the only life to circulate, however. At least two others existed, which offered a different perspective. See Robert Doran, *The Lives of Simeon Stylites* (Kalamazoo, MI: Cistercian Publications, 1992).

240. For example, Antony wrestles with the devil, Symeon endures the heat and cold of the desert, and Hilarion conquers lust. Ath., *V. Ant.* 8–12, Theodoret, *Life of St. Symeon* 22–23, and Jerome, *Life of St. Hilary [Vita S. Hilarionis]* 5 (J.-P. Migne, ed., PL 23).

241. Gregory, *Dia.* 2.1. Benedict is assisted by a monk (he receives the monastic garb), but this assistance is not spiritual.

242. Recall Symeon's fight to survive on his pillar or Martin's determination to sleep in a haunted cemetery.

243. Gregory, *Dia.* 2.12.

244. Gregory, *Dia.* 2.8.

245. Gregory, *Dia.* 2.8.

246. Gregory, *Dia.* 2.3.

247. "A superior ought to bear patiently with a community of evil men as long as it has some devout members who can benefit from his presence. When none of the members is devout enough to give any promise of good results, his efforts to help such a community will prove to be a serious mistake." Gregory, *Dia.* 2.3

248. Gregory, *Dia.* 2.16.

248. Gregory, *Dia.* 2.2.

250. Adalbert de Vogüé, "Benedict, Model of the Spiritual Life," in *Word and Spirit* (Still River, MA: St. Bede's Publications, 1981), 2:59–72.

251. Ath., *V. Ant.* 8–12.

252. E.g., Gregory, *Dia.* 2.10 and 2.12–14.

253. Gregory, *Dia.* 2.16.

254. Gregory, *Dia.* 2.16.

255. Gregory, *Dia.* 2.36.

Conclusion

1. Paul the Deacon, *Life of Gregory* 28–29; John the Deacon, *Life of Gregory* 4.69–80. See also P. A. B. Llewellyn, "The Roman Church in the Seventh Century: The Legacy of Gregory I," *Journal of Ecclesiastical History* 25 (1974): 365–66; and Dudden, *Gregory the Great,* 268–71.

2. John the Deacon, *Life of Gregory* 4.69.

3. Ibid.

4. See Llewellyn, "Roman Church," 365.

5. As Llewellyn has shown in "Roman Church," the papacy in the early seventh century oscillated for a time between supporters and detractors of Gregory's policies. With the death of Pope Honorius in 638, however, only one pope during the rest of the century (John IV, 640–42) had any monastic training at the time of his election. As a consequence, the old clerical establishment retained control in the Curia.

6. For more on Gregory's reputation in the East, see François Halkin, "Le Pape S. Grégoire le Grand dans l'hagiographie byzantine," *Orientalia Christiana Periodica* 21 (1955): 109–14.

7. Though Gregory makes no direct acknowledgment of them in the *Pastoral Rule,* the collective works of Augustine and John Cassian were also an important part of his theological formation. However, Gregory's appropriation of their ideas was not uncritical.

Bibliography

PRIMARY SOURCES

Ambrose. *On the Office [De officiis]*. Critical ed. Edited by Maurice Testard. Paris: Les Belles Lettres, 1984–92.

Ammonas. *Letters [Epistulae]*. Translated by Derwas J. Chitty and Sebastian T. Brock. In *The Letters of Ammonas: Successor to Saint Antony*. Oxford: SLG Press, 1979.

Antony. *Letters [Epistulae]*. Edited and translated by Samuel Rubenson. In *The Letters of St. Antony: Monasticism and the Making of a Saint*. Minneapolis: Fortress Press, 1995.

Apophthegmata Patrum. Edited by J.-P. Migne. PG 65.71–440.

Aristotle. *Rhetoric [Ars rhetorica]*. Critical ed. Edited by Rudolph Kassel. Berlin: De Gruyter, 1971.

Athanasius. *Against the Gentiles [Contra gentiles]*. Critical ed. Edited by P. Camelot. SC 18.

———. *Apology against the Arians [Apologia contra Arianos]*. Critical ed. Edited by Jan M. Szymusiak. SC 56.

———. *Apology to Constantine [Apologia ad Constantium]*. Critical ed. Edited by Jan M. Szymusiak. SC 56.

———. *Festal Index [Chronicon praevium]*. In *Histoire "acéphale" et Index syriaque des Lettres festales d'Athanase d' Alexandrie*. Critical ed. Edited and translated by Annik Martin and Marcelline Albert. SC 317.

———. *Festal Letters (preserved in Coptic) [Epistolae festales]*. Translated by David Brakke. In *Athanasius and Politics of Asceticism,* by David Brakke (Oxford: Clarendon Press, 1995), 320–34.

———. *Festal Letters (preserved in Greek) [Epistolae festales]*. Edited by J.-P. Migne. PG 26.

———. *First Letter to Monks [Ad monachos I]*. Edited by J.-P. Migne. PG 25b.

———. *Letter to Ammoun [Ad Amunem]*. Edited by J.-P. Migne. PG 26.

———. *Letter to Dracontius [Ad Dracontium]*. Edited by J.-P. Migne. PG 25b.

———. *Letter to Marcellinus [Ad Marcellinum]*. Edited by J.-P. Migne. PG 27.

———. *Letter to Rufianus [Ad Rufinianum]*. Edited by J.-P. Migne. PG 26.

———. *Letter to Serapion [Ad Serapionem]*. Edited by J.-P. Migne. PG 25b.

———. *Letters (preserved in Greek) [Epistulae]*. Edited by J.-P. Migne. PG 25–27.

———. *Letters to Virgins (preserved in Coptic) [Epistulae virginibus].* Translated by David Brakke. In *Athanasius and Politics of Asceticism,* by David Brakke (Oxford: Clarendon Press, 1995), 274–302.

———. *Life of Antony [Vita Antonii].* Critical ed. Edited by G. Bartelink. SC 400.

———. *On Sickness and Health [De morbo et valetudine].* Critical ed. Edited by Franz Diekamp. In *Analecta Patristica: Texte und abhandlungen zur griechischen patristik.* Rome: Pont. Institutum Orientalium Studorium, 1938.

———. *On the Incarnation [De incarnatione].* Critical ed. Edited by Charles Kannengiesser. SC 199.

———. *Second Letter to Horsisius [Epistola II ad Orsisium].* Edited by J.-P. Migne. PG 26.3.

———. *Second Letter to Monks [Ad monachos II].* Edited by J.-P. Migne. PG 26.

Augustine. *Against Cresconius the Grammarian [Contra Cresconium Grammaticum].* Critical ed. Edited by M. Petschenig. CSEL 52.

———. *Against Faustus the Manichean [Contra Faustum Manichaeum].* Critical ed. Edited by I. Zycka. CSEL 25.

———. *Against the Academics [Contra academicos].* Critical ed. Edited by W. M. Green. CCSL 29.

———. *Against the Letters of Petilian [Contra litteras Petiliani].* Critical ed. Edited by M. Petschenig. CSEL 52.

———. *Confessions [Confessiones].* Critical ed. Edited by L. Verheijen. CCSL 27.

———. *Lectures on the Gospel of John [In euangelium Ioannis tractatus].* Critical ed. Edited by R. Willems. CCSL 36.

———. *Letters [Epistulae].* Critical ed. Edited by A. Goldbacher et al. CSEL 34, 44, 57, 58, 88.

———. *Letters Recently Discovered [Epistolae ex duobus codicibus nuper in lucem prolatae].* Critical ed. Edited by Johannes Divjak. CSEL 88.

———. *On Baptism, against the Donatists [De baptismo].* Critical ed. Edited by Michael Petschenig. CSEL 51.

———. *On Catechizing the Ignorant [De catechizandis rudibus].* Critical ed. Edited by I. Bauer. CCSL 46.

———. *On Christian Teaching [De doctrina Christiana].* Critical ed. Edited by I. Martin. CCSL 32.

———. *On Correction and Grace [De correptione et gratia].* Edited by J.-P. Migne. PL 44.

———. *On Grace and Free Will [De gratia et libero arbitrio].* Edited by J.-P. Migne. PL 44.

———. *On Holy Virginity [De sancta virginitate].* Critical ed. Edited by I. Zycha. CSEL 41.

———. *On Marriage and Concupiscence [De nuptiis et concupiscentia].* Critical ed. Edited by C. F. Urba. CSEL 42.

———. *On Nature and Grace against Pelagius [De natura et gratia contra Pelagium].* Critical ed. Edited by C. F. Urba. CSEL 60.

———. *On Order [De ordine]*. Critical ed. Edited by W. M. Green. CCSL 29.

———. *On the Blessed Life [De beata vita]*. Critical ed. Edited by W. M. Green. CCSL 29.

———. *On the City of God [De civitate Dei]*. Critical ed. Edited by B. Dombart. CCSL 47–48.

———. *On the Good of Marriage [De bono coniugali]*. Critical ed. Edited by I. Zycha. CSEL 41.

———. *On the Good of Widowhood [De bono viduitatis]*. Critical ed. Edited by I. Zycha. CSEL 41.

———. *On the Grace of Christ and Original Sin [De gratia Christi et de peccato originali]*. Critical ed. Edited by C. F. Urba. CSEL 42.

———. *On the Guilt and Remission of Sins [De peccatorum meritis et remissione]*. Critical ed. Edited by C. F. Urba. CSEL 60.

———. *On the Morals of the Catholic Church [De moribus ecclesiae catholicae]*. Edited by J.-P. Migne. PL 32.

———. *On the Morals of the Manicheans [De moribus Manichaeorum]*. Edited by J.-P. Migne. PL 32.

———. *On the Usefulness of Believing [De utilitate credendi]*. Critical ed. Edited by I. Zycka. CSEL 25.

———. *On the Work of Monks [De opere monachorum]*. Critical ed. Edited by I. Zycha. CSEL 41.

———. *Retractions [Retractiones]*. Critical ed. Edited by A. Mutzenbecher. CCSL 57.

———. *Sermons [Sermones]*. Edited by J.-P. Migne. PL 38–39; PLS 2.

———. *Soliloquies [Soliloquiorum]*. Critical ed. Edited by W. Hörmann. CSEL 89.

———. *To Simplicianus [Ad Simplicianum]*. Critical ed. Edited by A. Mutzenbecher. CCSL 44.

———. *Unfinished Work against Julian [Contra Iuliani opus imperfectum]*. Critical ed. Edited by M. Zelzer. CSEL 85.

Basil. *Letters [Epistulae]*. Critical ed. Edited by Yves Courtonne. 3 vols. Paris: Les Belles Lettres, 1957, 1961, 1966.

———. *Longer Rules [Regulae fusius tractatae]*. In *Ascetic Works [Ascetica]*, edited by J.-P. Migne. PG 31.

———. *Morals [Moralia]*. In *Ascetic Works [Ascetica]*, edited by J.-P. Migne. PG 31.

———. *On the Holy Spirit [De Spiritu Sancto]*. Critical ed. Edited by B. Pruche. SC 17.

Bede. *Ecclesiastical History of the English People [Historia ecclesiastica gentis Anglorum]*. Critical ed. Edited by Bertram Colgrave. Oxford: Clarendon Press, 1969.

Benedict. *Rule of St. Benedict [Regula Benedicti]*. Critical ed. Edited by J. Neufville. SC 181–82.

Book of Pontiffs [Liber pontificalis]. Critical ed. Edited by Louis Duchesne. Paris, 1886–92.

Cassian, John. *Conferences [Conlationes]*. Critical ed. Edited by M. Petschenig. CSEL 13.

———. *Institutes [Institutiones]*. Critical ed. Edited by M. Petschenig. CSEL 17.

————. *On the Incarnation of the Lord, against Nestorius [De incarnatione Domini contra Nestorium]*. Critical ed. Edited by M. Petschenig. CSEL 17.

Cicero. *On the Making of an Orator [De optimo genere oratorum]*. Critical ed. Edited by A. S. Wilkens. In *M. Tulli Ciceronis rhetorica,* vol. 2. Oxford: Oxford University Press, 1903.

————. *On the Office [De officiis]*. Critical ed. Edited by M. Winterbottom. New York: Oxford University Press, 1994.

Didache. Critical ed. Edited by Adolf von Harnack. Reprinted in *Die Lehre der zwölf Apostel, nebst Untersuchungen zur ältesten Geschichte der Kirchenverfassung und des Kirchenrechts.* Berlin: Academie Verlag, 1991, vol. 2.

Didascalia Apostolorum. Edited and translated by R. H. Connolly. In *Didascalia Apostolorum: The Syriac Version Translated and Accompanied by the Verona Latin Fragments.* Oxford: Clarendon Press, 1929.

Epiphanius. *Refutation of All Heresies [Panarion/Adversus haereses]*. Critical ed. Edited by K. Holl and J. Dummer. GCS 25, 31, 37.

Evagrius of Pontus. *Praktikos.* Critical ed. Edited by A. Guillaumont and C. Guillaumont. SC 170.

Gennadius. *On the Lives of Illustrious Men [De viris illustribus]*. Critical ed. Edited by E. Richardson. Leipzig: J. C. Hinrichs, 1896.

Greek Life of St. Pachomius [Sancti Pachomii vitae graecae]. Critical ed. Edited by Francis Halkin. *Subsidia Hagiographica* 19 (1932).

Gregory I. *Book of Pastoral Rule [Liber regulae pastoralis]*. Critical ed. Edited by F. Rommel. SC 381–82.

————. *Dialogues [Dialogorum libri IV]*. Critical ed. Edited by Adalbert de Vogüé. SC 251, 260, 265.

————. *Homilies on the Gospels [Homiliae in Evangelia]*. Critical ed. Edited by R. Étaix. CCSL 141.

————. *Letters [Registrum epistularum]*. Critical ed. Edited by D. Norberg. CCSL 140–140A.

————. *Morals on the Book of Job [Moralia in Job]*. Critical ed. Edited by M. Adriaen. CCSL 143, 143A, 143B.

————. *On First Kings [In I Librum Primum Regum]*. Critical ed. Edited by P. Verbraken. CCSL 144.

————. *Responsa [Libellus responsionum]*. In Bede, *Ecclesiastical History of the English People [Historia ecclesiastica gentis Anglorum]*, critical ed., edited by Bertram Colgrave. Oxford: Clarendon Press, 1969.

Gregory Nazianzen. *Blessings of Various Lives [Variorum vitae generum beatitudines]*. Edited by J.-P. Migne. PG 37.

————. *Letters [Epistulae]*. Critical ed. Edited by P. Gallay. 2 vols. Paris: Les Belles Lettres, 1967.

————. *On God and Man: The Theological Poetry of St. Gregory Nazianzus.* Translated by P. Gilbert. Crestwood, NY: St. Vladimir's Seminary Press, 2001.

———. *On Himself and the Bishops [De seipso et de episcopis]*. Edited by J.-P. Migne. PG 37.

———. *On His Own Affairs [De rebus suis]*. Edited by J.-P. Migne. PG 37.

———. *On His Own Life [De vita sua]*. Edited by J.-P. Migne. PG 37.

———. *On the Different Walks of Life [De diversis vitae generibus]*. Edited by J.-P. Migne. PG 37.

———. *On the Incarnation against Apollinarius [De Incarnatione adversus Apolinarium]*. Edited by J.-P. Migne. PG 37.

———. *Orations 1–3 [Orationes 1–3]*. Critical ed. Edited by J. Bernardi. SC 247.

———. *Orations 4–5 [Orationes 4–5]*. Critical ed. Edited by J. Bernardi. SC 309.

———. *Orations 6–12 [Orationes 6–12]*. Critical ed. Edited by M.-A. Calvet-Sebasti. SC 405.

———. *Orations 13–19 [Orationes 13–19]*. Edited by J.-P. Migne. PG 35.

———. *Orations 20–23 [Orationes 20–23]*. Critical ed. Edited by J. Mossay. SC 270.

———. *Orations 24–26 [Orationes 24–26]*. Critical ed. Edited by J. Mossay. SC 284.

———. *Orations 27–31 [Orationes 27–31]*. Critical ed. Edited by P. Gallay. SC 250.

———. *Orations 32–37 [Orationes 32–37]*. Critical ed. Edited by C. Moreschini. SC 318.

———. *Orations 38–41 [Orationes 38–41]*. Critical ed. Edited by C. Moreschini. SC 358.

———. *Orations 42–43 [Orationes 42–43]*. Critical ed. Edited by J. Bernardi. SC 384.

———. *Poem of Lament over the Calamities Afflicting His Soul [De animae suae calamitatibus carmen lugubre]*. Edited by J.-P. Migne. PG 37.

———. *Prescriptions for Virgins [Praecepta ad virgines]*. Edited by J.-P. Migne. PG 37.

———. *St. Gregory Nazianzus: Three Poems*. Translated by D. Meehan. Fathers of the Church 75. Washington, DC: Catholic University Press, 1986.

———. *Theological Letters (101, 102, 202) [Epistulae]*. Critical ed. Edited by P. Gallay. SC 208.

Gregory of Tours. *History of the Franks [Historia Francorum]*. Critical ed. Edited by R. Buchner. Berlin, 1955.

Ignatius of Antioch. *Letters [Epistulae]*. Pt. 2, vols. 1–3 of *The Apostolic Fathers*. Critical ed. Edited by J. B. Lightfoot. 1885. Reprint, Peabody, MA: Hendrickson, 1989.

Irenaeus. *Against Heresies [Adversus haereses]*. Critical ed. Edited by A. Rousseau and L. Doutreleau. SC 100, 152–53, 210–11, 263–64, 293–94.

Jerome. *Against Jovinian [Aduersus Iouinianum]*. Edited by J.-P. Migne. PL 23.

———. *Life of St. Hilary [Vita S. Hilarionis]*. Edited by J.-P. Migne. PL 23.

John Chrysostom. *Against Those Men Who Cohabit with Virgins [Contra eos qui subintroductas habent virgines]*. Edited by J.-P. Migne. PG 47.

———. *Homilies on First Corinthians [Argumentum epistolae primae ad Corinthios]*. Edited by J.-P. Migne. PG 61.

———. *On Job [Fragmenta in beatum Job]*. Edited by J.-P. Migne. PG 51.

———. *On the Priesthood [De sacerdotio]*. Critical ed. Edited by A. M. Malingrey. SC 272.

John Climacus. *Ladder of Divine Ascent [Scala paradisi]*. Edited by J.-P. Migne. PG 88.

John the Deacon. *Life of Gregory [Vita Gregorii Magni]*. Edited by J.-P. Migne. PL 75.

Origen. *Commentary on the Gospel According to Matthew [Commentaria in Evangelium secundum Matthaeum]*. Edited by J.-P. Migne. PG 13.

———. *On First Principles [De principiis]*. Critical ed. Edited by Paul Koetschau. New York: Harper and Row, 1966.

Palladius. *Dialogue on the Life of John Chrysostom [Dialogus de vita Chrysostomi]*. Critical ed. Edited by A.-M. Malingrey. SC 341–42.

Paul the Deacon. *Life of Gregory [Vita Gregorii]*. Edited by J.-P. Migne. PL 75.

Plutarch. *On the Delays of the Divine Vengeance [De sera numinis vindicta]*. Critical ed. Edited by Robert Klaerr and Yvonne Vernière. In *Plutarch's Moral Works,* vol. 7. Paris: Les Belles Lettres, 1974.

Pomerius. *On the Contemplative Life [De vita contemplativa]*. Edited by J.-P. Migne. PL 59.

Porphyry. *Life of Pythagoras [Vita Pythagori]*. Critical ed. Edited by Édouard des Places. Paris: Les Belles Lettres, 1922.

Possidius. *Life of Augustine [Vita Augustini]*. Edited by J.-P. Migne. PL 32.

Procopius Caesariensis. *On the Wars [De belli]*. Critical ed. Edited by J. Haury. Teubner Series. Leipzig, 1905–13.

Prosper of Aquitaine. *Against the Conferencer [Liber contra collatorem]*. Edited by J.-P. Migne. PL 51.

Pseudo-Dionysius. *Ecclesiastical Hierarchy [De ecclesiastica hierarchia]*. Edited by J.-P. Migne. PG 3.

Rufinus. *Ecclesiastical History [Historia ecclesiastica]*. Critical ed. Edited by Theodore Mommsen. In *Die Kirchengeschichte*, vol. 2.2 of *Eusebius Werke,* revised by F. Winkelmann. Berlin: Akademie Verlag, 1999.

Rule of the Master [Regula magistri]. Critical ed. Edited by Adalbert de Vogüé. SC 105–7.

Siricius. *Letters [Epistulae]*. Edited by J.-P. Migne. PL 13.

Socrates Scholasticus. *Ecclesiastical History [Historia ecclesiastica]*. Critical ed. Edited by G. C. Hansen and M. Sirinjan. GCS, NF 1.

Sozomen. *Ecclesiastical History [Historia ecclesiastica]*. Critical ed. Edited by J. Bidez. Paris: Éditions du Cerf, 1983.

Sulpicius Severus. *Life of St. Martin of Tours [Vita Martini]*. Critical ed. Edited by J. Fontaine. SC 133–35.

Tertullian. *On Fasting, Against the Psychics [De jeiunio adversus Psychicos]*. Edited by Franciscus Oehler. In *Tertulliani quae supersunt omnia.* Liepzig: J. B. Hirschfeld, 1853.

———. *Prescription against Heretics [De praescriptione haereticorum]*. Critical ed. Edited by R. F. Refoulé. SC 46.

Theodoret of Cyrus. *Life of St. Symeon.* In his *History of the Monks of Syria [Historia religiosa]*. Critical ed. Edited by P. Canivet and A. Leroy-Molinghen. SC 234, 257.

SECONDARY SOURCES

Alexe, Stephan. "Le discernement selon saint Jean Cassien." *Studia Patristica* 30 (1997): 129–35.

Allen, Paul. "The Justinianic Plague." *Byzantion* 49 (1979): 5–20.

Anatolios, Khaled. *Athanasius: The Coherence of His Thought.* London: Routledge, 1998.

Anderson, Gary. "Celibacy or Consummation in the Garden? Reflections on Early Jewish and Christian Interpretations of the Garden of Eden." *Harvard Theological Review* 82 (1989): 121–48.

———. *The Genesis of Perfection: Adam and Eve in Jewish and Christian Imagination.* Louisville, KY: Westminster John Knox Press, 2001.

Appel, Regis. "Cassian's Discretio." *American Benedictine Review* 17 (1966): 20–29.

Arnold, Duane. *The Early Episcopal Career of Athanasius of Alexandria.* Notre Dame: University of Notre Dame Press, 1991.

Azkoul, Michael. "Peccatum Originale: The Pelagian Controversy." *Patristic and Byzantine Review* 3 (1984): 39–53.

Bacchi, Lee. "A Ministry Characterized by and Exercised in Humility: The Theology of Ordained Ministry in the Letters of Augustine of Hippo." In *Augustine: Presbyter Factus Sum,* edited by J. Leinhard. New York: Peter Lang, 1993.

Banniard, Michel. *Viva Voce.* Paris: Institut des Études Augustiniennes, 1992.

Barnard, Leslie. "The Letters of Athanasius to Ammoun and Dracontius." *Studia Patristica* 26 (1993): 354–59.

———. *The Monastic Letters of Saint Athanasius the Great.* Oxford: SLG Press, 1994.

———. "Two Notes on Athanasius." *Orientalia Christiana Periodica* 41 (1975): 348–49.

Barnes, Timothy. *Athanasius and Constantius: Theology and Politics in the Constantinian Empire.* Cambridge, MA: Harvard University Press, 1993.

Batiffol, Pierre. *Saint Grégoire le Grand.* Paris: J. Gabalda, 1928.

Bauer, Walter. *Orthodoxy and Heresy in Earliest Christianity.* Tübingen: Mohr, 1934.

Beck, Henry G. *The Pastoral Care of Souls in South-East France during the Sixth Century.* Rome: Apud Aedes Universitatis Gregorianae, 1950.

BeDuhn, Jason. *The Manichaean Body: In Discipline and Ritual.* Baltimore: Johns Hopkins University Press, 2000.

Behr, John. *The Way to Nicaea.* Crestwood, NY: St. Vladimir's Seminary Press, 2001.

Belche, Jean-Pierre. "Die Bekehrund zum Christentum nach Augustins Büchlein *De Catechizandis Rudibus.*" *Augustiniana* 27 (1977): 26–69.

Bernard, R. "La prédestination du Christ total selon saint Augustin." *Recherches Augustiniennes* 3 (1956): 1–58.

Bonner, Gerald. "Pelagianism and Augustine." *Augustinian Studies* 23 (1992): 34.

Brachtendorf, Johannes. "Cicero and Augustine on the Passions." *Revue des Études Augustiniennes* 43 (1997): 289–308.

Brakke, David. *Athanasius and the Politics of Asceticism.* Oxford: Clarendon Press, 1995. Reprint, Baltimore: Johns Hopkins University Press, 1998.

————. "Canon Formation and Social Conflict in Fourth-Century Egypt: Athanasius of Alexandria's Thirty-ninth Festal Letter." *Harvard Theological Review* 87 (1994): 395–419.

————. "The Egyptian Afterlife of Origenism: Conflicts over Embodiment in Coptic Sermons." *Orientalia Christiana Periodica* 66 (2000): 277–93.

————. "The Making of Monastic Demonology." *Church History* 70 (2001): 19–48.

Brechter, Heinrich. *Die Quellen zur Angelsachsenmission Gregors des Grossen.* Münster: Aschendorff, 1941.

Bright, Pamela. "The Combat of the Demons in Antony and Origen." In *Origeniana Septima,* edited by W. Bienert and U. Kühneweg, 339–43. Leuven: Leuven University Press, 1997.

Brown, Peter. *Augustine of Hippo.* Berkeley: University of California Press, 1967.

————. *The Body and Society: Men, Women and Sexual Renunciation in Early Christianity.* New York: Columbia University Press, 1988.

————. *Cult of the Saints: Its Function in Latin Christianity.* Chicago: University of Chicago Press, 1981.

————. "Eastern and Western Christendom in Late Antiquity: A Parting of the Ways." In *Society and the Holy in Late Antiquity,* 166–95. Berkeley: University of California Press, 1982.

————, ed. *The Philosopher and Society in Late Antiquity: Protocol of the Colloquy.* Center for Hermeneutical Studies in Hellenistic and Modern Culture, Protocol Series. Berkeley, CA: Center for Hermeneutic Studies, 1980.

————. *Power and Persuasion.* Madison: University of Wisconsin Press, 1992.

————. "The Rise and Function of the Holy Man in Late Antiquity." *Journal of Roman Studies* 61 (1971): 80–101.

————. *The Rise of Western Christendom: Triumph and Diversity, 200–1000.* Cambridge: Blackwell, 1996.

————. "The Saint as Exemplar in Late Antiquity." In *Saints and Virtues,* edited by J. S. Hawley, 3–14. Berkeley: University of California Press, 1987.

————. "St. Augustine's Attitude to Religious Coercion." *Journal of Religious Studies* 54 (1964): 107–16.

————. "Sorcery, Demons and the Rise of Christianity from Late Antiquity into the Middle Ages." In *Witchcraft: Confessions and Accusations,* edited by M. Douglas, 17–45. London: Tavistock, 1970.

Brown, T. S. "The Interplay between Roman and Byzantine Traditions and Local Sentiment in the Exarchate of Ravenna." In *Settimane di Studio del Centro Italiano di Studi sull'Alto Medioevo* 36 (1988): 127–60.

Burtchaell, James. *From Synagogue to Church: Public Services and Offices in the Earliest Christian Communities.* Cambridge: Cambridge University Press, 1992.

Burton-Christie, Douglas. "Scripture, Self-Knowledge and Contemplation in Cassian's *Conferences.*" *Studia Patristica* 25 (1993): 339–45.

————. *The Word in the Desert.* New York: Oxford University Press, 1992.

Cameron, Averil. *Christianity and the Rhetoric of Empire: The Development of Christian Discourse.* Berkeley: University of California Press, 1994.

Campenhausen, Hans von. "Polykarp und die Pastoralen." In *Aus der Frühzeit des Christentums: Studien zur Kirchengeschichte des ersten und zweiten Jahrhunderts,* 197–252. Tübingen: Mohr, 1963.

Camplani, Alberto. *Le Lettere festali di Atanasio di Allessandria: Studio storico-critico.* Rome: C.I.M., 1989.

Casiday, Augustine. "Cassian against the Pelagians." *Studia Monastica* 46 (2004): 7–23.

Cavadini, John C., ed. *Gregory the Great: A Symposium.* Notre Dame: University of Notre Dame Press, 1995.

Chadwick, Henry. *Expectations of Justice in the Age of Augustine.* Philadelphia: University of Pennsylvania Press, forthcoming.

————. "The New Sermons of St. Augustine." *Journal of Theological Studies,* n.s., 47 (1996): 69–91.

————. *Priscillian of Avila: The Occult and the Charismatic in the Early Church.* Oxford: Clarendon Press, 1976.

————. *The Role of the Christian Bishop in Ancient Society.* Protocol Series of the Colloquies of the Center 35. Berkeley: Center for Hermeneutical Studies in Hellenism and Modern Studies, 1979.

Chadwick, Owen. "Euladius of Arles." *Journal of Theological Studies* 46 (1945): 200–205.

————. *John Cassian: A Study in Primitive Monasticism.* Cambridge: Cambridge University Press, 1950.

Chéné, Jean. "Les origines de la controverse semi-pélagienne." *L'Année Théologique Augustinienne* 14 (1953): 56–109.

Chitty, Derwas. *The Desert a City.* London: Oxford University Press, 1966.

Christopher, Joseph. *St. Augustine: The First Catechetical Instruction.* Westminster, MD: Newman Bookshop, 1946.

Chryssavgis, John. *Soul Mending: The Art of Spiritual Direction.* Brookline, MA: Holy Cross Orthodox Press, 2000.

Clark, Elizabeth. "'Adam's Only Companion': Augustine and the Debate on Marriage." *Recherches Augustiniennes* 21 (1986): 139–62.

————. "Asceticism." In *Augustine through the Ages,* edited by Allan Fitzgerald. Grand Rapids, MI: Eerdmans, 1999.

————. *Jerome Chrysostom and Friends.* New York: Edwin Mellon Press, 1979.

————. *The Origenist Controversy: The Cultural Construction of an Early Christian Debate.* Princeton: Princeton University Press, 1992.

————. "Patrons, Not Priests: Gender and Power in Late Ancient Christianity." *Gender and History* 2 (1990): 253–73.

————. *Reading Renunciation: Asceticism and Scripture in Early Christianity.* Princeton: Princeton University Press, 1999.

———. "Theory and Practice in Late Ancient Asceticism: Jerome, Chrysostom and Augustine." *Journal of Feminist Studies in Religion* 5 (1989): 25–46.

———. "Vitiated Seeds and Holy Vessels: Augustine's Manichaean Past." In *Ascetic Piety and Women's Faith.* New York: E. Mellon Press, 1986.

Clark, Francis. *The Pseudo-Gregorian Dialogues.* Leiden: E. J. Brill, 1987.

Colish, Marcia L. "Cicero, Ambrose, and the Stoic Ethics: Transmission of Transformation?" In *The Classics in the Middle Ages,* edited by A. Bernardo and S. Levin, 95–112. Binghamton, NY: Center for Medieval and Early Renaissance Studies, 1990.

Courcelle, Pierre. *Latin Writers and Their Greek Sources.* Translated by H. Wedeck. Cambridge, MA: Harvard University Press, 1969.

Coyle, J. K. "Mani, Manicheanism." In *Augustine through the Ages,* edited by Allan Fitzgerald, 520–25. Grand Rapids, MI: Eerdmans, 1999.

Crespin, Rémi. *Ministère et sainteté: Pastorale du clergé et solution de la crise donatiste dans la vie et la doctrine de S. Augustin.* Paris: Études Augustiniennes, 1965.

Cunningham, Lawrence S. "Cassian's Hero and Discernment." In *Finding God in All Things,* edited by Michael J. Himes and Stephen J. Pope, 231–43. New York: Crossroad, 1996.

Dagens, Claude. "Grégoire le Grand et le monde Oriental." *Revista di Storia e Letteratura Religiosa* 17 (1981): 243–52.

———. "L'église universelle et le monde oriental chez saint Grégoire." *Istina* 4 (1975): 457–75.

———. "Saint Grégoire le Grand, Consul Dei: La mission prophétique d'un pasteur." In *Gregorio Magno e il suo tempo,* Studia Ephemeridis "Augustinianum" 33–45. Rome: Institutum Patristicum Augustinium, 1991.

———. *Saint Grégoire le Grand: Culture et expérience chrétiennes.* Paris: Études Augustiniennes, 1977.

Damian, Theodor. "Some Critical Considerations and New Arguments Reviewing the Problem of St. John Cassian's Birthplace." *Orientalia Christiana Periodica* 57 (1991): 257–80.

Davidson, I. J. "'De Officiis' and the Intellectual Climate of the Fourth Century." *Vigiliae Christianae* 49 (1995): 313–33.

Davis, Raymond. *The Book of Pontiffs.* Liverpool: Liverpool University Press, 1989.

Deanesly, Margaret, and Paul Grosjean. "The Canterbury Edition of the Answers of Pope Gregory I to St. Augustine." *Journal of Ecclesiastical History* 10 (1959): 1–49.

Decret, François. *L'Afrique manichéenne: Étude historique et doctrinale.* Paris: Études Augustiniennes, 1978.

Demacopoulos, George. "Ambivalence in Athanasius's Approach to Spiritual Direction." *Studia Patristica,* forthcoming.

———. "Leadership in the Post-Constantinian Church According to St. Gregory Nazianzen." *Louvain Studies* 30 (2005): 223–39.

————. "Liturgical Calendar in the East." In *Dictionary of the Middle Ages,* edited by William Chester Jordan, 14:327–30. New York: Charles Scribner's Sons, 2004.

————. "A Monk in Shepherd's Clothing: Pope Gregory I and the Asceticizing of Pastoral Direction." PhD diss., University of North Carolina at Chapel Hill, 2002.

————. "The Soteriology of Pope Gregory I: A Case against the Augustinian Interpretation." *American Benedictine Review* 54 (2003): 312–27.

Diesner, Hans-Joachim. "Possidius and Augustinus." *Studia Patristica* 6 (1962): 350–65.

Doran, Robert. *The Lives of Simeon Stylites.* Kalamazoo, MI: Cistercian Publications, 1992.

Dudden, Frederick H. *Gregory the Great.* New York: Longmans Green, 1907.

Elm, Susanna. "The Diagnostic Gaze: Gregory of Nazianzus' Theory of Orthodox Priesthood in His Orations 6 *De Pace* and 2 *Apologia de fuga sua.*" In *Orthodoxy, Christianity, History,* edited by S. Elm, É. Rebillard, and A. Romano, 83–100. Rome: École Française de Rome, 2000.

————. "Evagrius Ponticus' *Sententiae ad Virginem.*" *Dumbarton Oaks Papers* 45 (1991): 97–120.

————. "Hellenism and Historiography: Gregory of Nazianzus and Julian in Dialogue." In *The Cultural Turn in Late Ancient Studies: Gender, Asceticism and History,* edited by D. Martin and P. Cox Miller, 258–77. Durham: Duke University Press, 2005.

————. "Perceptions of Jerusalem Pilgrimage as Reflected in Two Early Sources on Female Pilgrimage (3rd and 4th Century AD)." *Studia Patristica* 20 (1989): 219–23.

————. "A Programmatic Life: Gregory of Nazianzus' *Orations* 42 and 43 and the Constantinopolitan Elites." *Arethusa* 33 (2000): 411–27.

————. *Virgins of God: The Making of Asceticism in Late Antiquity.* Oxford: Clarendon Press, 1994.

Eno, Robert. *St. Augustine: Letters 1*–29.* Washington, DC: Catholic University Press, 1989.

Ferrari, Leo. "Saint Augustine's Conversion Scene: The End of a Modern Debate?" *Studia Patristica* 20 (1989): 235–50.

Fitzgerald, Allan, ed. *Augustine through the Ages.* Grand Rapids, MI: Eerdmans, 1999.

Fleming, Julia. "By Coincidence or Design? Cassian's Disagreement with Augustine Concerning the Ethics of Falsehood." *Augustinian Studies* 29 (1998): 19–34.

Folliet, Georges. "Aux origines de l'ascétisme et du cénobitisme africain." *Studia Anselmiana* 46 (1961): 25–44.

————. "Le monachisme en Afrique de saint Augustin à saint Fulgence." In *Il monachesimo occidentale,* Studia Ephemerides Augustinianum 62, 291–316. Rome: Institutum Patristicum Augustinianum, 1998.

Fontaine, Jacques. "Valeurs antiques et valeurs chrétiennes dans la spiritualité des grands propriétaires terriens à la fin du IVe siècle occidental." In *Epektasis: Mélanges J. Daniélou,* edited by Jacques Fontaine and Charles Kannengiesser, 571–95. Paris: Beauchesne, 1972.

Ford, David. "The Interrelationship of Clergy and Laity within the Church According to St. John Chrysostom." *St. Vladimir's Theological Quarterly* 36 (1992): 329–53.

Frazee, Charles. "Anatolian Asceticism in the Fourth Century: Eustathios of Sebastea and Basil of Caesarea." *Catholic Historical Review* 66 (1980): 16–33.

Fredricksen, Paula. "Paul and Augustine: Conversion Narratives, Orthodox Traditions, and the Retrospective Self." *Journal of Theological Studies,* n.s., 37 (1986): 3–34.

Frend, W. H. C. *The Donatist Church.* Oxford: Clarendon Press, 1952.

Gessel, Wilhelm M. "Reform am Haupt: Die Pastoralregel Gregors des Grossen und die Besetzung von bischofsstühlen." In *Papsttum und Kirchenreform: Historische Beiträge. Festschrift für Georg Schwaiger zum 65,* edited by Manfred Weitlauff and Karl Hausberger, 17–36. St. Ottilien: EOS Verlag Ezabtei, 1990.

Giet, Stanislas. *Sasimes: Une méprise de saint Basile.* Paris: Librairie Lecoffre, 1941.

Glad, Clarence. *Paul and Philodemus: Adaptability in Epicurean and Early Christian Psychagogy.* Leiden: E. J. Brill, 1995.

Godding, Robert, ed. *Bibliografia di Gregorio Magno, 1890–1989.* Rome: Città Nuova, 1990.

———. "Les Dialogues . . . de Grégoire le Grand. A propos d'un livre récent." *Analecta Bollandiana* 106 (1988): 201–29.

Goehring, James. *Ascetics, Society and the Desert: Studies in Early Egyptian Monasticism.* Harrisburg, PA: Trinity International Press, 1999.

———. "The Dark Side of Landscape: Ideology and Power in the Christian Myth of the Desert." In *The Cultural Turn in Late Ancient Studies: Gender, Asceticism and History,* edited by D. Martin and P. Cox Miller, 136–49. Durham: Duke University Press, 2005.

———. "The Encroaching Desert: Literary Production and Ascetic Space in Early Christian Egypt." *Journal of Early Christian Studies* 1 (1993): 281–96.

Greeley, Dolores Lee. "John Chrysostom, 'On the Priesthood': A Model for Service." *Studia Patristica* 22 (1989): 121–28.

Griffe, Élie. "Cassien a-t-il été prêtre d' Antioche?" *Bulletin de Littérature Ecclésiastique* 55 (1954): 240–44.

Guillaumont, Antoine. *Les "Kephalaia gnostica" d'Evagre le Pontique et l'histoire de l'origénisme chez les Grecs et chez les Syriens.* Paris: Éditions du Seuil, 1962.

Guy, Jean-Claude. *Recherches sur la tradition grecque des Apophthegmata Patrum.* Subsidia Hagiographica 36. Brussels: Société des Bollandistes 1962.

Hadot, Pierre. *Philosophy as a Way of Life: Spiritual Exercises from Socrates to Foucault.* Edited by Arnold I. Davidson. Translated by Michael Chase. Oxford: Blackwell, 1995.

Hägg, T., and P. Rousseau, eds. *Greek Biography and Panegyric in Late Antiquity.* Berkeley: University of California Press, 2000.

Halkin, François. "Le pape S. Grégoire le Grand dans l'hagiographie byzantine." *Orientalia Christiana Periodica* 21 (1955): 109–14.

Harmless, William. *Augustine and the Catechumenate.* Collegeville, MN: Liturgical Press, 1995.

Harries, Jill. *Law and Empire in Late Antiquity.* Cambridge: Cambridge University Press, 1999.

Harrison, Verna. "Poverty, Social Involvement, and Life in Christ According to Saint Gregory the Theologian." *Greek Orthodox Theological Review* 39 (1994): 151–64.

Hauben, Hans. "The Melitian 'Church of the Martyrs': Christian Dissenters in Early Egypt." In *Ancient History in a Modern University,* edited by T. W. Hillard, 2:329–49. Grand Rapids, MI: Eerdmans, 1998.

Hausherr, Irénée. "La théologie du monachisme chez saint Jean Climaque." In *Théologie de la vie monastique,* 385–410. Paris: Aubier, 1961.

———. "The Monastic Theology of St. John Climacus." *American Benedictine Review* 38 (1987): 381–407.

———. *Spiritual Direction in the Early Christian East.* Translated by A. Gythiel. Kalamazoo, MI: Cistercian Publications, 1990. Originally published as *Direction spirituelle en orient autrefois.* Rome: Pont. Institutum Orientalium Studiorum, 1955.

Heinz, Hanspeter. "Der Bischofsspiegel des Mittelalters zur Regula Pastoralis Gregors des Grossen." In *Sendung und Dienst im bischöflichen Amt,* edited by J. Stimpfle, 113–35. St. Ottilien: EOS Verlag Erzabtei St. Ottilien 1991.

Herrin, Judith. *The Formation of Christendom.* Princeton: Princeton University Press, 1987.

Hillgarth, J. N. "Modes of Evangelization of Western Europe in the Seventh Century." In *Ireland and Christendom,* edited by P. Ni Chatháin and M. Richter, 311–31. Stuttgart: Klett-Cotta, 1987.

Holman, Susan. *The Hungry Are Dying: Beggars and Bishops in Roman Cappadocia.* Oxford: Oxford University Press, 2001.

Holtzen, Thomas. "The Therapeutic Nature of Grace in St. Augustine's *De gratia et libero arbitrio.*" *Augustinian Studies* 31 (2000): 93–115, esp. 108–9.

Holze, Heinrich. "Die Bedeutung der *experientia* in der monastischen Theologie Johannes Cassians." *Studia Patristica* 20 (1989): 256–63.

Hombert, Pierre-Marie. *Nouvelles recherches de chronologie augustinienne.* Paris: Institut d'Études Augustiniennes, 2000.

Hunter, David. "Augustinian Pessimism? A New Look at Augustine's Teaching on Sex, Marriage and Celibacy." *Augustinian Studies* 25 (1994): 153–77.

———. "Clerical Celibacy and the Veiling of Virgins." In *The Limits of Ancient Christianity: Essays on Late Antique Thought and Culture in Honor of R. A. Markus,* edited by William E. Klingshirn and Mark Vessey, 139–52. Ann Arbor: University of Michigan Press, 1999.

———. "Rereading the Jovinianist Controversy: Asceticism and Clerical Authority in Late Ancient Christianity." In *The Cultural Turn in Late Ancient Studies: Gender, Asceticism and History,* edited by D. Martin and P. Cox Miller, 119–35. Durham: Duke University Press, 2005.

Jenal, Georg. "Gregor der Grosse und die Stadt Rom (590–604)." In *Herrschaft und Kirche: Beiträge zur Enstehung und Wirkungsweise episcopaler und monastischer Organisationsformen,* edited by Friedrich Prinz, 123–30. Stuttgart: A. Hiersemann, 1988.

Jones, A. H. M. *The Later Roman Empire, 284–602.* 2 vols. 1964. Reprint, Baltimore: Johns Hopkins University Press, 1986.

Judic, Bruno. "La Bible miroir de pasteurs dans la Règle pastorale de Grégoire le Grand." In *Le monde latin antique et la Bible,* edited by Jacques Fontaine and Charles Pietri, 455–73. Paris: Beauchesne, 1985.

———. "Structure et fonction de la 'Regula Pastoralis.'" In *Grégoire le Grand,* edited by Jacques Fontaine, 409–17. Paris: Éditions du CNRS, 1986.

Kannengiesser, Charles. "Athanasius of Alexandria and the Ascetic Movement of His Time." In *Asceticism,* edited by Vincent L. Wimbush and Richard Valantasis, 479–92. Oxford: Oxford University Press, 1995.

———. "St. Athanasius of Alexandria Rediscovered: His Polemical and Pastoral Achievement." *Coptic Churches Review* 9 (1988): 68–74.

Kaufman, Peter I. "Augustine, Macedonius, and the Courts." *Augustinian Studies* 34 (2003): 67–82.

———. "Augustine, Martyrs and Misery." *Church History* 63 (1994): 1–14.

———. *Church, Book and Bishop.* Boulder, CO: Westview Press, 1996.

———. "The Lesson of Conversion: A Note on the Question of Continuity in Augustine's Understanding of Grace and Human Will." *Augustinian Studies* 11 (1980): 49–64.

———. *Redeeming Politics.* Princeton: Princeton University Press, 1992.

Klingshirn, William E., and Mark Vessey, eds. *The Limits of Ancient Christianity: Essays on Late Antique Thought and Culture in Honor of R. A. Markus.* Ann Arbor: University of Michigan Press, 1999.

Konstan, David. "How to Praise a Friend." In *Greek Biography and Panegyric in Late Antiquity,* edited by Tomas Hägg and Philip Rousseau, 160–79. Berkeley: University of California Press, 2000.

Krupp, R. A. *Shepherding the Flock of God: The Pastoral Theology of John Chrysostom.* New York: P. Lang, 1991.

Laistner, M. L. W. *Thought and Letters in Western Europe.* 2nd ed. Ithaca: Cornell University Press, 1966.

Lamberigts, Mathijs. "A Critical Evaluation of the Critics of Augustine's View of Sexuality." In *Augustine and His Critics: Essays in Honor of Gerald Bonner,* edited by Robert Dodaro and George Lawless, 176–97. London: Routledge, 2000.

Lamoreaux, John. "Episcopal Courts in Late Antiquity." *Journal of Early Christian Studies* 3 (1995): 143–67.

Lancel, Serge. *Actes de la Conférence de Carthage en 411.* 4 vols. Paris: Éditions du Cerf, 1972.

Lanzoin, F. *Le origini delle diocesi antiche d'Italia: Studio critico.* Studies and Texts 35. Rome: Tip. Poliglotta Vaticana, 1923.

Laporte, Jean. "Gregory the Great as a Theologian of Suffering." *Byzantine and Patristic Review* 1 (1982): 22–31.

Lawless, George. *Augustine of Hippo and His Monastic Rule.* Oxford: Clarendon Press, 1987.

———. "Augustine of Hippo as Preacher." In *St. Augustine the Bishop: A Book of Essays,* edited by F. LeMoine and C. Kleinhenz, 13–37. New York: Garland, 1994.

———. "Augustine's Decentring of Asceticism." In *Augustine and His Critics: Essays in Honor of Gerald Bonner,* edited by Robert Dodaro and George Lawless, 142–63. London: Routledge, 2000.

Levko, John. "The Relationship of Prayer to Discernment and Spiritual Direction for John Cassian." *Saint Vladimir's Theological Quarterly* 40 (1996): 155–71.

Leyser, Conrad. *Authority and Asceticism from Augustine to Gregory the Great.* Oxford: Oxford University Press, 2000.

———. "Expertise and Authority in Gregory the Great: The Social Function of *Peritia.*" In *Gregory the Great: A Symposium,* edited by John C. Cavadini, 38–61. Notre Dame: University of Notre Dame Press, 1995.

———. "'This Sainted Isle': Panegyric, Nostalgia, and the Invention of Lerinian Monasticism." In *The Limits of Ancient Christianity: Essays on Late Antique Thought and Culture in Honor of R.A. Markus,* edited by William E. Klingshirn and Mark Vessey, 188–206. Ann Arbor: University of Michigan Press, 1999.

Lienhard, Joseph. "On 'Discernment of Spirits' in the Early Church." *Theological Studies* 41 (1980): 505–29.

———. "St. Basil's 'Asceticon Parvum' and the 'Regula Benediti.'" *Studia Monastica* 22 (1980): 231–42.

Lieu, Samuel. *Manichaeism in the Later Roman Empire and Medieval China: A Historical Survey.* Manchester: Manchester University Press, 1985.

Lizzi, Rita. "La traduzione greca delle opere di Gregorio Magno: Dalla Regula pastoralis ai Dialoghi." In *Gregorio Magno e il suo tempo,* Studia Ephemeridis "Augustinianum" 33–34, 41–57. Rome: Institutum Patristicum Augustinium, 1991.

Llewellyn, P.A.B. "The Roman Church in the Seventh Century: The Legacy of Gregory I." *Journal of Ecclesiastical History* 25 (1974): 363–80.

Lochbrunner, Manfred. *Über das Priestertum: Historische und systematische Untersuchung zum Priesterbild des Johannes Chrysostomus.* Bonn: Borgengässer, 1993.

Lossky, Vladimir. *The Mystical Theology of the Eastern Church.* Crestwood, NY: St. Vladimir's Seminary Press, 1976.

Malingrey, Anne-Marie, ed. *Jean Chrysostome: Sur le sacerdoce.* Paris: Éditions du Cerf, 1980.

Maraval, Pierre. "Gregoire le Grand et les lieux saints d'Orient." In *Gregorio Magno e il suo tempo,* Studia Ephemeridis "Augustinianum" 33–34, 65–76. Rome: Institutum Patristicum Augustinium, 1991.

Markus, Robert. "The Chronology of the Gregorian Mission to England: Bede's Narrative and Gregory's Correspondence." *Journal of Ecclesiastical History* 14 (1963): 16–30.

———. *Conversion and Disenchantment in Augustine's Spiritual Career.* Villanova: University of Villanova Press, 1989.

———. *The End of Ancient Christianity.* Cambridge: Cambridge University Press, 1990.

————. "Gregory the Great and a Papal Missionary Strategy." *Studies in Church History* 6 (1970): 29–38.

————. *Gregory the Great and His World.* Cambridge: Cambridge University Press, 1998.

————. "Gregory the Great on Kings: Rulers and Preachers in the Commentary on 1 Kings." *Studies in Church History,* 2nd ser., 9 (1991): 7–21.

————. "Gregory the Great's *Rector* and Its Genesis." In *Grégoire le Grand,* edited by Jacques Fontaine, 137–45. Paris: Éditions du Centre National de la Recherche Scientifique, 1986.

————. "The Jew as a Hermeneutic Device: The Inner Life of a Gregorian Topos." In *Gregory the Great: A Symposium,* edited by John C. Cavadini, 1–15. Notre Dame: University of Notre Dame Press, 1995.

————. "The Legacy of Pelagius: Orthodoxy, Heresy and Conciliation." In *The Making of Orthodoxy: Essays in Honour of Henry Chadwick,* edited by R. Williams, 215–35. Cambridge: Cambridge University Press, 1989.

————. "The Sacred and the Secular: From Augustine to Gregory the Great." *Journal of Theological Studies,* n.s., 36 (1985): 84–96.

Marrou, Henri. "Jean Cassien à Marseille." *Revue du Moyen Âge Latin* 1 (1945): 5–26.

————. "La patrie de Jean Cassien." *Orientalia Christiana Periodica* 13 (1947): 588–96.

Martin, D., and P. Cox Miller, eds. *The Cultural Turn in Late Ancient Studies: Gender, Asceticism and History.* Durham: Duke University Press, 2005.

McCready, William D. *Signs of Sanctity: Miracles in the Thought of Gregory the Great.* Toronto: Pontifical Institute of Medieval Studies, 1989.

McCulloh, John M. "The Cult of Relics in the Letters and 'Dialogues' of Pope Gregory the Great: A Lexicographical Study." *Traditio* 32 (1976): 145–86.

McGuckin, John. "Autobiography as Apologia in St. Gregory Nazianzus." *Studia Patristica* 37 (2001): 160–77.

————. *St. Gregory Nazianzus.* Crestwood, NY: St. Vladimir's Seminary Press, 2001.

McLynn, Neil. *Ambrose of Milan: Church and Court in a Christian Capital.* Berkeley: University of California Press, 1994.

————. "Gregory Nazianzen's Basil: The Literary Construction of a Christian Friendship." *Studia Patristica* 37 (2001): 178–93.

————. "A Self-Made Holy Man: The Case of Gregory Nazianzen." *Journal of Early Christian Studies* 6 (1998): 463–84.

Merdinger, Jane. *Rome and the African Church in the Time of Augustine.* New Haven: Yale University Press, 1997.

Meyendorff, John. *Byzantine Theology: Historical Trends and Doctrinal Themes.* New York: Fordham University Press, 1974.

————. *Imperial Unity and Christian Divisions: The Church, 450–680.* Crestwood, NY: St. Vladimir's Seminary Press, 1989.

Meyvaert, Paul. "Diversity within Unity: A Gregorian Theme." *Heythrop Journal* 4 (1963): 141–62.

———. "The Enigma of Gregory the Great's Dialogues: A Response to Francis Clark." *Journal of Ecclesiastical History* 39 (1988): 335–81.

———. "Gregory the Great and the Theme of Authority." *Spode House Review* 3 (1966): 3–12.

———. "Le libellus responsionum à Augustin de Cantorbéry: Une oeuvre authentique de saint Grégoire le Grand." In *Grégoire le Grand,* edited by Jacques Fontaine, 543–50. Paris: Éditions du CNRS, 1986.

Miles, Margaret. *Augustine on the Body.* Missoula, MN: Scholars Press, 1979.

Munz, Peter. "John Cassian." *Journal of Ecclesiastical History* 11 (1960): 1–22.

Muyser, Jacob. "Contribution à l'étude des listes épiscopales de l'Église copte." *Bulletin de la Société d'Archéologie Copte* 10 (1944): 115–76.

Norris, Frederick. "Your Honor, My Reputation: St. Gregory of Nazianzus's Funeral Oration on St. Basil the Great." In *Greek Biography and Panegyric in Late Antiquity,* edited by Tomas Hägg and Philip Rousseau, 140–59. Berkeley: University of California Press, 2000.

Norris, Frederick, and Lionel Wickham. *Faith Gives Fullness to Reason.* Leiden: E. J. Brill, 1991.

O'Connell, R. J. "The *De Genesi contra Manichaeos* and the Origin of the Soul." *Revue des Études Augustiniennes* 39 (1993): 129–41.

O'Laughlin, Michael. "Closing the Gap between Antony and Evagrius." In *Origeniana Septima,* edited by W. Bienert and U. Kühneweg, 345–54. Leuven: Leuven University Press, 1997.

———. "New Questions Concerning the Origenism of Evagrius." In *Origeniana Quinta,* edited by R. Daly. Leuven: Leuven University Press, 1989.

Olphe-Galliard, M. "Vie contemplative et vie active d' après Cassien." *Revue d'Ascètique et de Mystique* 16 (1935): 252–88.

Oort, Johannes Van, Otto Wermelinger, and Gregory Wurst, eds. *Augustine and Manichaeism in the Latin West: Proceedings of the Fribourg-Utrecht Symposium of the International Association of Manichaean Studies.* Leiden: E. J. Brill, 2001.

Paronetto, Vera. "Une presence augustinienne chez Grégoire le Grand: Le *De catechizanis rudibus* dans la *Regula pastoralis.*" In *Grégoire le Grand,* edited by Jacques Fontaine, 511–19. Paris: Éditions du CNRS, 1986.

Petersen, Joan M. *The Dialogues of Gregory the Great in the Late Antique Cultural Background.* Toronto: Pontifical Institute of Medieval Studies, 1984.

———. "Did Gregory the Great Know Greek?" In *Orthodox Churches and the West,* edited by D. Baker, 121–34. Oxford: Basil Blackwell, 1976.

———. "Greek Influences upon Gregory the Great's Exegesis of Luke 15: 1–10 in His Homelia in Evang. II. 34." In *Grégoire le Grand,* edited by Jacques Fontaine, 522–29. Paris: Editions du CNRS, 1986.

———. "'Homo omnino Latinus'? The Theological and Cultural Background of Pope Gregory the Great." *Speculum* 62/63 (1987): 529–51.

Pettersen, Alvyn. *Athanasius and the Human Body.* Bristol: Bristol Press, 1990.

Pietri, Charles. "La Rome de Grégoire." In *Gregorio Magno e il suo tempo,* Studia Ephemeridis "Augustinianum" 33–34, 9–32. Rome: Institutum Patristicum Augustinium, 1991.

Pricoco, Salvatore. *L'isola dei santi: Il cenobio di Lerino e le origini del monachesimo gallico.* Rome: Edizioni dell'Ateneo and Bizzarri, 1978.

Prinz, Friedrich. *Frühes Mönchtum im Frankenreich: Kultur und Gesellschaft in Gallien, den Rheinlanden und Bayern am Beispiel der monastischen Entwicklung, 4. bis 8. Jahrhundert.* 2nd ed. Munich: R. Oldenbourg, 1988.

Quasten, Johannes. *Patrology.* Vol. 3. 1950. Reprint, Westminster, MD: Christian Classics, 1992.

Raikas, Kauko. "*Audientia Episcopalis*: Problematik zwischn Staat und Kirche bei Augustin." *Augustinianum* 37 (1997): 476–77.

Ramsey, Boniface. Introduction to *John Cassian: The Conferences,* translated by Boniface Ramsey. Ancient Christian Writers Series 57. Mahwah, NJ: Newman Press, 1997.

———. "Two Traditions on Lying and Deception in the Ancient Church." *Thomist* 49 (1985): 504–33.

Rapp, Claudia. "The Elite Status of Bishops in Late Antiquity in Ecclesiastical, Spiritual and Social Contexts." *Arethusa* 33 (2000): 379–99.

———. "'For Next to God, You Are My Salvation': Reflections on the Rise of the Holy Man in Late Antiquity." In *The Cult of the Saints in Late Antiquity and the Middle Ages: Essays on the Contribution of Peter Brown,* edited by J. Howard-Johnston and P. Hayward, 63–81. Oxford: Oxford University Press, 1999.

———. *Holy Bishops: The Nature of Christian Leadership in an Age of Transition.* Berkeley: University of California Press, 2005.

Rentinck, Pietro. *La cura pastorale in Antiochia nel IV secolo.* Rome: Università Gregoriana Editrice, 1970.

Richards, Jeffrey. *Consul of God: The Life and Times of Gregory the Great.* London: Routledge and Kegan Paul, 1980.

———. *The Popes and the Papacy in the Early Middle Ages, 476–752.* London: Routledge and Kegan Paul, 1979.

Riché, Pierre. *Écoles et enseignement dans le Haut Moyen Age.* Paris: Aubier Montaigne, 1979.

———. *Education et culture dans l'occident barbare, VIe–VIIIe siècles.* 2nd ed. Paris: Editions du Seuil, 1973.

Rist, John. *Augustine: Ancient Thought Baptized.* Cambridge: Cambridge University Press, 1994.

———. "Augustine on Free Will and Predestination." *Journal of Theological Studies,* n.s., 20 (1969): 420–27.

Rousseau, Philip. "Antony as Teacher in the Greek *Life*." In *Greek Biography and Panegyric in Late Antiquity,* edited by Tomas Hägg and Philip Rousseau, 89–109. Berkeley: University of California Press, 2000.

————. *Ascetics, Authority and the Church in the Age of Jerome and Cassian.* Oxford: Oxford University Press, 1978.

————. *Basil of Caesarea.* Berkeley: University of California Press, 1994.

————. "Cassian, Contemplation and the Coenobitic Life." *Journal of Ecclesiastical History* 26 (1975): 113–26.

————. "Christian Asceticism and the Early Monks." In *Early Christianity: Origins and Evolution to 600. In Honour of W.H.C. Frend,* edited by Ian Hazlett, 112–22. London: SPCK, 1991.

————. *Pachomius: The Making of a Community in Fourth-Century Egypt.* Berkeley: University of California Press, 1985.

————. "The Spiritual Authority of the 'Monk-Bishop': Eastern Elements in Some Western Hagiography of the Fourth and Fifth Centuries." *Journal of Theological Studies,* n.s., 23 (1971): 380–419.

Rousselle, Aline. *Porneia: On Desire and the Body in Antiquity.* Translated by F. Pheasant. Oxford: Basil Blackwell, 1988.

Russell, Frederick. "Augustine: Conversion by the Book." In *Varieties of Religious Conversion in the Middle Ages,* edited by J. Muldoon. Gainesville: University Press of Florida, 1997.

————. "Only Good Can Be Evil: The Genesis of Augustine's Secular Ambivalence." *Theological Studies* 51 (1990): 698–716.

Scheppard, Carol. "The Transmission of Sin in the Seed: A Debate between Augustine of Hippo and Julian of Eclanum." *Augustinian Studies* 27 (1996): 99–108.

Schmitt, Emile. "Le mariage dans la controverse pélagienne (412–430)." In *Le mariage chrétien dans l' oeuvre de saint Augustin: Une théologie baptismale de la vie conjugale.* Paris: Études Augustiniennes 1983.

Schöllgen, Georg. *Die Anfänge der Professionalisierung des Klerus und das kirchliche Amt in der syrischen Didaskalia.* Münster: Ashendorffe Verlagsbuchhandlung, 1988.

Simson, Otto von. *Sacred Fortress: Byzantine Art and Statecraft in Ravenna.* Chicago: University of Chicago Press, 1948.

Solignac, A. "Julien Pomère." In *Dictionnaire de spiritualité ascétique et mystique,* vol. 8. Paris: G. Beauchesne et Ses Fils, 1937–95.

Stancliffe, Clare. "Kings and Conversion: Some Comparisons between the Roman Mission to England and Patrick's to Ireland." *Fruhmittelalterliche Studien* 14 (1980): 59–94.

Stead, G. C. "Athanasius' Earliest Written Work." *Journal of Theological Studies,* n.s., 39 (1988): 76–91.

————. "Rhetorical Method in Athanasius." *Vigiliae Christianae* 30 (1976): 121–37.

Sterk, Andrea. "On Basil, Moses, and the Model Bishop: The Cappadocian Legacy of Leadership." *Church History* 67 (1998): 227–53.

————. *Renouncing the World yet Leading the Church: The Monk-Bishop in Late Antiquity.* Cambridge, MA: Harvard University Press, 2004.

Stewart, Columba. *Cassian the Monk.* Oxford: Oxford University Press, 1998.

Straw, Carol. *Gregory the Great: Perfection in Imperfection.* Berkeley: University of California Press, 1988.

Stuhlfarth, Walter. *Gregor I, der Große: Sein Leben bis zu seiner Wahl zum Papste nebst einer Untersuchung der ältesten Viten.* Heidelberg: C. Winter, 1913.

Summa, Gerd. *Geistliche Unterscheidung bie Johannes Cassian.* Studien zur systematischen und spirituellen Theologie 7. Würzburg: Echter, 1992.

Testard, Maurice. "Le *De officiis* de Ambroise: Observations philologiques et historique sur le sens et le contexte du traité." *Recherches Augustiniens* 28 (1995): 3–35.

Tilley, Maureen. "No Friendly Letters: Augustine's Correspondence with Women." In *The Cultural Turn in Late Ancient Studies: Gender, Asceticism and History,* edited by D. Martin and P. Cox Miller, 40–62. Durham: Duke University Press, 2005.

Trout, Dennis. *Paulinus of Nola: Life, Letters and Poems.* Berkeley: University of California Press, 1999.

Tuilier, André. "Grégoire le Grand et le titre de patriarche oecuménique." In *Grégoire le Grand,* edited by Jacques Fontaine, 69–82. Paris: Éditions du CNRS, 1986.

Uhalde, Kevin. *Expectations of Justice in Christian Society in the Age of Augustine.* Philadelphia: University of Pennsylvania Press, forthcoming.

Van Dam, Raymond. *Family and Friends in Late Roman Cappadocia.* Philadelphia: University of Pennsylvania Press, 2003.

Van Der Meer, F. *Augustine the Bishop: The Life and Work of a Father of the Church.* Translated by B. Battershaw and G. R. Lamb. New York: Sheed and Ward, 1961.

Vinson, Martha. *Gregory Nazianzen, Select Orations.* Washington, DC: Catholic University Press, 2003.

Vivian, Tim. "'Everything Made by God Is Good.'" *Église et Théologie* 24 (1993): 75–108.

Vogüé, Adalbert de. "Benedict, Model of the Spiritual Life." In *Word and Spirit,* 2:59–72. Still River, MA: St. Bede's Publications, 1981.

———. "Cassien, le Maître et Benoît." In *Commandements du Seigneur et libération évangélique,* ed. J. Gribomont, Studia Anselmiana 70, 223–35. Rome: Editrice Anselmiana, 1977.

———. "De Cassien au Maître et à Eugippe." *Studia Monastica* 23 (1981): 247–61.

———. "Les débuts de la vie monastique à Lérins." *Revue de l'Histoire des Religions* 88 (1993): 5–53

———. "Les mentions des oeuvres de Cassien chez saint Benoît et ses contemporains." *Studia Monastica* 20 (1978): 275–85.

———. *Les règles des saints Pères.* Paris: Éditions du Cerf, 1982.

———. "Un morceau célèbre de Cassien parmi des extraits d' Evagre." *Studia Monastica* 27 (1985): 7–12.

Wallace-Hadrill, J. M. *The Long-Haired Kings.* London: Methuen, 1962.

Ward, Benedicta, trans. *The Sayings of the Desert Fathers.* Kalamazoo, MI: Cistercian Publications, 1975.

Ware, Kallistos. Introduction to *John Climacus, Ladder of Divine Ascent,* translated by C. Luibheid and N. Russell. New York: Paulist Press, 1982.

Weaver, Rebecca H. *Divine Grace and Human Agency: A Study of the Semi-Pelagian Controversy.* Patristic Monograph Series 15. Macon, GA: Mercer University Press, 1996.

Weber, Hans-Oskar. *Die Stellung des Johannes Cassianus zur ausserpachomianischen Mönchstradition: Eine Quellenuntersuchung.* Münster: Aschendorff, 1961.

Wermelinger, Otto. *Rom und Pelagius: Die theologische Position der römischen Bischöfe im pelagianischen Streit in den Jahren 411–432.* Stuttgart: A. Hiersemann, 1975.

Will, Elisabeth. *Saint Apollinaire de Ravenne.* Paris: Les Belles Lettres, 1936.

Wilson-Kastner, Patricia. "Grace as Participation in the Divine Life in the Theology of Augustine of Hippo." *Augustinian Studies* 7 (1976): 149–50.

Wimbush, Vincent. Introduction to *Ascetic Behavior in Greco-Roman Antiquity,* 1–11. Minneapolis: Fortress Press, 1990.

Winslow, Donald. "Gregory of Nazianzus and the Love for the Poor." *Anglican Theological Review* 47 (1965): 348–59.

Wisse, F. "Gnosticism and Early Monasticism in Egypt." In *Gnosis: Festschrift für Hans Jonas,* edited by B. Aland. Göttengen: Vandenhoeck und Ruprecht, 1978.

Index

GEORGE E. DEMACOPOULOS

is assistant professor of historical theology at Fordham University.